# THE GAYELORD HAUSER
# COOK BOOK

# The Gayelord Hauser
# COOK BOOK

*Good Food*
*Good Health*
*Good Looks*

A Perigee Book

Perigee Books
are published by
G. P. Putnam's Sons
200 Madison Avenue
New York, New York 10016

Library of Congress Catalog Card Number 79-92173

ISBN 0-399-50475-3

Ten Previous Printings

First Perigee Printing, 1980

PRINTED IN THE UNITED STATES OF AMERICA

# Introduction

*What we eat today*
*Walks and talks tomorrow.*
—Slavic Proverb

TENDER YOUNG MEATS deliciously broiled; bright-colored vegetables, fresh, plump, and succulent with their own juices; salads crisp yet suave, aromatic with herbs; nutlike breads made from freshly ground whole-grain flours—what cook does not aspire to serve such meals? These are the foods which delight the gourmet the world over, and these are the foods which build good health and bestow good looks.

Good cooks are born, not made, they say. But I believe that anyone who will use his intelligence—and his five senses—can be a superb cook; for of all the creative arts none requires the use of the senses more than the art of cooking. Rigidly following a recipe will not insure a gastronomic delight unless the senses of taste, smell, touch, and sight are sensitive and alive during its preparation. Even hearing has its uses in cooking, as well as that sixth sense of "flare" and "timing." Because the "proof of the pudding is in the eating" the dish must be several times sampled. From the delicious smells which emanate from it the cook can judge its progress. The sense of touch tells when a mixture is of the right consistency, and the sense of sight will be evidenced in the attractiveness of the dish when it is finally served.

Although cooking is an art, it is in no sense a secret or mysterious art. Some of the most delicious dishes I have ever eaten were prepared by the simplest people with the crudest equipment. I remember a wonderful goulash I once ate at the edge of a small lake in the hills of northern Rumania. A peasant woman had prepared it, and her young daughter carried it on her back up a narrow trail from her mother's kitchen and delivered it to us steaming hot in a large iron canister. Another occasion I will never forget is the time I shared a roast lamb with a group of shepherds camped on a little-traveled road on the plains of Yugoslavia. The lamb, heavily spiced with garlic, had been roasted on a spit over an open fire.

Certainly it was neither elaborate equipment nor esoteric knowledge which made these dishes so delicious that they linger in my memory. It was simply native intelligence about food and the use of the five senses. The same thing is true of the omelets I have eaten in the North of France. They were prepared before my eyes with absolutely no effort, yet their taste rivaled anything I had ever eaten. I remember with pleasure the wonderful stuffed cabbage and stuffed peppers served in Hungarian restaurants; also the pheasant cooked in sauerkraut and champagne which Baroness Lili Hatvany served for luncheon in Budapest when that city was the world capital of gracious living.

The delicious *pastas* and the vegetables fried in egg batter which have been served to me in the villages of Italy make me rebel at the products of most of the so-called Italian restaurants in this country. A salad bowl of crisp greens dressed with nutty-flavored olive oil which one finds everywhere in the South of France puts to shame the traditional American salad of tasteless hearts of lettuce and unripe tomatoes, further degenerated by the addition of a revolting sour pink dressing which seems to be standard equipment in restaurants from coast to coast.

No wonder we in America must look to pills for vitamins and minerals which we ought to get in the foods we eat daily. What a pity it is that in nearly all restaurants and in the majority of homes vegetables are still cooked to the point where they are completely colorless and devoid of all appeal to the appetite as well as their nutrients. There is a saying, "Heaven sends us good foods, but the devil sends us bad cooks." It seems particularly true of this country, for America has a richer abundance than any other country of fresh, first-quality foods.

When you peel, pickle, cook to death, or throw away the best parts of food, you are nourishing the kitchen sink and starving your family. When you use the new-style cookery described in this book, you preserve the life-giving vitamins and minerals. The peelings of most vegetables, the outside dark-green leaves, and the tops of many vegetables are treasure houses of minerals. Don't waste them.

The care and cooking of different kinds of foods are discussed in the various chapters of this book, but one cardinal rule applies to all foods—*never overcook*. The best method of cooking any food is the method which cooks it in the least time. Second, never throw away any liquid in which vegetables have been cooked. A cookbook which tells you to "drain" is a relic of the horse-and-buggy days. Preferably there should be no liquid left when the vegetables are short-cooked, as described in Chapter 1. But if there is a little left, save it.

Never overcook and never throw away nutritious juices—these are the fundamentals of my new-style cookery. Unless you have some special problem of diet, this is practically all you need to know in order to serve healthful meals.

It is my hope that from this book you will learn to cook with all your five senses and intelligence: There is no reason why you, your family, and your guests cannot enjoy the delights of really excellent cooking such as I have known in my travels throughout the world, and such as thousands of my students enjoy daily.

The "something new which has been added" in this book consists in the elimination of unhealthy methods and ingredients. Refined white flour, a "foodless food," has of course been eliminated. In its place we use natural flour and grains with all their goodness left intact. Dead white sugar, probably the greatest curse in our American dietary, is replaced with natural brown sugar, black molasses, and honey. In place of irritating too-hot condiments we use pungent herbs and flavorsome vegetable salt which makes your meals even more interesting. (See Chapter 24 for information about these foods.) Vitamin-rich lemon juice has it all over ordinary vinegar; and of course fresh pork and lard have no place in a healthful regime. Otherwise we use all the foods which you and your family could possibly wish for. Meals prepared by the new-style cookery can be gastronomic triumphs—and in addition will insure good health, good looks, and a longer life.

GAYELORD HAUSER

*Beverly Hills, California*
*April 1946*

# Contents

# Contents

# CHAPTER 1

# *Vegetable Cookery*

IN NO OTHER DEPARTMENT of cookery are care and intelligence so necessary as in the cooking of vegetables. And yet good vegetable cookery is really a simple, time-saving matter. It actually takes less time and trouble to do it right than to turn out flat, lifeless, overcooked vegetables.

Just as surely as sugar dissolves in water, the vital elements of vegetables dissolve in cooking water. The principle of the new-style cookery is to save those rich food elements—by cooking in as little time as possible, in as little liquid as possible, and never throwing away any liquid which remains. Never use soda to keep vegetables green, and never peel, scrape, or pare when the scrubbing brush will do as well.

## SHORT-COOKING VEGETABLES

The greatest loss of vitamins occurs between the time when the food is put on the fire and the time when it reaches the boiling point. Therefore have your cooking pot—one small enough so your vegetables will fill it to the top—piping hot before the food is put in. In the bottom put two or three tablespoons of Hauser Broth, bring it to the boil, and when the kettle is filled with steam put in the vegetables.

3

*To Speed the Cooking Time:* As the cell walls break down while the vegetables cook, the nutrients pass into the cooking water. Therefore fewer nutrients are lost when the cooking time is short. If you shred, dice, or chop the vegetables, then cook them in small pots with tight lids to keep the air out and the steam in, you can greatly reduce the time necessary for cooking, hence save minerals and vitamins.

## EQUIPMENT FOR SHORT-COOKING

*Pots:* Heavy steel, glass, or pottery pots which distribute the heat from the bottom to the sides and lid of the pan give best results because the vegetables can be cooked in a very little liquid, just enough to start the steam. There is a vogue nowadays for pottery. If you're in the money you can get lovely French pottery. If you're not, the less expensive Mexican pottery will serve the same purpose. If you are devoted to herbs, try seasoning your pottery cooking vessels by boiling

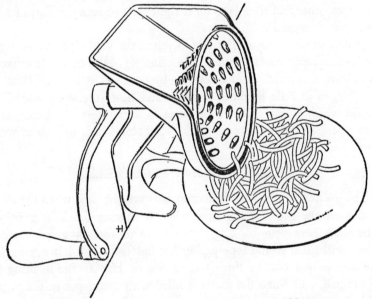

THE SNITZLER, A HANDY GADGET FOR SHREDDING VEGETABLES.

herbs in them for several hours—on the same principle as seasoning an iron frying pan with grease. Then everything you cook in the seasoned pot will have a delicate nuance of herb flavor.

*Snitzler:* I discovered that there is a great waste of time in shredding and dicing vegetables and fruits, so a clever gadget called the snitzler was invented. So far it is only in the homes of my students, but I hope in the future it will be available in department stores. In the meantime, if you cannot get hold of one, use a coarse shredder to prepare vegetables for short-cooking—one that does not mash, but cuts in thin slices. And remember that vitamin C deteriorates upon exposure to air, so the shredding should be done at the last moment before cooking.

*Clock:* Short-cooking is a matter of minutes. You will need a clock convenient to your range, a clock with a large round face on which you can tell the minutes accurately.

## BOILED VEGETABLES

If you have no heavy waterless cooking pots and don't wish to buy new ones, you can still save minerals and vitamins by this method: Bring the water to a rolling boil, add vegetable salt, then the food, and bring to a boil again as quickly as possible. Use just enough water barely to cover the vegetables.

## TO KEEP THE COLOR OF VEGETABLES

All vegetables taste better cooked in a little Hauser Broth. To keep the color in them without the use of soda, add a few drops of lemon to the liquid. Sooner or later some progressive manufacturer will produce a vitamin C tablet to enrich the cooking water and keep in the natural color of vegetables. Until that day lemon juice will have to do.

## SELECTING YOUR VEGETABLES

Choose young, tender vegetables, as fresh as possible in this day of commercial farming. See that the colors are bright, the vegetables firm and crisp in texture. Destruction of vitamins begins the moment a vegetable is pulled from the earth or plucked from the plant. There is nothing you can do about the care the vegetable receives before it reaches you, but you can tell something about which have had the best treatment by their appearance. Fortunately, the vegetables which look the best usually have the best flavor and the highest vitamin content.

Green leafy vegetables such as spinach and lettuce should be crisp when you buy them—and so also should peas, string beans, and all seed or pod vegetables. Roots, tubers, bulbs, and fruits—carrots, onions, tomatoes, etc.—should be firm with unwrinkled skins. Onions and potatoes should not have sprouts.

*Canned and Frozen Vegetables:* Garden-fresh vegetables are highest in vitamin content, of course. But because quick-frozen vegetables are processed the same day they are picked, they often have better food value than fresh vegetables shipped to distant markets. Quick-frozen vegetables put up by well-known firms are uniformly reliable. But look with suspicion upon cellophane bags of quick-frozen vegetables without familiar labels. They may or may not be good.

Once you let frozen vegetables thaw, cook them quickly. If you let them lie around, they will lose their vitamin C just as fast as fresh vegetables. It is a good plan to follow directions on package.

Federal food laws demand that canned goods be labeled according to grade—A, B, and C. This is for your protection, to indicate the quality of the vegetables in the can. Buy grades A and B rather than C.

## HOW TO CARE FOR YOUR VEGETABLES

Wash all vegetables thoroughly. Scrub roots and tubers with a brush. If they are young, they need not be peeled, but blemishes, eyes, mold, etc., should be removed.

Greens, flowers, and heads should be thoroughly washed in several waters. Pick over greens and remove any wilted leaves before you put them in water. It is easier to handle them when they are dry. Shake and drain in a colander or sieve. Remove stem ends, stalks, or cores from heads.

# Vegetable Cookery 7

All vegetables to be eaten raw should be crisped in a hydrator. Never cut or otherwise break the skin of a vegetable until you are ready to use it because destruction of vitamin C begins the moment the cut surface is exposed to the air.

Store mushrooms and pod vegetables without washing in a tightly covered container in the refrigerator. Root vegetables should be stored in a cool place, preferably a vegetable bin where they can be spread out so they do not touch each other.

Potatoes and dry onions keep for some time without serious loss of vitamins, but all other vegetables should be used as soon as possible.

## ARTICHOKES

Wash the artichokes thoroughly and remove any discolored outer leaves. Cut off the spiny tips of the leaves with scissors and chop off the stem about ½ inch below the base of the leaves. Drop into 2 inches of boiling water in a heavy kettle. As soon as the water boils again, cover the kettle tightly. Cook 20-30 minutes, until the outer leaves come away easily from the stalk. Serve whole with melted butter or Hollandaise sauce.

NOTE: The water in which artichokes are cooked is astringent and has an unpleasant taste. Don't save it for your Hauser Broth.

## ASPARAGUS

Wash the stalks under running water. Cut off all of the stem which is hard and woody. If the asparagus is very sandy, scrape the large scales from the stalks, taking care not to bruise or knock off the tips. Tie the stalks together in bunches easy to handle with white cotton string. Place the bunches stem end down in the bottom of a double boiler containing 2 inches of boiling water or Hauser Broth. Cover with the upper part of the double boiler, inverted, and cook 12-20 minutes, until tender. Add salt just before removing from the heat. Lift the bunches from the liquid, remove the string, and dress with melted butter or Hollandaise sauce.

## LIMA BEANS

Shell the beans just before cooking. Wash the shelled beans and drop them into 1 inch of boiling Hauser Broth. When the liquid reaches a rolling boil again, cover the utensil and cook about 20 minutes, depending upon the freshness and quality of the beans. Add salt just before removing from the heat. Serve with butter.

## STRING BEANS

Young tender green or yellow beans are shredded lengthwise and placed in a heavy, hot cooking utensil. Cover the bottom with hot broth and keep the utensil tightly covered. Cook for about 8 minutes. When tender, add a bit of vegetable salt and some butter or vegetable oil.

## BEETS, CARROTS, AND TURNIPS

Select young vegetables. Thoroughly wash but do not peel. Shred on a medium shredder blade. Use a heavy pan, small enough so the vegetables will fill it. Heat the pan and put 2 or 3 tablespoons of water—better still, Hauser Broth—in the bottom. Add the shredded vegetable when the liquid is steaming. Cover tightly to keep in the steam and short-cook 5-10 minutes, depending on the quantity you are cooking. Shake occasionally to prevent sticking.

As soon as the shreds are done, add some vegetable salt and a lump of butter or a bit of vegetable oil.

## BEETS IN BUTTER

Use butter instead of water in the above recipe. Melt the butter in the pan, put in the shredded beets, and cook slowly over a low flame, stirring frequently, for 5-10 minutes. Add vegetable salt and serve. The nutlike flavor of these beets will be a pleasant surprise.

## NESTED BEETS

Shred the crisp leaves of young beets, which contain good food value, and short-cook them about 4 minutes in butter. Make a nest of these leaves on a plate and serve short-cooked beets in the center.

## BEET GREENS

Remove any coarse, wilted, or discolored leaves and stems. Wash in several waters to remove all traces of sand. Place in a kettle containing ½ inch of boiling Hauser Broth. When the broth reaches a rolling boil again, cover the kettle and cook about 7 minutes, until tender. Season with salt just before removing from the fire. Chop and add butter. Serve with lemon wedges.

## BROCCOLI

Discard the largest and heaviest leaves and any woody part of the stem. Separate the flowers into portions for serving and wash well. Tie into bunches with white cotton string. Split the stems lengthwise to make them cook faster and place the bunches stem down in the bottom of a double boiler containing 3 inches of boiling Hauser Broth. When the broth reaches a rolling boil again, invert the top of the double boiler over it as a cover and cook 15-30 minutes, until tender. Add salt just before removing from the fire. Lift the bunches from the broth, remove the string, and dress with butter or Hollandaise sauce.

## BRUSSELS SPROUTS

Remove any wilted stems and leaves. Cut into quarters and wash well. Soaking is not necessary and destroys valuable vitamins. Drop the quartered sprouts into enough boiling Hauser Broth to cover and add 1 teaspoon of minced onion to 1 quart of sprouts. Cook 8-10 minutes with the kettle uncovered. Add salt and 2 tablespoons of minced parsley just before removing from the fire. Dress with butter, lemon butter, or thin cream.

## CABBAGE

White or red cabbage contains the greatest food value raw. However, it is permissible to prepare cabbage short-cooked. Shred and short-cook for 2 to 5 minutes, in either butter or oil. In reality, this is a hot raw salad, and is easily digested, especially if a bit of lemon juice is sprinkled over the cabbage after heating. Adding a bit of cream to the cabbage makes a welcome change.

## RED CABBAGE AND APPLES

3 cups finely shredded red cabbage
2 cups sliced tart apples
3 cups boiling water

3 tbsp. natural brown sugar
1 tsp. vegetable salt
3 tbsp. lemon juice

Combine the cabbage, apples, and water. Simmer uncovered over medium heat 10-15 minutes, until just tender. Put a piece of stale bread over the top of the cabbage to prevent the odor from spreading. Add the salt, sugar, and lemon juice just before removing from the fire. Serve in individual dishes with a dab of butter if desired.

## CARROTS

Carrots retain most of their good qualities when cooked in the new manner, but they are most healthful when eaten raw. Never peel the carrots, but wash them with a stiff brush and shred them. Add just a few tablespoons of Hauser Broth to start the steam. Cook slowly about 5 minutes and season with a bit of vegetable salt.

Delicious shredded carrots are prepared by melting butter over a slow fire, stirring in the shredded carrots, and letting them cook about 5 minutes. Season with a bit of vegetable salt and sprinkle some finely chopped parsley over the carrots before serving.

## CARROTS IN CREAM

Use cream instead of butter and short-cook shredded carrots over a slow flame for 5 minutes. Season with vegetable salt and sprinkle some finely chopped parsley over the carrots before serving.

## CARROTS AND TURNIPS

Shred equal parts of carrots and turnips and cook as above. When turnips are young and tender, they should not be peeled. Use a medium shredder. This combination is delicious.

## BAKED CAULIFLOWER

Short-cook shredded cauliflower. Place in a baking dish with alternate layers of freshly grated American cheese. Cover the top with cheese and a few lumps of butter, and brown under a broiler flame for just a few minutes. You will find this to be a delicious dish, and it does not require more than about 10 minutes of actual cooking time.

## LEMON CAULIFLOWER

Short-cook the cauliflower, then cool. Pour over it French dressing to which has been added 1 tablespoon of minced parsley and 1 tablespoon of minced chives. Let stand in the refrigerator at least an hour. Serve with roasts or steaks.

## CORN ON THE COB

Corn should be freshly picked—the fresher the better. Select well-filled ears with fresh green husks. The kernels should be soft and milky; if they are hard and glazed-looking the corn is too old. Remove the husks, silk, and stem ends, and the unfilled tips if necessary. Place in boiling salted water to cover. Cook 6 to 10 minutes. Add a bit of marjoram to the water for improved flavor. If the corn is old, a little sugar in the water will help. Two tablespoons of milk or the juice of half a lemon will keep its color.

## CORN OFF THE COB

Select young, fresh-picked corn. Husk and score each row of kernels and scrape from the cob with a sharp knife. Place this pulp in the top of a double boiler. Add a few tablespoons of water and season with butter. Cook in the double boiler until the corn is heated through. Just a pinch of marjoram gives it a lift.

## EGGPLANT

Select tender vegetables. Wash thoroughly but do not peel. Shred on a medium shredder blade. Cook in a heavy pot in 2 tablespoons of Hauser Broth for 8-10 minutes. When tender, add a bit of vegetable salt and some butter.

## STEWED OKRA

Use only very young okra pods. Remove the stems and boil very slowly until tender—20 minutes or more. Season with salt, butter, and freshly ground black pepper. Some add a few peeled chopped tomatoes 10 minutes before the okra is done.

## PEAS

Wash the pods before shelling the peas. Shell and put the pods through a juice extractor. Simmer the peas in the pea-pod juice over low heat for 5 minutes. Season with sweet cream and vegetable salt after you turn off the heat. Thyme improves peas.

## SPINACH

Remove all dead, crushed leaves before wetting the spinach. After you have removed the undesirable parts, put the spinach into a large pan of cold water and let it stand a few minutes to loosen the sand. Allow water to run through it until it is clean. Spinach contains an abundance of water and will always cook in its own juices. Shred large leaves with scissors. Place these shredded leaves in a hot cooking utensil. No water is needed. When leaves are thoroughly wilted (usually 3 minutes), add a bit of vegetable salt and butter or vegetable oil. Serve piping hot. A bit of onion, horse-radish, or rosemary improves spinach.

Another good way to prepare spinach is to shred it and add it to a pan in which a few finely chopped onions have been cooked for a minute or two. Short-cook the spinach for about 4 minutes; add butter and a bit of vegetable salt. For variety a bit of sweet cream may be added instead of butter, but the flame must be turned off before the cream is added to avoid curdling.

Do not make the preparation of this important vegetable a drudgery. Spinach can be prepared deliciously and easily in many ways. Grind it through a coarse food chopper and short-cook 4 minutes in butter. Add some thoroughly beaten eggs and scramble.

## ACORN SQUASH

Either cut the squash in two lengthwise or cut off the top to form a cup. Remove the seeds and strings, season with salt and paprika, place a nubbin of butter in each, and bake in a hot oven about 50 minutes, or until tender, basting the inside from time to time with melted butter.

## BAKED HUBBARD SQUASH

Cut the squash into wedge-shaped pieces, remove seeds and strings. Sprinkle each piece with salt and paprika, dot with butter, and bake in a moderate oven (350°F.) 1 hour, or until soft.

## ZUCCHINI

Select small, tender zucchini. Scrub with a brush, taking care to remove all the sand. Do not peel. Slice thin or shred on a coarse snitzler blade. Shredding seems to give a milder flavor. Add a little water to start the steam, and cook for 8 to 10 minutes over a slow flame. For variety other flavors may be added—parsley, garlic, onion, etc.

## FRENCH-FRIED VEGETABLES

Many an overzealous health enthusiast deprives himself of the pleasure of having French-fried vegetables occasionally. It is true that food fried in the ordinary manner is more difficult to digest; especially if things are fried too hard and where a mixture of fats is used. Pure vegetable fats or oils such as peanut oil, corn oil, cottonseed oil are permissible. But the fats must be pure—that is, no mixture of animal and vegetable fats as in some margarines.

For French-frying in the healthful manner, use pure vegetable fats, and only fry the vegetables until they are a light golden brown and still soft.

I ate some of the most delicious French-fried cauliflower and carrots in the famous Bircher-Benner diet sanatorium in Zurich, Switzerland. They surprise you there every once in a while with some delicious French-fried vegetables. This cuts the monotony of some rigid diets.

So the next time you have a yen for delicious French-fried vegetables, try these. Remember to use only pure vegetable fats. Have a thermometer handy to watch the heat, or your vegetables will shrivel away to nothing. When your vegetables are still piping hot, sprinkle a bit of vegetable salt over them and serve at once.

### FRENCH-FRIED CARROTS

Cut unpeeled scraped carrots into fingers. Fry in pure vegetable fat at 385°F. for about 8 minutes, or until a golden brown. Drain on absorbent paper and sprinkle with vegetable salt.

### FRENCH-FRIED ONION RINGS

Dip onions in batter made with egg and whole-wheat flour. Fry only a few rings at a time to prevent sticking together. Fry in pure vegetable fat at about 340°F. for 6 minutes, or until golden brown and tender. Drain on absorbent paper and sprinkle with vegetable salt. Serve hot.

### FRENCH-FRIED RUTABAGAS

Cut unpeeled rutabagas into fingers. Fry in pure vegetable fat at 340°F. for about 10 minutes. Drain on absorbent paper and sprinkle with vegetable salt.

### FRENCH-FRIED PARSNIPS

Cut chilled parsnips and fry in deep vegetable fat at 300°F. Watch your heat carefully, as parsnips shrivel and burn easily. Fry about 8 minutes and drain, sprinkle with vegetable salt, and serve piping hot.

## FRENCH-FRIED POTATOES

Cut unpeeled potatoes about ⅓ inch thick. When the thermometer reads 360°F. put potatoes into a heated basket. Then raise the heat to about 380°F. After a minute or two cut the heat down to 340°F. If you want potatoes to be nice and brown, be sure to keep the temperature up.

## SHOESTRING POTATOES

Cut unpeeled potatoes into shoestrings. Fry in deep vegetable fat at 360°F. Sprinkle with vegetable salt and serve hot.

## SWEET POTATO CHIPS

Slice one chilled unpeeled yam or sweet potato and place in hot vegetable fat at 350°F. Fry until nice and golden brown. Then continue with another potato. It takes about 6 minutes for yams and 15 minutes for sweet potatoes. Sprinkle with vegetable salt and serve hot.

## POTATOES

The best potatoes are firm and clean, have shallow eyes and no cuts, decay, or green spots. For mashed or baked potatoes, use a mealy, flaky variety. For salads, creaming, and the like, use firm, waxy potatoes that hold their shape. To get the most food value from potatoes, always cook them in their jackets. Potatoes give an excellent form of natural starch accompanied by good alkalinizing minerals. Cooked in the modern manner, they are a splendid alkalinizing food.

## STEAMED POTATOES

Wash the potatoes and scrub with a brush. Place in a perforated pan over boiling water, cover, and steam until tender—30-45 minutes. The length of cooking time varies depending upon size, age, and variety of potatoes used. New potatoes take longer than old ones; mealy potatoes cook more quickly than waxy ones.

Or cook in a heavy kettle in very little water.

## MASHED POTATOES

Steam white potatoes with the jackets on, using only a little water to start the steam. Be sure all the water is absorbed. Peel and mash, then add a large handful of finely chopped greens—parsley, green onions, or chives. Add a lump of butter, some vegetable salt, and hot milk. Beat until fluffy. Adding the shredded vegetables further helps to alkalinize the potatoes and makes them delicious.

Try these in place of the ordinary "smashed potatoes."

## BAKED POTATOES

Select smooth, evenly shaped potatoes of a mealy variety—Idaho, Green Mountain, and Maine potatoes are good. Scrub clean and rub the skins with butter or oil. Bake in a hot oven (450°F. or more) about 45 minutes. When the potatoes are soft, remove from the oven and cut in half. Scoop out the potato from the shells and mash. Add a large handful of your favorite garden greens, finely chopped—parsley, green onions, chives, or mint. Add a lump of butter, some vegetable salt, and a little milk. Beat until very fluffy and replace in the shells. Brown in the oven or under the broiler.

## IRISH POTATO CRISPS

Scrub the potatoes thoroughly. Cut lengthwise strips ½ inch wide and ⅛ inch thick. Place on a buttered baking sheet and bake in a very hot oven (500°F) for a few minutes until they puff up. Serve instead of crackers or bread. Delicious on restricted diets.

## CREAMED POTATOES

Dice steamed potatoes and place in a heavy skillet. Pour thin cream over them—enough to just cover the potatoes. Add a lump of butter and vegetable salt to taste. Cook over low heat, stirring frequently, until thick—about 15 minutes.

Flavor with onion or any of your favorite herbs, or add paprika.

## HASHED BROWN POTATOES

Melt 1 heaping tablespoon of vegetable shortening in a heavy iron skillet. Add 2 cups of minced boiled potatoes and ¼ cup of minced onion. Season with ½ teaspoon of vegetable salt and a good dash of paprika. Add 3 tablespoons of milk and cook easily without stirring until browned on the bottom. Fold like an omelet and serve garnished with fresh parsley.

## FRIED POTATOES

Scrub and slice thinly 4 medium-sized unpeeled potatoes. Place in a heavy skillet with 1 heaping tablespoon of vegetable oil, some minced onion or chives, a little chopped parsley, and vegetable salt to taste. Sauté easily for 15 minutes, or until browned, turning from time to time. Cover and cook slowly another 15 minutes.

## SCALLOPED POTATOES

| | |
|---|---|
| 2 cups sliced raw unpeeled potatoes | 1 tbsp. grated onion |
| ½ tsp. vegetable salt | 1 tbsp. butter |
| 1 tbsp. whole-wheat flour | 1 cup milk |

Wash and pare the potatoes and slice thin. Put half of them in a buttered baking dish and sprinkle them with half the vegetable salt, flour, and onion. Repeat for the second layer. Add the milk—enough so it can just be seen between the top slices. Cover and bake in a moderate oven (350°F.) about 30 minutes. Remove the cover and continue baking another 30 minutes, or until the potatoes are tender and brown.
Each layer may be sprinkled with cheese if desired.

## NEW POTATOES AND BASIL

Thoroughly scrub the potatoes but do not peel. Add enough water to steam them, with a pinch of basil in the water. When tender, dress with melted butter and vegetable salt. Any of your favorite herbs can be used.

## PARSLEY POTATOES

Scrub new potatoes thoroughly. Cut into inch squares without peeling. Barely cover with boiling water, and add a little vegetable salt. Cook over low heat until tender and the water is absorbed. Dress with melted butter and chopped parsley.

## SWEET POTATOES

*Baked:* Select even-sized potatoes and wash thoroughly. Dry and rub the skins with oil or butter if you like a soft shell. Put in a hot oven (400°F.) for 35 to 45 minutes, depending on size.
*Boiled:* Wash the potatoes thoroughly and cook in boiling salted water for 20 minutes, or until soft. Peel, and serve with butter.

*Mashed:* Boil the potatoes and peel them. Mash, and for each potato add 1 teaspoon butter, a pinch of salt, and 1 teaspoon of warm milk or cream. Beat briskly and place in a warmed dish.

*Candied:* 4 sweet potatoes

1 cup natural brown sugar

¼ cup water

Vegetable salt

Butter

Juice of 1 orange

Boil the potatoes in their jackets. Drain and peel, cut in halves lengthwise. Make a syrup by boiling the brown sugar and water together. Sprinkle each slice of potato with salt and cinnamon or nutmeg if desired; dip it into the syrup, and place it in a buttered baking dish. Arrange the potatoes so they do not touch each other. Dot with butter, pour on the rest of the syrup, and bake in a hot oven (450°F.) until the tops are brown. Shortly before removing from the oven, sprinkle the juice of an orange over the potatoes.

## SWEET POTATOES AND APPLES

6 boiled sweet potatoes

3 red apples

¼ cup orange juice

½ cup butter

½ cup natural brown sugar

¼ tsp. nutmeg

Slice the potatoes and the unpeeled apples. Add the orange juice. Butter a casserole and arrange in it alternate layers of sweet potatoes and apples. Blend together the butter, sugar, and nutmeg and spread over the top of the dish. Bake in a moderate oven (375°F.) about 20 minutes, until the apples are tender and the top browned.

# CHAPTER 2

# *Salads*

THE BEST WAY to make sure that every member of your family gets sufficient health protection is to *start* your meal with a salad. Also, it stimulates the appetite and makes the whole meal more delicious.

## A COURSE IN SALAD MAKING

The secret of good salads is to select fruits and vegetables which are full of life and sunshine. They should be as young and as freshly picked as possible. They should be crisp, with leaves a rich green from abundant sunlight. Handle them as little as possible in preparation so as to prevent bruising or bleeding, with consequent loss of vital juices.

*Care of Salad Materials:* Chill salad greens in a tightly covered pan in the refrigerator. When ready to use, wash thoroughly and dry on a clean towel. Parsley is quickly revived by sprinkling with cold water, putting in an airtight jar, and keeping in the refrigerator.

Keep salad mixtures light and fluffy. The best and simplest way to do this is to shred finely the non-juicy vegetables such as carrots, beets, celery root, turnips, cauliflower, squash, etc. Cut juicier vegetables and fruits with a stainless steel knife. Leaves are least bruised when cut with scissors.

If it becomes necessary to revive any prepared salad material, sprinkle it with just enough water to be absorbed. Too much water will leach the valuable minerals out of the plant tissues. Never leave cut vegetables soaking.

*To Prevent Loss of Vitamin C:* Since vitamin C is lost with exposure to air, slice or dice fruits and vegetables at the last moment before serving. Cut salad greens at the last moment, preferably with scissors.

*Things to Remember:* When making salads, remember the following points:

1. Make them look attractive. Most people eat with their eyes.

2. Make them delicious so the digestive juices will be stimulated to flow freely.

3. Never serve the same combination twice in the same week. Variety gives spice to your menus.

## UNLIMITED VARIETY IN VEGETABLE SALADS

It will be useful to the salad maker to have the various salad materials divided into groups as follows:

*Foundation Vegetables:* Vegetables having color, mild flavor, bulk, and juice. They are the best base for blending flavors and textures.

Carrot
Celery
Celery root
Cabbage—red, white, Chinese, Savoy
Salad greens—lettuce, romaine, chickory, escarole, French endive, etc.

In special salads one of the above vegetables will predominate. But for general use in mixed salads, juice-laden cabbage and celery make an excellent foundation to which other vegetables may be added in varying proportions.

*Accessory Vegetables:* These are the vegetables which are added to the foundation vegetables. Four or five vegetables should make a full-flavored salad, and sometimes others may be added for special flavoring and garnishing. For weak digestion, it is best to stick to a simple combination of two or three vegetables.

| | |
|---|---|
| Radish | Sweet potato |
| Beet | Shallots |
| Parsnip | Leeks |
| Rutabaga | Bean sprouts |
| Turnip | Asparagus tips |
| Jerusalem artichoke | Mushrooms |
| Onions, bulb and top | Globe artichoke bottoms |
| Chives | Parsley |
| Scallions | Cucumber |
| Nasturtium leaves, green pods | Chayote |
| Cress, water and garden | Sweet pepper, green and ripe |
| Celery leaves | Tomato |
| Tender leaves of any green leafy | Okra |
| vegetable | Kohlrabi |
| Fennel | Cauliflower |
| Young sweet corn | Broccoli |
| Squash, summer and winter varieties | Cabbage, core |
| ties | Cauliflower, core |
| Pumpkin | Broccoli stems |

Never discard a bit of salad material unless imperfect or decayed. Use it for soup stock instead. The coarse outer leaves of every salad green make a delicious cooked vegetable; or, if they are too tough, cut with scissors into narrow ribbonlike strips and use in your Hauser Broth. As a rule, the greener the leaf, the greater the content of organic salts.

You will soon learn what basic combinations your family likes especially, and with ingenuity you can serve delicious variations of these combinations that will keep up their interest daily in this most valuable health aid. Once in a while try adding certain highly flavored ingredients in small quantities. A number of these flavor combinations are listed below to assist you in providing changes of flavor in salad

making. And always use parsley and water cress, for their food value
as well as their appearance.

Beet and shredded lemon peel
Bitter leaves and sweet fruits—chicory and raisin or apple, etc.
Cabbage and ripe olives
Cabbage and pineapple
Carrot and orange, including a little peel
Celery and olives
Cucumber and dill
Tomato and basil
Water cress and orange

When in need of a finishing touch, look through the following suggestions for a flavor or garnish which will add to the combination.

Herbs—basil, chervil, dill, marjoram, mint, tarragon, thyme
Celery seed
Garlic seasoning, powdered
Horse-radish
Olives
Shredded rind of orange or lemon
Chips of orange or lemon with peel
Candied peel
Crystallized ginger
Sweet dried fruits—unsulphured figs, raisins, dates, prunes
Ripe fruits not too soft—pear, apple, grape, orange, pineapple,
    kumquat, banana, melon, persimmon

Once you have started to experiment, many favorite combinations
can be made with cooked vegetables also. For variety try these:

Green peas with raw carrots
Baked potato with raw beet and onion
String beans with raw celery
Legumes with raw cauliflower
Beet with raw cauliflower
Soybeans with green pepper and radish

The salad vies with the soup course in possibilities for making left-over vegetables count. Practically any cooked vegetable may be added in small proportions to the raw mixed salad; but string beans, shell beans, soybeans—all dried legumes and potato make a special contribution in flavor and consistency.

The following salads are favorites with thousands of my students. Just so the salad is fresh and large, you may select one of these or follow your own chemical appetite.

## ALL-IN-ONE SALAD

2 carrots  
2 young beets  

¼ medium-sized cabbage  
½ cup celery  

Shred very fine and serve in a nest of lettuce leaves with French dressing.

## BRIGHT-EYE SALAD

Select very fresh young green turnip leaves, wash and chill. Serve on a plate with stuffed egg, a slice of raw tomato, and olive-oil dressing.

## CABBAGE AND WATER-CRESS SALAD

Shred very fine the cabbage and add a bit of onion. Just before serving, add a dressing of two-thirds thick, sour cream and one-third lemon juice with a bit of vegetable salt.

## CABBAGE SALAD RUSSE

Shred fine young tender cabbage and add one-third as much chopped water cress. Serve on lettuce or romaine with French dressing.

## COTTAGE CHEESE SALAD I

½ cup cottage cheese  
½ cup sliced small radishes  
½ cup diced celery  

2 tbsp. chopped green pepper  
Pinch of vegetable salt  

Mix the vegetables and chill. Add the cottage cheese to any desired salad dressing and fold this into the mixed vegetables.

## COTTAGE CHEESE SALAD II

½ cup cottage cheese
¼ tsp. vegetable salt
2 tsp. minced onions or chives

1 tbsp. minced parsley
Paprika to taste

Combine the cheese, salt, onion or chives, and parsley. (If the cheese is the dry kind, add a little cream.) Pack in a cup or ramekin and chill until firm—half an hour or more. Unmold onto a plate, sprinkle with paprika, and trim with shredded lettuce or cabbage. Pour French dressing over the lettuce and garnish with sliced cucumber and radish if desired.

## CAULIFLOWER SALAD

Shred fine a young head of cauliflower and mix with salad dressing. Celery root may be combined with it. Serve on a bed of green leaves.

## CELERY-NUT SALAD

4 stalks celery, chopped
1 green sweet pepper, chopped
2 large tomatoes, cut in wedges

4 tbsp. French dressing
½ cup grated nuts
Water cress

Saturate thoroughly the celery, green pepper, and tomato with dressing. Arrange on beds of lettuce, sprinkle with nuts, and garnish with cress.

Serves 4.

## COMPLEXION SALAD

1 cup carrots, finely shredded
8 tbsp. pineapple juice
1 cup celery, finely chopped

1 cup cabbage, finely shredded
¾ cup red apples, diced

Saturate the ingredients with pineapple juice. When cold, arrange on crisp leaves of lettuce or escarole and garnish with sprigs of water cress.

## FAMILY SALAD

3 cups finely shredded cabbage
1 green pepper, chopped

1 small onion, chopped
1½ cups mayonnaise

Combine the chopped vegetables with the mayonnaise. Serve in a large bowl lined with your favorite salad greens.

## HOLLYWOOD SALAD

2 cups finely shredded cabbage
10 large ripe olives cut in pieces

2 cups shredded tart apples
4 tbsp. French dressing

Mix with dressing and place in a nest of crisp lettuce leaves. Garnish with radishes and parsley.

## MIXED VEGETABLE SALAD

Shred coarsely equal parts of young cabbage and celery. To this add chopped cucumber, onion, tomato, and a bit of sweet green pepper. Chill and serve on crisp lettuce leaves with French dressing.

## OLIVES ITALIAN

Allow ripe olives to marinate overnight in a small bowl of yellow olive oil to which has been added a clove or two of garlic.

## ONE-TWO-THREE SALAD

Shred finely equal parts of carrots, apples, and cabbage. To this add pineapple juice enough to moisten, which makes a delicious nonfattening dressing.

## PARTY SALAD

2 tsp. gelatine
1/4 cup cold water
3 tbsp. raw sugar
3 tbsp. lemon juice
1/3 tsp. vegetable salt

2/3 cup boiling water
3 tbsp. pimento
1/3 cup cabbage
2/3 cup celery

Soak the gelatine in the cold water for 5 minutes. Mix the sugar, lemon juice, and salt with the hot water and pour over the gelatine. Stir until the gelatine is thoroughly dissolved. Set aside to cool. When the gelatine begins to thicken, add chopped vegetables. Turn into molds, chill, and serve on lettuce with olive-oil mayonnaise.

## PINEAPPLE AND CABBAGE SALAD

Combine finely shredded young cabbage and unsweetened raw pineapple. For the dressing use unsweetened pineapple juice and a bit of cream cheese.

# Salads

## SALAD SANTÉ

1 cup finely shredded cabbage
1 cup chopped celery
1 cup finely shredded carrots

½ sweet green pepper, chopped
4 tbsp. French dressing
1 cup unsweetened pineapple juice

Mix the vegetables with the dressing and pineapple juice and chill. When ready to serve, place on crisp lettuce leaves and garnish with water cress.

## SNAPPY SALAD

1 cup finely shredded cabbage
1 cup finely shredded celery
1 cup finely chopped apples

½ cup chopped water cress
4 tbsp. pineapple Fruit-Juice Dressing

Mix the vegetables and marinate in pineapple dressing. Serve on a bed of lettuce. Garnish with small radishes and sprigs of parsley.

## SPRING SALAD BOWL

Cut up water cress, tender leaves of lettuce, young radishes, green onions, chopped fine, 1 large tomato, sliced, 2 cucumbers and 2 carrots finely shredded. Put all in a salad bowl and mix with French dressing.

## STUFFED TOMATOES

Remove the centers from 4 tomatoes, keeping the juice for the dressing. Chop up the centers, ½ cup celery, ½ cup unpeeled cucumbers, and ⅛ cup radishes. Use also a little garlic and water cress. Fill the tomatoes and garnish. Serve in nests of lettuce.

## SOUR-CREAM SALAD

1 cup thick sour cream
1 small onion, finely chopped
½ tsp. vegetable salt

4 tbsp. lemon juice
2 unpeeled cucumbers, finely shredded

Beat the cream and add the onion, salt, and lemon juice. Pour over crisp cucumbers.

## SUMMER SALAD

Mix equal parts of finely shredded cabbage, sliced tomatoes, and sliced cucumber. Season with lemon juice, a little vegetable salt, and a bit of onion. Serve cold.

### THREE-IN-ONE SALAD

Finely shred equal parts of raw cabbage, carrots, and celery. Serve cold and garnish with parsley or water cress. Serve with French dressing.

### TOMATO, CUCUMBER, AND CELERY SALAD

Arrange lettuce hearts and two or three slices of chilled sliced tomato. Coarsely shred equal parts of cucumber and celery and season with chopped green onions. Mix these chopped vegetables with mayonnaise dressing. Serve a large spoonful of this mixture on the tomato. Sprinkle with a bit of paprika.

### TURNIP AND CARROT SALAD

Finely shred young turnips and carrots. To equal parts of this add a little chopped celery. Mix and serve in lettuce-heart cups. Add a bit of water cress and serve with French dressing.

### CARROT-RAISIN SALAD

Soak ½ cup of washed seeded raisins in ¼ cup of lemon juice. When the raisins are plump, combine with 1½ cups of shredded carrots, moisten with mayonnaise, and serve on lettuce leaves or beds of shredded cabbage.

### RAW CHEF'S SALAD

| | |
|---|---|
| 2 cups shredded cauliflower | 1 tsp. chopped onion or onion juice |
| ½ cup chopped green pepper | Pinch of vegetable salt |
| ½ cup chopped water cress | |

Combine all ingredients and moisten with mayonnaise. Arrange on lettuce leaves and serve with extra mayonnaise.

### METCHNIKOFF'S SALAD

Mix equal parts of cottage cheese and shredded carrots. Mix with mayonnaise and a teaspoon of lemon juice. Serve on beds of chopped or shredded lettuce.

### CELERY-ROOT SALAD

| | |
|---|---|
| 4 medium-sized celery roots | ½ tsp. vegetable salt |
| 1 qt. Hauser broth | |

Scrub and peel the celery roots. Chop up the tops and boil all in Hauser Broth until soft. Then slice the roots thinly and marinate with French dressing. Serve on lettuce and sprinkle with paprika. Be sure and save the broth.

Raw or cooked celery roots make a delicious addition to all sorts of salads.

## VEGETABLE GELATINE FROM THE SEA

A species of sea green, sometimes called vegetable gelatine and other times agar-agar, is derived from a sea algae and contains iodine. Dried agar-agar swells to many times its normal size when it reaches the intestines, and for that reason is used as a bulk food.

For cooking, agar-agar must first be dissolved in hot water. It can be eaten with cereals, in desserts instead of ordinary gelatine, or alone as a jelly. Powdered agar-agar makes delicious aspic and gelatine salads and desserts. For their low calorie value, agar-agar foods are included in many reducing diets.

¼ oz. agar-agar                              2½ or 3 cups boiling water
  1 cup cold water

Soak the agar-agar in the cold water until it is transparent. Drain off this water and pour on the boiling water—2½ cups if you wish to serve the jelly unmolded, 3 cups if molded. Let the agar-agar boil until thoroughly dissolved. Strain and add any fruit juice desired as a flavoring. When the jelly begins to set, add chopped fruits or vegetables.

## FRUIT SALADS

You can make delicious mixed raw salads with fresh ripe fruits by giving attention to freshness, texture, taste, and arrangement of the fruits. The choice of fruits which blend well is a matter of individual taste, limited only by what the market affords. The best fruits are always those which are in season, preferably those ripened in the sun. A combination of no more than four, one of which should be of the citrus group, makes a more palatable mixture than the hodge-podge of more fruits.

Here is a partial list of the variety of materials which may be added to fruits, either as part of the salad or as a garnish, to liven up the mixture:

| | |
|---|---|
| Mild cheese | Shredded rind of orange or lemon |
| Nuts | Crystallized ginger |
| Pimento | Candied peel |
| Water cress | Shredded coconut |
| Mints—spearmint, apple, orange, etc. | Sweet dried fruits |

Some of the best combinations are listed below, and they include the exceptions to the rule that citrus and sweet dried fruits do not combine well.

| | |
|---|---|
| Apple and mint | Persimmon and orange |
| Avocado and citrus | Pear and cream cheese |
| Banana and raisins or dates | Pineapple and cream cheese |
| Orange and ripe banana | Pineapple and date |
| Orange and black mission figs | Pineapple and mint |
| Orange and onion | Pineapple and strawberry |

Among fruits, orange and apple are basic ingredients. They supply sweet juiciness, crisp substance, and color. Orange has the added advantage of lending itself to preparation in various shapes—slices, whole or cubed, skinned sections, or small wedges cut across the sections from the core out.

The flavors and textures of fruits are so individual that when any mixture has combined to make a flavorsome blend, the matter of consistency will have been taken care of. The fruit should be prepared in large, neat slices, cubes, wedges, or balls—and with only the sharpest of tools—to avoid crushing or tearing. Include at least one fruit which will give a touch of harmonizing color, or use as a garnish a few cherries, grapes, berries, or a spoonful of a bright jelly or conserve. Always chill cut fruit and do not mix until just before serving time.

For the sake of health and time, do not pare fruits. Remove only that part of the coating which will peel off. When fruits must be pared before using, give special attention to those like apples and pears which darken on exposure to air. Oxidation will be delayed if the pieces of fruit are covered with acid fruit juices—citrus, pineapple. Oxidation is a visible illustration of what happens to all cut fruit upon exposure to air.

Keep the fruit chilled, and remember that the living values of a fruit start to diminish from the moment it is cut. That is why fruit juices should never be allowed to stand.

## FLORIDA SALAD

1 qt. fresh strawberries
1 fresh pineapple or 1 can pineapple

1 cup grated coconut

Cut the pineapple into cubes. Add the coconut to the strawberries and pineapple and mix with French dressing. Serve on crisp lettuce.

## GRAPEFRUIT AND STRAWBERRY SALAD

2 grapefruit
Honey to taste

1 pt. box strawberries
Water cress

Cut the grapefruit in halves. Loosen the pulp from the skin and remove the center stem after loosening each section on all three sides. Cut a hole in the center and fill with strawberries. Serve on beds of lettuce and garnish with water cress. Use a bit of honey for sweetening if any is desired.

## ORANGE MINT SALAD

Cut 4 large oranges in small pieces, add honey to taste and 2 tablespoons of finely chopped mint. Flavor with 1 tablespoon of lemon juice mixed with 1 teaspoon of honey and trim with leaves of fresh mint.

## PEACH SALAD

Remove the stones from large freestone peaches. Arrange on lettuce and fill the centers with finely chopped nuts. Top with ripe berries and garnish with fresh mint. Serve with fresh lime juice sweetened with honey.

## PEAR SALAD

1 cup diced pears
⅛ cup cut-up oranges

¾ cup diced unpeeled apples
2 tbsp. cream dressing

Mix all ingredients thoroughly and serve in nests of lettuce.

## TROPICAL SALAD

Arrange alternately, on lettuce or Romaine, half-slices of fresh or canned pineapple and sections of oranges. Serve with pineapple Fruit-Juice Dressing.

## WALDORF SALAD

2 red-skinned eating apples  
2 tbsp. lemon juice  
1 cup diced celery

⅓ cup chopped walnuts or almonds  
¼ tsp. vegetable salt

Dice the apples, leaving the skins on. Sprinkle the lemon juice over them to keep them white, add the celery and chopped nuts, and mix with mayonnaise to which the vegetable salt has been added. Serve in lettuce nests or on beds of shredded salad greens.

## CREAM-CHEESE FRUIT SALAD

Take a 3-oz. package of cream cheese and divide it into about 6 parts. Shape each piece into a ball and roll it in minced parsley. Pile the balls in the hollows of pear or peach halves or canned pineapple slices. Arrange in nests of lettuce leaves or on beds of shredded cabbage. Serve French dressing in a separate dish.

## SIMPLE SALAD COMBINATIONS

Salads offer unlimited opportunities of creative approach, but some of the simpler mixtures have been found to excel in certain definite proportions. Here are a few suggestions:

Apple and parsnip  
Cabbage, water cress, and raisin  
Carrot, apple, and raisin  
Carrot and pineapple—equal parts  
Celery and apple with dates or figs, or raisins and nuts  
Cooked peas, carrots, and celery  
Head lettuce, escarole, and French endive  
Tomatoes, green peppers, parsley, and onions  
Apples, cabbage, celery, and fresh mint  
Cucumber, artichokes, radishes, and water cress  
Carrots, celery root, and water cress

Shredded red cabbage and red apples
Shredded young beets, green peas, and onions
Shredded Romaine lettuce, grated cauliflower, and radishes
Shredded carrots, green peppers, parsley, and celery
Young spinach, cabbage, and water cress
Shredded fresh or unsweetened canned pineapple, red cabbage, and parsley
Shredded Swiss chard, grated carrots, and onions
Thinly sliced Spanish onion, chickory, and spinach
Green apples, radishes, and water cress
Cucumbers, tomatoes, and young green peas
Chopped endive, sliced beets, and water cress
Cabbage, carrots, celery, and sweet peppers

# CHAPTER 3

# *Salad Dressings*

———

THE THREE BASIC salad dressings—French, mayonnaise, and cooked dressing—are all descendants of the happy blend of lemon juice and olive oil which the ancient Romans used on their garden greens. Whether you like a tart dressing or a bland one, the zest of onion or its stronger cousin, garlic, the simple French dressing can be adapted to your taste.

## FRENCH DRESSINGS

In a real French dressing the proportion of olive or vegetable oil to lemon juice is 4 to 1, but experiment will show whether you prefer a little less oil. It will depend partly upon your taste and partly on the quality of the oil you use—and, of course, on the "shape" you're in.

To make a tossed green salad according to the mystic rites of French and Italian chefs, have your greens crisp and chilled, but perfectly dry. Rub a gashed clove of garlic over the inside of a wooden salad bowl. Pile the greens in lightly. Then drop by drop pour the oil over the leaves, lightly tossing them with a wooden spoon and fork. The idea ·is to have every leaf coated with oil, but not too much. A good thef considers himself disgraced if there is a drop of dressing left on the plate after the salad is eaten. Then drop by drop add the lemon juice, sprinkle with vegetable salt and paprika, and serve immediately. When you are expert enough to judge the amount of oil and lemon juice with the eye, you can mix your salad at the table. There is no quicker way to gain a reputation as an epicure.

And don't forget that all the sweet herbs can be used to point up a salad. Use them dried at any season, or in the summer put among your greens a few tender young leaves of anise, dill, borage, sweet marjoram, chopped rue—whatever you fancy.

French dressings can, however, be made up ahead of time and kept in the refrigerator. Crush a clove of garlic—if you use garlic—and put it in a fruit jar or any vessel which can be tightly covered and shaken. Put in the rest of the ingredients, shake well, and set away to chill. Remember, though, to take out the garlic after an hour or two. And shake up the dressing again when you are ready to use it because the oil and lemon will have a tendency to separate.

If you prefer onion to garlic, use 2 teaspoons of onion juice to 1 cup of salad oil. Last but not least, all dressings taste better, and are better, when some sweet is added. A good thing to remember in the preparation of any salad dressing is the five ingredients:

*Sweet:*
   Honey or natural brown sugar
*Sour:*
   Lemon is the best
*Salt:*
   Vegetable salt
*Oil:*
   Olive oil, if you are in the money; otherwise, peanut and corn oil
   are next best.
*Flavor:*
   This is where the herbs and your imagination come in.

### MY BASIC FRENCH DRESSING

| | |
|---|---|
| 1 clove garlic, crushed, or 2 tsp. onion juice | ½ tsp. paprika |
| 4 tbsp. lemon juice | 1 tsp. dry mustard |
| 1 tsp. honey (or to taste) | 1 cup olive or vegetable oil |
| 1 tsp. vegetable salt | |

Place the ingredients in a covered fruit jar and shake well.

## FRUIT FRENCH DRESSING

4 tbsp. grape juice
2½ tbsp. olive or vegetable oil
1 tbsp. lemon juice

½ tsp. vegetable salt
⅛ tsp. paprika

Put all the ingredients in a covered fruit jar and shake well. Serve with fruit salads.

## SWEET FRENCH DRESSING

½ cup lemon juice
½ cup honey
3 tbsp. olive or vegetable oil
1 tbsp. finely shredded onion

2 tbsp. minced green pepper
2 tbsp. minced celery
1 tsp. vegetable salt
½ tsp. paprika

Mix all the ingredients in a bowl. Add a small piece of ice and beat until thickened—about a minute. Serve with cabbage, combination, green, or tomato salads.

## TARRAGON FRENCH DRESSING

1 cup olive or vegetable oil
¼ cup lemon juice
2 tbsp. honey

½ tsp. vegetable salt
Few tarragon leaves, fresh or dried crushed

Put all the ingredients in a covered fruit jar and shake well. Let stand in the refrigerator at least half a day before using and shake well before serving. This dressing improves with standing.

## CHILI FRENCH DRESSING

6 tbsp. olive or vegetable oil
2 tbsp. lemon juice
1 tbsp. honey

¾ tsp. grated horse-radish
½ tsp. paprika
½ tsp. vegetable salt

Put all the ingredients in a covered fruit jar and shake well. Chill to thicken and serve with egg, avocado, or green salad.

## HERB FRENCH DRESSING

Add about 3 tablespoons of minced fresh herbs to a cup of dressing. Parsley, chives, tarragon, basil, sweet marjoram, and thyme are a few suggestions to start with. Use them mixed or all one kind. If you use dried herbs instead of fresh, add only 1 tablespoon of herbs.

## AVOCADO FRENCH DRESSING

1 medium-sized avocado                    ½ tsp. vegetable salt
2 tbsp. mayonnaise                        Dash of paprika
½ cup French dressing (about)

Peel a ripe avocado and mash the pulp until smooth. Add the mayonnaise and then beat in enough French dressing to give the mixture the thickness of heavy whipped cream. Add salt and paprika to taste.

## OTHER VARIATIONS OF FRENCH DRESSING

Variety is the secret of getting your husband to eat two helpings of your salads. There are so many varieties of salad dressings, try not to have the same salad dressing twice in the same week. Following are some suggestions of ingredients which can be added to either the Basic French Dressing or to the Tarragon French Dressing. Your own tastes and imagination will suggest others. The quantities given here are based on dressing made with 1 cup of olive or vegetable oil.

For *Sweet Fruit Salads:*
Add ½ cup cream cheese and blend well.
Add 4 tbsp. chopped water cress and 4 tbsp. chili sauce. (This is particularly good with pear salad.)

For *Tomato Salads:*
Add ½ cup cream cheese, 2 tbsp. chopped unpeeled cucumber, 2 tbsp. chopped green pepper, and 2 tbsp. chopped water cress.
Add 4 tbsp. Roquefort or bleu cheese, crumbled. (Your rich relatives will love this.)

For *Meat Salads:*
Add 2 tbsp. horse-radish.
Add ¼ cup chili sauce and ½ tsp. soy sauce.
Add 2 tbsp. minced sweet onion, 3 tbsp. minced parsley, and 1 tbsp. minced pimento.

For *Fish and Chicken Salads:*
Add 4 tbsp. chopped green olives.

For *Green Salads:*
Add 4 tbsp. crumbled Roquefort or bleu cheese.
Add 2 tbsp. golden wheat germ, 1½ tbsp. minced parsley, 1½ tbsp. minced chives.

*For Vegetable Salads:*

To the Tarragon French Dressing add 3 tbsp. more lemon juice, 1 tbsp. chopped green olives, 1 tbsp. chopped pimento. This dressing can also be served hot over cabbage.

## HOLIDAY DRESSING

4 tbsp. olive or vegetable oil
4 tbsp. juice from sweetened stewed cranberries

1 tsp. lemon juice (or to taste)
¼ tsp. vegetable salt

Put the ingredients in a bowl and beat until thoroughly blended. Serve this tasty red dressing with any fruit salad.

## ENERGY DRESSING

½ cup olive or vegetable oil
¼ cup tomato juice
4 tbsp. lemon juice
2 tbsp. honey

¼ tsp. vegetable salt
1 egg yolk
2 tbsp. chopped garden greens

Combine the oil, juices, honey, and salt in a bowl. Beat the egg yolk into this mixture, and just before serving add the chopped greens. Serve immediately.

## SOUR-CREAM DRESSING

1 cup heavy cream, well soured
2 tbsp. lemon juice
½ tsp. vegetable salt

1 tbsp. honey
¼ tsp. paprika

Mix all the ingredients thoroughly and beat until foamy. Serve with either fruit or vegetable salads. Especially good with cabbage. Add 1 tbsp. chopped chives and ½ tsp. grated horse-radish for vegetable salads.

## PINEAPPLE CREAM-CHEESE DRESSING

1 3-oz. package cream cheese
Pinch of vegetable salt

⅓ cup pineapple juice (about)

Break up the cream cheese with a fork, then cream until soft. Work in the vegetable salt and about 4 tablespoons of pineapple juice. Then with an egg beater whip until the cheese is the consistency of whipped cream, adding more pineapple juice as you whip. But be sure not to get the mixture too thin. Serve with fruit salads or cabbage.

## ALMOND CREAM DRESSING

Thin 2 tablespoons of almond butter (very finely ground almonds) with 3 tablespoons of fruit juice, milk, or cream.

## PEANUT-BUTTER DRESSING

Thin 2 tablespoons of fresh peanut butter with 3 tablespoons of pineapple juice to a smooth creamy consistency. Excellent over carrot and raisin salad.

## DRESSINGS FOR REDUCING DIETS

### FRUIT-JUICE DRESSING

Cover your greens, or saturate fruit and shredded vegetables, with fruit juice. Use orange, pineapple, lemon, or lime juice seasoned with a pinch of vegetable salt and a bit of honey.

Apples, celery, carrots, and cabbage are particularly delicious when saturated with fruit juices.

### VEGETABLE REDUCING DRESSING

½ cup finely chopped vegetables
1 cup liquid from canned okra
Juice of 1 lemon
1 cup tomato

½ tbsp. honey
¼ tsp. vegetable salt
Dash of garlic

Use celery, parsley, onion, and green pepper for the chopped vegetables, or any other vegetables in season. Add the okra liquid and thin with lemon juice and tomato pulp. Season with honey and vegetable salt and add a dash of garlic—onion if you prefer, unless onions are among your chopped vegetables.

### YOGURT REDUCING DRESSING

½ cup yogurt
¼ tsp. honey

⅛ tsp. vegetable salt
½ tsp. lemon juice
Grated rind of ¼ lemon

Beat all the ingredients together. Serve with any raw-vegetable salad. Vary by including a few chopped green olives, 1 tablespoon of chopped water cress or chives. Tastes like sour-cream dressing.

## BUTTERMILK DRESSING

½ cup thick buttermilk
¼ tsp. honey
⅛ tsp. vegetable salt

½ tsp. lemon juice
Grated rind of ¼ lemon

Beat all the ingredients together in a bowl. Serve with shredded cabbage or any vegetable combination. For variety, add chopped green olives, water cress, or parsley.

## MAYONNAISE DRESSINGS

The secret of making mayonnaise lies in adding the oil gradually. At first add it a drop at a time or the oil will float on top of the finished dressing. Don't give up if this happens. Beat your batch of dressing into another egg yolk as if you were starting a new batch.

After about a quarter of the oil has been beaten in, you can add the rest in slightly larger doses.

A whole egg can be used instead of an egg yolk, but it makes a thinner dressing.

## MAYONNAISE

1 egg yolk
1 cup olive or vegetable oil
2 tbsp. lemon juice

½ tsp. vegetable salt
½ tsp. honey

Slightly beat the egg yolk. Add the oil drop by drop, beating briskly the while with a rotary egg beater. After the first ¼ cup has been beaten in, you can add the oil faster. Thin with lemon juice until the dressing is of the consistency and tartness you want. Fold in the salt and honey. Store in a covered jar in the refrigerator. (Don't let the jar rest against the freezing unit or the oil will float to the top.)

## VARIATIONS OF MAYONNAISE

To 1 cup of mayonnaise, add any one of the following:

*For Vegetable Salads:*
   Thick buttermilk, about 1 cup. More buttermilk makes a thinner dressing.
      Delicious on mixed vegetable salads.
   ⅓ cup French dressing.

# Salad Dressings 39

1 cup chili sauce, 1 cup minced celery, 2 tsp. minced chives, 2 tsp. minced parsley.

⅓ cup condensed tomato soup.

½ cup chopped olives, ⅓ cup chili sauce, 2 chopped hard-cooked eggs.

*For Fish Salads:*
½ cup finely chopped unpeeled cucumbers.
2 to 4 tbsp. chopped chives.

*For Meat Salads:*
4 tbsp. horse-radish.
Mild mustard to taste.

*For Fruit Salads:*
2 tbsp. orange juice and 2 tbsp. pineapple juice, first mixed with 2 tbsp. honey.

4 tbsp. jelly. Beat together until smooth.

1 cup heavy cream. Mash 2 3-oz. packages of cream cheese and stir in smoothly. Add 1 cup crumbled Roquefort or bleu cheese and 2 tbsp. lemon juice. Good with all fruits and also lettuce and tomato. Let your figure be your guide!

½ cup heavy cream, whipped. Fruit may also be added to this whipped cream dressing. For instance:

1 cup crushed strawberries or raspberries sweetened with 2 tbsp. honey.

2 tsp. grated orange rind and ⅓ cup orange juice.

⅔ cup drained crushed pineapple and 1 tbsp. lemon juice.

## CREAM-CHEESE MAYONNAISE

1 3-oz. package cream cheese
2 tbsp. lemon juice
¼ tsp. onion juice
½ tsp. honey
½ tsp. paprika
¾ tsp. vegetable salt
4 tbsp. olive or vegetable oil

Cream the cheese until soft and smooth. Work in the lemon juice and seasonings, then gradually beat in the salad oil. Beating in another tablespoon of oil will make a thicker dressing.

This dressing, which does not have the oily texture of a true mayonnaise, can be served with any vegetable or fruit salad for which mayonnaise is appropriate. And the same savory ingredients used to enhance the flavor of mayonnaise can also be added to Cream-Cheese Mayonnaise.

## THOUSAND-ISLAND DRESSING

To 1 recipe Mayonnaise, add:
4 hard-cooked eggs, chopped
½ cup sieved tomato pulp
1 sweet green pepper, minced

½ cup minced celery
¼ cup minced onion

## DELECTABLE CREAM AND HONEY DRESSINGS

Some of the most delicious and unusual salad dressings are those made of cream, cheese, or honey. Although it is true that most salad dressings belong to one of the three main families—French, mayonnaise, and cooked—some of the best dressings are orphans which belong to no family. Don't let your imagination stop short with the well-known dressings. Adopt some of these dressings and watch the salad-haters in your family fall into line.

## AVOCADO CREAM DRESSING

1 cup avocado pulp
Pinch of vegetable salt

2 tbsp. honey
1 cup heavy cream

Rub the avocado through a sieve or fruit press. Add the salt and honey and mix thoroughly. Whip the cream and fold in the avocado pulp. Serve with fruit salads. Especially delicious on molded grapefruit.

## DATE CREAM DRESSING

½ cup pitted soft dates
Pinch of vegetable salt

1 cup heavy cream

You must have soft dates for this dressing because they are rubbed through a sieve or fruit press. Mix the salt in thoroughly. Whip the cream and fold in the date pulp. Serve with fruit salads.

## HONEY CREAM DRESSING

2 tbsp. honey
5 tbsp. heavy cream

5 tbsp. lemon juice
Pinch of vegetable salt

Mix all ingredients thoroughly and serve with fruit salads.

## LEMON HONEY DRESSING

Mix the juice and grated rind of 1 lemon with 6 tbsp. of honey. Serve with apple and parsnip salad or any sweet one.

## ENGLISH DRESSING

2 egg yolks
1 can condensed milk
½ cup lemon juice

1 tsp. vegetable salt
¼ cup melted butter
1 tsp. mustard
1 tsp. vegetable salt

Place the unbeaten egg yolks in a small mixing bowl. Add the milk, stirring constantly. Add the lemon juice, mustard, and salt, then the melted butter. Set aside to stiffen, then place in a covered jar and keep in the refrigerator.

## PEANUT DRESSING

1½ cups fine dry whole-wheat bread crumbs
½ cup finely chopped peanuts
½ cup heavy cream

2 or 3 tbsp. melted butter
Vegetable salt to taste
Dash of paprika

Mix the bread crumbs and chopped peanuts with the cream. Add the salt and paprika to the melted butter and combine with the rest to a smooth, creamy consistency.

CHAPTER 4

# Soups in the Modern Manner

THICK OR THIN, cold or hot, soups are delicious to the taste and start the digestive juices flowing. A good hot soup, even a thin broth, gives an immediate feeling of nourishment, which encourages slower eating and discourages overeating during the rest of the meal. All these things promote better digestion and better dispositions.

Soups range from clear broths, bouillons, and consommés to chowders, bouillabaisse, minestrone, and *petite marmite,* any one of which is a meal in itself. Jellied soups refresh the jaded palate in summer; cold fruit soups are just beginning to come into favor in this country. All these soups have one purpose in common—to supply nourishment in liquid form. Hence the basic principle in soup cookery is to draw out the life from the ingredients used, and to accomplish this cold water is best. Excess heat is the enemy of good soup, for hot water seals the food elements into the meat or vegetables, or whatever you are using for stock, and toughens the fibers so that the juices do not all get into the liquid.

Start soups in cold water, bring them to the simmering point, and continue to cook at simmering temperature, so that only the faintest ripple disturbs the surface of the liquid. Add vegetable salt when the foods are tender, a few minutes before the soup has finished cooking. Salt tends to draw out juices, which is what we want in soup making, contrary to the usual procedure.

Avoid cabbage, cauliflower, and other foods rich in sulphur. If you want these foods for flavor, add them finely shredded about 3 minutes before turning off the heat. If sulphur foods are cooked with the stock they may cause discomfort.

The finer you cut your soup ingredients and the less you cook them, the more delicate the flavor. If at all possible buy, borrow, or steal one of those handy gadgets called the "snitzler." It shreds vegetables into delectable little shreds for broths and salads, and saves your hands. It also reduces cooking time to a minimum.

*Sherry in Soups:* For festive occasions or when you entertain your pompous relatives, you may want to use a bit of sherry in your soups; 2 teaspoons of sherry to a serving gives an elegant and distinct flavor. Don't let the sherry cook, however; add it just before you remove the soup from the heat. You will probably like it, especially in black bean soup—the favorite of the Duchess of Windsor. Use sherry in cream of mushroom or asparagus soup, or add a bit to your oyster stew the next time you entertain that man.

## HOW TO MAKE GOOD HAUSER BROTH

Get yourself two empty milk bottles, preferably the square kind. Keep one of them filled with my good broth, and into the other pour every bit of vegetable water, or pot liquor, you can lay your hands on. Remember that the water in which vegetables have been cooked is full of good food elements, including vitamins B and C. At least half the money you spend for vegetables goes down the sink whenever you throw away any of these juices. I go so far as to tell my students that if they must throw away something, they should throw out the vegetables and drink the juice.

My simple vegetable broth has given nourishment and comfort to thousands of people during the past twenty-five years. You can drink it hot or cold, winter or summer, and any time of the day or night. Drink all you want when you are on a restricted diet, or on my Seven-Day Elimination Diet. Hauser Broth is alkaline, low in calories, and starts healthy digestion when taken at the beginning of a meal.

By making Hauser Broth a few times, you will discover the mixtures of flavors which most appeal to you. Simply use the basic recipe as a foundation, then let your imagination and experience guide you in combining various vegetables.

*In any recipe which calls for water,* use Hauser Broth or your saved-up collection of vegetable waters. Sauces, gravies, cocktails, and stews take on new character; otherwise flat-tasting vegetables are twice as good when cooked in broth. You good ladies who still make your own bread, muffins, and other baked goods can make them even better by using Hauser Broth in place of water. Keeping those two milk bottles filled with broth and pot liquor will save you much money and help to keep you on the sunny side of life.

Here is the famous recipe:

### HAUSER BROTH

1 cup finely shredded carrots
1 cup finely shredded celery, leaves and all
½ cup shredded spinach
1 tbsp. chopped parsley

1 large onion, chopped
1 large celery root, chopped (whenever you can get it)
1 heaping tsp. vegetable salt
1 qt. water

Put all these shredded vegetables in cold or warm—not hot—water. Simmer over a low flame for not more than 30 minutes. Then turn off the heat, add your heaping teaspoonful of vegetable salt, and let stand 10 minutes. Strain.

This gives you the basic stock from which you can concoct endless varieties of vegetable broth. In my house we add a small can of tomatoes, or when fresh tomatoes are fat and ripe we cut up a few and add them to the broth. The onion and celery root give body and flavor to the soup and should always be used whatever else you have. For more spice, add a chopped green pepper or 2 tablespoons of chives. A handful of fresh okra or ½ can of canned okra is especially good for the inner man.

A pinch (be careful) of old-fashioned garden herbs can entirely change the character of the broth. Try a bit of basil, savory, thyme, or marjoram—and of course a bit of garlic now and then, but ever so little. The Italian saying is, "Garlic keeps colds away"; but I say, "Garlic keeps everybody away—if you use too much."

Keep a supply of freshly dried herbs on your shelves, a jar of pure garlic powder, and a big shaker of vegetable salt. Those who like the meat flavor in broth can add a tablespoonful of that wonderful yeast extract which used to come only from Switzerland but now is available here.

## VEGETABLE BROTH FOR LAZY PEOPLE

If you live in Alaska, or in a climate where fresh vegetables are not always available—or if you're just plain lazy—you can buy a good prepared vegetable broth which comes from sunny California. All you do is put a teaspoonful of this powdered broth in a cup of very hot water. Or, still better, add a teaspoonful of the powder to a cup of hot tomato juice. Sprinkle a little fresh parsley or chives over the top to make the broth more attractive and give it added nourishment.

## SPRING VEGETABLE SOUP

Take any clear broth or vegetable water you may have in your refrigerator and add very finely chopped vegetables. Simmer for 10 minutes. The vegetables will be crisp and colorful, not dull and mushy as so many vegetables in soups are.

## OTHER VEGETABLE SOUPS

### CREAM OF GREEN PEA SOUP

Put 1 cup of shelled fresh peas through the fine knife of a food chopper or into a Fletcherizer. Add 1 pint of cold Hauser Broth, bring slowly to the simmering point, and simmer 5 minutes. Season and remove from the fire. Then add ½ cup of sweet cream and serve without reheating.

### CREAM OF ALMOND SOUP

| | |
|---|---|
| ½ cup blanched almonds | 1 cup Hauser Broth |
| 1 tbsp. butter | ¾ tsp. vegetable salt |
| 1 medium onion, chopped fine | 2 tsp. minced green pepper or |
| 1 tbsp. whole-wheat flour | finely chopped cucumber |
| 1 cup milk | 1 egg yolk, beaten |

Put the almonds through the fine knife of a food chopper or pulverize in an electric Fletcherizer, adding a bit of milk to make a smooth paste. Melt the butter in the top of a double boiler and cook the onion in it until transparent. Add the flour and cook a minute while stirring. Moisten with a tablespoon of broth, stir in the almond paste, and by degrees add the rest of the milk, stirring all the while. Bring to the boiling point, place over hot water, and cook for 10 minutes. Add the broth and seasonings and heat thoroughly but do not cook. Mix the beaten egg yolk with a little milk and add to the hot soup, stirring it in thoroughly. Taste to make sure the seasoning is right and serve immediately with crisp croutons.

## DUCHESS OF WINDSOR BEAN SOUP

| | |
|---|---|
| 2 cups black beans | 1 tsp. vegetable salt |
| 1½ cups cold Hauser Broth | Dash of paprika |
| 1 small onion, sliced | Juice of 1 lemon |
| 1 cup diced celery | 1 tbsp. whole-wheat flour |
| 2 tbsp. butter | 1 tbsp. sherry |
| 1 small bay leaf | |

Cover the beans with cold water and soak overnight. Most of the water will be absorbed by the beans; if some is left, do not drain, but reduce the Hauser Broth to 1 cup. Brown the onion and celery in 1 tablespoon of the butter until they are golden brown. Add to the beans with the bay leaf. Let simmer for about 2 hours; by then the beans should be soft. Be sure to keep plenty of liquid on the beans while they are cooking; add more broth as it boils away. Put the beans through a fine sieve and reheat. Add the vegetable salt, paprika, and lemon juice. Thicken with the other tablespoon of butter browned with the whole-wheat flour. Let cook another 5 minutes, turn off the heat, and add the sherry. Serve piping hot garnished with a thin slice of lemon or some hard-boiled egg yolk forced through a sieve. Your most blasé relatives will like this soup.

## LENTIL AND VEGETABLE SOUP

| | |
|---|---|
| ½ cup dried lentils | ¼ cup butter |
| 2½ cups Hauser Broth (about) | ½ tsp. vegetable salt |
| 1 medium-sized onion, chopped | ½ tsp. celery seed |
| 1 clove garlic, minced | ½ tsp. natural brown sugar |
| 1 small carrot, finely shredded | ¼ cup butter |
| 3 outside stalks celery with leaves | Pinch of thyme or shredded lemon |
| 1 cup canned tomato | rind |
| 1 sprig parsley | |

Wash the lentils carefully and put to soak in 1 cup of water in the pan you intend to cook them in. In the morning add 1 cup of Hauser Broth and bring to the boiling point. Reduce the heat and simmer until the lentils are soft enough to mash—about 1 hour.

Meanwhile prepare the vegetables. Brown the onion and garlic in a little vegetable oil. Slice the celery stalks thin across the grain. Chop the celery leaves with the parsley.

Mash the lentils and add all the vegetables with enough Hauser Broth to cover—about 1½ cups. Bring to the boil, reduce the heat, and simmer gently until the vegetables are done—about 20 minutes. Add the butter and seasonings and let simmer another 10 minutes to blend the flavors, stirring occasionally. Taste before serving and add whatever is needed.

## MUSHROOM BROTH

| | |
|---|---|
| ½ cup minced mushrooms | 2¼ cups Hauser Broth |
| ¼ tsp. vegetable salt | 2 tbsp. minced parsley |
| 1½ tbsp. chopped onion | Grated nutmeg to taste |
| 2 tsp. butter | |

Sprinkle the minced mushrooms with the vegetable salt. Melt the butter in the top of a double boiler over direct heat and cook the onion in it until golden brown. Add the mushrooms, cover, and simmer until the juice is extracted—about 10 minutes—stirring occasionally. Add the Hauser Broth and place the pan over hot water. Let the soup heat through, then add seasonings. Keep over hot water, but not boiling, for at least 15 minutes to blend the flavors.

## PUREED LEGUME SOUP

| | |
|---|---|
| ½ cup dried legumes (lima beans, lentils, green split peas, etc.) | 1½ cups Hauser Broth |
| 1 small onion, chopped | ¼ tsp. vegetable salt |
| 3 tsp. butter | Basil, thyme, or garlic to taste |
| 1 outside stalk celery with leaves, chopped | ¼ cup finely chopped spinach or parsley |

Wash the peas or beans, pick over, and put to soak in the pan you expect to cook them in with 1 cup water. In the morning add another cup of water. Bring to the boiling point, reduce the heat, and simmer until the legumes are soft enough to mash—about 1 hour.

Meanwhile prepare the vegetables, add them to the soup, and simmer until all the vegetables are done—about 20 minutes more. If you like a smooth consistency, rub through a fine colander. To this purée add the broth, butter, vegetable salt, and seasonings. Heat through but do not boil. Stir in the chopped greens just before serving. (Garlic goes well with lima beans, basil with split peas, and thyme with lentils.)

## SOYA TOMATO SOUP

⅜ cup chopped onions
1 tbsp. butter
1½ cups tomato juice or puréed tomato pulp
1 small leaf basil, crumbled
1 tsp. vegetable salt

2 tbsp. vegetable oil
3 tbsp. soya flour
1 tbsp. minced celery leaves
1 tbsp. minced spinach
1½ cups Hauser Broth

Sauté the onion in the butter until golden brown. Add the tomato juice or pulp, basil leaf, and vegetable salt. Start over low heat. Meanwhile mix the oil and soya flour to a paste. Add hot soup by degrees, stirring thoroughly after each addition, until the mixture is thin enough to pour. Pour the mixture into the soup and stir thoroughly until the boiling point is reached. Let boil for a few minutes to cook the flour, then reduce the heat and simmer for 15 minutes. Add the chopped leaves and Hauser Broth. Taste for correct seasoning and sweeten with natural brown sugar if desired. Heat thoroughly before serving, but do not allow to cook again. Garnish each serving with plenty of chopped parsley.

## CREAM OF CARROT PURÉE

½ cup mashed cooked carrots
½ cup rich cream
1½ cups Hauser Broth
½ tsp. vegetable salt

½ tsp. butter
1 tbsp. chopped parsley, chives, water cress, or any desired green

Mix the carrots, broth, salt, and butter in a saucepan and heat thoroughly. Season as desired with celery salt, onion juice, garlic seasoning, nutmeg, or whatever you like. Just before serving add the cream, but do not let boil. Sprinkle with a bit of paprika.

## CREAM OF GREENS SOUP

1 medium-sized onion
3 tbsp. butter
½ bunch water cress, or ⅛ lb. sorrel, spinach, lettuce, or escarole
2 large outer leaves lettuce
1 tbsp. whole-wheat flour

¾ cup milk
¾ cup Hauser Broth
⅜ tsp. vegetable salt
Grated nutmeg, celery salt, basil, or chervil to taste
1 egg yolk, beaten

Chop the onion fine and cook in 2 tablespoons of the butter in the top of a double boiler for 5 minutes without browning. Add the greens and lettuce leaves cut into thin shreds with scissors. Cover and cook slowly, stirring occasionally, until the leaves are wilted—about 5 minutes. Add the flour and stir for a minute to mix it thoroughly into the butter. Slowly add the milk, stirring constantly, and bring the mixture to the boil. Cook another 10 minutes, then add the Hauser Broth, vegetable salt, and the remaining butter. Heat through but do not cook. Just before serving, pour the hot soup over the beaten yolk of egg, stir thoroughly, and serve with crisp croutons.

## SOYA SOUP

3 tbsp. butter
½ cup soya flour
⅔ cup hot water
2 cups Hauser Broth
¼ tsp. vegetable salt
⅛ tsp. curry powder

½ tsp. natural brown sugar
½ tsp. vegetable salt
Pinch of basil or 2 tsp. Chinese soy
   sauce
2 tbsp. finely chopped parsley, chives,
   or any desired leafy vegetable

Melt the butter in the top of a double boiler. Add the soya flour and cook a few minutes, stirring to blend thoroughly. By degrees stir in the hot water and let simmer until very thick—about 15 minutes. It will need stirring to keep from sticking, so watch it. Add the broth, place the pan over boiling water, and bring to the boiling point. Add the curry, sugar, chopped vegetables, and the desired seasoning. Taste to see if the seasoning is right and remove from the heat. Serve with crisp croutons.

Almost any leftover cooked vegetable can be chopped and added to the soup up to ¾ cup. But first taste the combination you have in mind to be sure it will make a palatable blend.

## TOMATO AND CELERY SOUP

½ cup fresh raw celery juice
1½ cups canned tomato or tomato juice
¾ tsp. finely shredded onion
½ tsp. garlic seasoning or ½ clove
   garlic, minced

½ tsp. vegetable salt
2 tsp. butter
½ tsp. natural brown sugar
1 tbsp. chopped parsley
Pinch of basil

Put all the ingredients in a saucepan and heat thoroughly but do not boil. Taste to make sure the seasoning is right. Just before serving, add 1 tablespoon of minced green pepper for flavor and garnish.

## ONION SOUP

6 onions, sliced
3 tbsp. fresh butter
6 cups Hauser Broth

1 tsp. vegetable salt
4 slices whole-wheat toast
Grated Parmesan cheese to taste

Sauté the onions in the butter until golden brown. Add the Hauser Broth and bring to the boil. Let simmer over low heat for 10 or 15 minutes, just until the onions are tender. Pour into individual earthenware ramekins or *petite marmite* dishes. Cut the toast into rounds and put a slice on top of each dish of soup. Sprinkle grated cheese on top of the toast and put under the broiler or in a hot oven until the cheese is melted and slightly brown. Serve hot, hot, in the baking dishes.

## ONION SOUP FOR REDUCERS

A delicious vegetable soup stock for clear bouillon, cream soup, or vegetable soup is made as follows:

Shred 2 medium-sized onions finely, cutting crosswise with a very sharp knife. Place in a heavy skillet with only enough water to start the steam. Place over a low flame and allow to cook until the water is evaporated and the onions browned down to the pan. Add 1 pint of Hauser Broth and cook about 5 minutes. The liquid will be a golden brown. Season with vegetable salt and serve strained or with the onions in, as preferred. This is a satisfying broth when on a reducing diet or the elimination diet.

## ENERGY POTATO SOUP

Here at last is a recipe where you throw the potato away and use the peelings! Scrub the potatoes thoroughly, then peel them with peelings ½ inch thick. Dice the peelings.

| | |
|---|---|
| 1 cup diced potato peels | ½ tsp. vegetable salt |
| 1 cup Hauser Broth | ½ cup sweet cream |
| ½ tbsp. butter | 2 tbsp. minced parsley |
| 1 cup finely shredded onion | |

Simmer the potato peels in the broth for 15 minutes. Melt the butter in a heavy skillet and cook the onions until golden brown. When the potato peels are tender, add the onion, blend for a minute over the flame, and add the vegetable salt. Turn off the heat, add the sweet cream and minced parsley, and serve without reheating.

## BORSCH

| | |
|---|---|
| 4 small young beets, chopped fine | 2 tbsp. butter |
| 1 onion, chopped | 1 qt. Hauser Broth |
| 1 potato, sliced | ½ pt. sour cream, lightly whipped, |
| 2 tbsp. natural brown sugar | or yogurt |
| Juice of 2 lemons | Vegetable salt and paprika to taste |

Put the beets, onion, potato, and butter in 1 pint of water and bring to the boil. Reduce the heat and simmer, tightly covered, for 20 minutes. Add the broth, lemon juice, sugar, salt, and paprika. Bring to the boil again, then simmer for half an hour. Serve hot or cold, topped with whipped sour cream or thick yogurt.

## LEEK AND POTATO SOUP

½ clove garlic, minced
1 medium leek, chopped (about 1¼ cups)
½ tbsp. vegetable oil
½ lb. potatoes
1½ cups boiling water
½ small green pepper, minced

¾ tsp. vegetable salt
1 tbsp. butter
¾ cup milk, or Hauser Broth mixed with 2 tbsp. heavy cream
1 tbsp. chopped chives or green onion tops

Sauté the garlic and leek in the vegetable oil until slightly browned—5 to 10 minutes. Cut washed but not peeled potatoes into slices ⅛ inch thick. Pour in the boiling water and simmer until the potatoes are done—about 20 minutes.

Mash the potatoes with a fork and add the remaining ingredients. Heat through but do not let boil again. Taste and complete the seasoning with grated onion, garlic seasoning, salt, cream, celery salt, nutmeg, or grated cheese as desired.

## OTHER VEGETABLE AND POTATO SOUPS

Other vegetables can be used in the recipe for Leek and Potato Soup. Substitute, for instance, turnip, celery, onion, or spinach for the leeks. In the case of spinach soup, add finely chopped raw spinach 10 minutes before the potatoes are done. Mash but do not strain.

## GUMBO

Gumbos, so popular in the South, are soups thickened with okra, either fresh, canned, or powdered. Be careful of the powdered okra—a little goes a long way. One-half teaspoon of okra powder will thicken 1 pint of soup.

Mock gumbos can be thickened by other means. For a very heavy soup, use natural brown rice flour, 1 level tablespoon to each cup of liquid. Or use 1 tablespoon of gelatin to 1 pint of soup.

A word of warning—cook gumbos in glass or enamel pots. They may turn black in a metal one.

## RAW VEGETABLE SOUPS

Uncooked soups made of raw fresh vegetable juice are a new vogue. They add a pleasing flavor to the menu, are very nourishing and easily digested. The vegetable juices should preferably be freshly made. Heat quickly, but do not let them reach the boiling point. Overheating destroys the color, flavor, and food values.

Try any of your favorite vegetable juices mixed with milk (half and half). Especially desirable for children and "skinnies."

### CREAM OF RAW VEGETABLE SOUP

1½ cups Hauser Broth  
¼ tsp. vegetable salt  
⅛ tsp. finely chopped onion  
Pinch of natural brown sugar

½ tsp. butter  
½ cup fresh vegetable juice  
¼ cup heavy cream

Put the broth, salt, onion, sugar, and butter into a saucepan and heat through. Just before serving add the vegetable juice—celery, spinach, beet, or tomato—and the cream. Do not boil after the vegetable juice and cream have been added. Garnish with finely chopped parsley or chives.

### OLD-FASHIONED SOUP STOCKS

Stock is the basic soup made from the original ingredients. Sometimes it is clarified and served as bouillon, broth, or consommé. Sometimes it is used as a part of more elaborate soups. Brown stock usually means stock made from beef, and the beef is browned before the cold water is added. White stock is made from chicken or veal or both. And vegetable stock is an extract of vegetable juices, as described under Hauser Broth.

If you are not serving stock immediately as broth, strain it, cool it quickly, and store it in the refrigerator. When ready to use meat stock, remove the layer of fat congealed on the surface, strain through several thicknesses of cheesecloth, and clarify.

## TO CLARIFY MEAT STOCK

For each quart of stock, use the white and shell of 1 egg. Beat the white slightly, crush the shell, and mix with 2 tablespoons of cold water. Add to the cold stock, bring slowly to a boil, and boil 5 minutes, stirring constantly. Add ½ cup of cold water and let stand 10 minutes, then strain again through several thicknesses of cheesecloth.

## PREPARED SOUP STOCKS

Time was when every housewife had a soup kettle simmering on the back of the stove. Nowadays not everyone has the time to prepare stock. You can buy canned bouillons and consommés, or bouillon cubes and pastes which make a soup with the addition of hot water. If you like the flavor of meat stock but do not wish to use it, you can buy in any health store meatless bouillon which can be kept on hand. Put a teaspoonful into a cup and add hot water, and you will have a basic stock which can be served clear or built into a variety of soups with the addition of herbs, vegetables, or cream. You can also buy prepared vegetable stocks, such as the Hauser Broth, which will give you an instant delicious soup to be served as is or combined with other ingredients just as you would use stock made from fresh vegetables.

In any of the recipes in this chapter, you may substitute Hauser Broth for meat stock, or vice versa, according to your preference.

## OLD-FASHIONED BROWN STOCK

| | |
|---|---|
| 1 lb. cracked soup bones | 2 sprigs parsley, chopped |
| 4 lb. shin of beef cut in small pieces | 1 bay leaf |
| 3 qt. cold water | ¼ tsp. marjoram |
| ⅓ cup chopped celery | ¼ tsp. thyme |
| ⅓ cup diced carrots | 1 tbsp. vegetable salt |
| ⅓ cup chopped onion | |

Scrape the marrow from the bones into a heavy kettle. Brown the meat in the marrow fat, add the bones and cold water, cover, and bring slowly to the simmering point. Remove the scum which forms on top the water. Add the vegetables and herbs and simmer gently for 3 to 4 hours, periodically removing the scum. Add the vegetable salt shortly before removing from the heat. Strain, cool, remove fat, and clarify.

## WHITE STOCK

Prepare as for Brown Stock, using veal knuckle, fowl, or a combination of both instead of beef.

## BUTTER DUMPLINGS

| | |
|---|---|
| 1 tbsp. butter, creamed | ½ tsp. brown sugar |
| 1 egg, beaten | ½ tsp. vegetable salt |
| 2 tbsp. sifted whole-wheat flour | 1 tsp. chopped parsley or chives |

Cream the butter, add the egg, then the flour, sugar, salt, and chopped parsley. Stir the mixture until it is light and smooth. Drop from the tip of a teaspoon into boiling hot broth. Cover the kettle and let boil for about 15 minutes. Delicious in chicken broth.

## BOUILLON

Bouillon is simply Brown Stock clarified and reheated. If desired, add 1 cup of tomato or celery juice to each cup of bouillon, top with whipped cream, and sprinkle with parsley.

Most canned bouillons will not jelly without the addition of gelatine (see Jellied Consommé).

## CONSOMME

Consommé is a mixture of brown and white stock, made by following the recipe for Brown Stock, using 2 pounds of beef and 2 pounds of veal knuckle. Brown 1 pound of the beef but not the rest of the meat.

Various garnishes and additional ingredients enhance the flavor of consommé and bring changes upon the basic theme. Add 1 tablespoon each of finely chopped chicken and blanched almonds to each cup of consommé. For special occasions add ¼ cup of claret wine to each cup and garnish with finely chopped parsley. Top each serving of consommé with a spoonful of whipped cream and sprinkle with grated Parmesan cheese and paprika. Finely chopped vegetables should be added to each serving—carrots, celery, leeks, onions, and turnips are excellent and make for a better-balanced soup.

## JELLIED CONSOMMÉ

Homemade consommés—and some canned ones—will jelly when placed in the refrigerator. Store overnight.

If a consommé will not jelly by itself, use 1 teaspoon of gelatine to each cup of consommé. Soak the gelatine 5 minutes in a little cold water, add the hot consommé, and stir until the gelatine is dissolved. Season to taste, pour into a pan, and set in the refrigerator until firm. Just before serving, break up the consommé lightly with a fork.

## RICH BOUILLON

1½ tbsp. butter
¼ cup chopped onion
2 cups Hauser Broth

1 tsp. vegetable salt
2 tbsp. cream cheese

Melt the butter in a pan and cook the onion in it until golden brown. Add ¼ cup of the broth, cover, and simmer gently until tender—about 10 minutes. Add the rest of the broth and the vegetable salt. Stir and simmer a few minutes to blend the flavors. Before filling the soup cups, put some riced cream cheese in the bottom. Garnish with any minced green or with a sprinkling of paprika.

## MINESTRONE

The story goes that minestrone comes from the gypsy habit of throwing into one pot anything handy to eat, which perhaps explains why minestrone is different everywhere you eat it. You will doubtless work up your own version of this soup, but here is a starting recipe:

1 cup dried marrowfat or yellow-eye beans
6 cups Hauser Broth or 3 cans consommé
4 tbsp. olive oil or butter
1 clove garlic, minced
2 carrots, sliced
1 onion, diced

2 tbsp. chopped parsley
1 cup chopped cabbage
1 cup cooked whole-wheat spaghetti, chopped
1 stalk celery, sliced
1 cup canned Italian tomatoes
1 tsp. vegetable salt
Grated Parmesan cheese

Soak the beans overnight in 2 cups of water in the utensil in which you plan to cook them. In the morning add 2 cups more of water and bring to the boil. Reduce the heat and simmer for 2 hours. Put the broth in a large kettle and bring to the boil. Add the olive oil or butter, carrots, onion, garlic, parsley, cabbage, salt, and beans. Simmer until all the vegetables are tender—about 20 minutes. Add the tomatoes and spaghetti and cook 10 minutes more. Add grated cheese to taste just before serving.

## CHICKEN SOUP WITH WINE

4-lb. fowl
1 tbsp. vegetable salt
3 qt. cold water
1 carrot, sliced
1 onion, sliced

2 stalks celery, chopped
1 bay leaf
Chopped parsley to taste
2 tbsp. dry white wine

Have the fowl cut in pieces. Place in the water with the vegetable salt. Bring slowly to a boil, then simmer for an hour and a half, removing the scum at intervals. Add the vegetables and spices and simmer for another hour. Cool, remove the fat, and strain the soup.

Reheat 1 quart of broth. Just before serving, add the wine.

The leftover chicken can be made tasty by serving it in curry sauce.

## CLAM BROTH

Scrub 12 large clams with a stiff brush under running water. Steam as directed on page 89. Pour the broth through several thicknesses of cheesecloth. Reheat and serve as is if you like a strong broth; diluted with milk or Hauser Broth if you like it milder. Season with a little celery salt and garnish with a dash of paprika or a spoonful of whipped cream.

## CHOWDERS

Chowder comes from the coast of France, where the *chaudière* is the large pot in which the fisherman's wife cooks various mixtures of fish. Strictly speaking, chowders should always be fish soups; but we have come to use the word loosely enough to embrace any hearty milk soup with onions and potatoes in it. In New England the fish chowder is made strictly with milk; farther down the coast tomatoes are used with clams. One school of chowder makers favors a little thyme; the other insists upon caraway seeds.

## FISH CHOWDER

2 lb. cod or haddock, whole or
  filletted
3 tbsp. vegetable shortening
1 cup diced onion
2 cups cubed unpeeled potatoes
1½ to 2 cups Hauser Broth

1 qt. rich milk
2 tbsp. butter
1½ tsp. vegetable salt
⅛ tsp. paprika
⅛ tsp. thyme or caraway seed if
  desired

If you buy the fish whole, simmer it in a little water until the flesh will part from the bones. The old recipes insisted that the whole fish was the only way to make chowder. But the trick in fish chowder is to get the fish flavor thoroughly into the milk without cooking the fish into shreds, and it is easier to do this if you use filleted fish.

Melt the vegetable shortening in a heavy skillet and brown the onion in it. Meanwhile parboil the cubed potato for 10 minutes, drain, and add to the onion. When the potatoes are slightly brown, pour Hauser Broth into the frying pan to cover the vegetables. (If you are using whole fish, use the water in which the fish was cooked for this.) Cover and simmer gently until the vegetables are nearly done. Meanwhile put the milk in a large kettle with the butter and seasonings. Heat the milk slowly but do not let it boil. If you have cooked your fish, cut it into sizable chunks, removing the skin and bones. If you are using filleted fish, lay the fish over the top of the cooking vegetables and in a few minutes it will steam through. Then break into chunks with a fork. This is much easier than trying to chop up the raw fish—and far simpler to clean up after.

When the vegetables and fish are done, add them to the hot milk. Cover and allow to heat through without boiling. Another 10 minutes over the flame should do it.

If there is any chowder left, reheat it the next day over a gentle flame so that it simmers but never boils. Some people think that chowder is even better the second day because the flavors are more thoroughly blended.

## CLAM CHOWDER

3 tbsp. vegetable shortening
1 onion, chopped
1 pt. shelled clams, with juice
2 medium unpeeled potatoes, diced
2 cups boiling Hauser Broth
3 cups milk

2 tbsp. butter
1 cup cream
1 tsp. vegetable salt
Paprika
Thyme if desired

Melt the vegetable shortening in a heavy kettle, add the onion, and sauté until golden brown. Drain the clams, setting aside the juice. Clean the clams, chop them, and add to the onions. Boil the potatoes 5 to 10 minutes, depending on the size of the cubes, and add to the clam mixture. Pour the boiling broth over all and simmer gently until the potatoes are done.

Scald the milk and cream together with the butter and seasonings. Heat the clam juice and add it slowly to the milk to prevent curdling. Put the clam and potato mixture in a hot tureen, pour the milk and clam juice over it, and bring to the table.

## MANHATTAN CLAM CHOWDER

Use tomatoes in place of milk and cream. Add ¼ cup diced celery, a little minced garlic, and 1 tablespoon of Worcestershire sauce to the recipe for Clam Chowder.

## OYSTER STEW

1 pt. shelled oysters
¼ cup butter
¼ cup Hauser Broth

1 qt. scalded milk
½ tsp. vegetable salt
Dash of paprika

Clean and pick over the oysters, saving the liquor. Heat the butter, add the oysters, oyster liquor, and broth, and simmer gently until the edges of the oysters begin to curl. Add the scalded milk and seasonings and serve at once. Garnish with a dash of paprika.

For a richer stew, use part cream instead of milk.

## THE NEW FRUIT SOUPS

Yes, soups made from fruits—over here it is a new idea; but if you have been to Sweden or Norway you no doubt have enjoyed some of these exotic soups. They are served hot or cold; hot when the rest of the meal is cold as for Sunday-night supper. In the summertime fruit soups are thoroughly chilled and served cold. If you want to serve something different at your next luncheon, serve a fruit soup; the ingredients are all wholesome—fruits, spices, natural sugar, a bit of wine. For thickening purposes, half a teaspoonful of powdered agar-agar or seaweed is ideal, but you can also use a bit of gelatine, okra, or cornstarch. Do not use too much—fruit soups must never be thick like puddings. After you have served the following soups, you can make any number of other soups with your favorite fruits.

## CHERRY SOUP

2½ cups canned sour cherries
3½ cups water
1 1-inch stick cinnamon
2 tbsp. natural brown sugar
½ tsp. vegetable salt

½ tsp. powdered agar-agar or 2 tbsp. cornstarch
2 tbsp. lemon juice
½ cup red wine if desired

Combine the cherries, with juice, and the water. Add the cinnamon stick and sugar, then the cornstarch dissolved in 2 tablespoons of cold water or the agar-agar dissolved in hot water. Place over low heat and cook until clear, stirring constantly. Press through a sieve, chill, and add lemon juice. Just before serving, add the wine. Top each serving with whipped cream if desired.

NOTE: To use fresh cherries instead of canned, increase the water to 4 cups and stew the cherries with the cinnamon stick until tender; add sugar to taste and proceed as above.

### BERRY SOUP

| | |
|---|---|
| 1 pt. berries | 1/4 tsp. vegetable salt |
| 3 1/2 cups water | 1/2 tbsp. powdered agar-agar or 2 |
| 2 cups apple juice | tbsp. cornstarch |
| Honey to taste | 1/4 cup lemon juice |
| 1/8 tsp. nutmeg | |

Make this soup with any berries you like—blueberries, raspberries, strawberries, etc. The amount of sweetening will depend upon the kind of berries. Cook the berries in the water in a saucepan. Bring to a boil, cover, and cook 10 minutes or until soft. Press through a sieve. Add the apple juice, salt, nutmeg, and honey, then the cornstarch dissolved in 2 tablespoons of cold water, or the agar-agar dissolved in hot water. Cook over low heat until clear, stirring constantly. Chill and add lemon juice. Top each serving with whipped cream if desired; sprinkle with chopped mint.

### BERRY CREAM SOUP

After chilling, add 1 cup of thick sour cream to Berry Soup.

### APPLE SOUP

| | |
|---|---|
| 1/4 tsp. powdered agar-agar or | 2 cups loganberry juice |
| 1 tbsp. cornstarch | 2 tsp. grated lemon rind |
| 2 1/2 cups applesauce | 2 tbsp. lemon juice |
| 1/4 tsp. vegetable salt | 1/3 cup white wine if desired |

Dissolve the cornstarch in 2 tablespoons of cold water or the agar-agar in hot water. Add the applesauce, salt, loganberry juice, and lemon rind. Place over low heat and cook until clear, stirring constantly. Add a little honey if desired. Chill and add the lemon juice. Just before serving add the white wine. Sprinkle each serving with grated nutmeg.

## FRUIT-JUICE SOUP

1½ cups water
½ cup natural brown sugar
1 1-inch stick cinnamon
1½ cups cranberry juice

3 cups fruit juice—plum, peach, pineapple, etc.
2 tbsp. granulated tapioca

Combine the water, sugar, and cinnamon in a saucepan. Bring to the boil, then simmer 5 minutes. Add the cranberry juice and fruit juices and bring to the boil again. Gradually add the tapioca, stirring constantly. Simmer 5 minutes, stirring occasionally. Chill thoroughly. Garnish each serving with a thin slice of lemon.

## RHUBARB SOUP

1 lb. rhubarb cut in pieces
1 qt. water
¼ cup natural brown sugar

¼ tsp. powdered agar-agar or 1 tbsp. cornstarch
1 egg yolk, beaten
½ cup cream

Cook the rhubarb and water in a covered pan until the rhubarb is soft. Press through a sieve. Add sugar and the cornstarch dissolved in 2 tablespoons of cold water, or the agar-agar dissolved in hot water. Cook over low heat until clear, stirring constantly. Slowly add some of the hot liquid to the egg yolk until it is thin enough to pour. Return to the hot soup, mix thoroughly, and chill.

When ready to serve, whip the cream and either fold it into the soup or top each serving with it.

# CHAPTER 5

# *Beef, Lamb, and Veal*

THE BEST METHOD OF cooking any meat is the one which cooks it in the least time. This will depend upon the kind and cut of meat, of course. Veal should be cooked longer than beef and lamb. Tender cuts should be cooked by dry heat under the broiler, on top the stove in a sizzling skillet, or roasted uncovered in the oven with no liquid added. Tougher cuts demand braising or stewing—methods in which the meat is first seared to keep the juices in, then slowly simmered, never boiled, in liquid, very little for braising, more for stewing. Marinating in lemon juice before cooking also helps to reduce the time by breaking down the tough fibers of the meat (see p. 72).

*Care of Meat:* Remove the meat from the paper in which it is wrapped the moment it comes from the market. Store it in an uncovered dish in the refrigerator in the spot where the temperature is lowest. Let quick-frozen meats thaw slowly in the refrigerator before you take off the wrapper. If there is not time for thawing, allow a little extra time for cooking. But if you want a nice brown crust, be sure the meat is thoroughly thawed and dry before you try to sauté it.

## BEEF

Good beef has a smooth, glossy grain and is well marbled or streaked with fat. The outer fat should be thick and firm and creamy in color.

*Cuts for Roasting:* The best cuts for roasting come from the sixth to twelfth ribs. The sirloin, which is tender solid meat, is also roasted for big groups. The tenderloin, smaller and more expensive, is solid meat and makes an elegant roast which is sliced thin against the grain when served. You've eaten it under the name of London Broil. The chuck, which comes from the fifth rib, can be rolled, larded, and roasted, but the meat is not as tender as the other roasts and usually is better pot-roasted.

*Cuts for Broiling:* Broiling is the best way to cook meat in that it takes the least time. Unhappily, only the choicest and most expensive cuts are suitable for broiling unless the meat is chopped or otherwise tenderized. Porterhouse, tenderloin, sirloin, and top round are the cuts of beef suitable for broiling. Tenderloin steak, or *filet mignon,* is the aristocrat of the beef family and costs the most. Club steaks and Delmonico steaks are simply small cuts of porterhouse. Minute steaks are thin slices from the top round. Cube steaks, a fairly recent discovery, are thin slices of the round cut almost through the tendons by a machine to make them tender.

*Cuts for Pot-Roasting and Stewing:* The tougher cuts of meat need to be cooked by wet heat rather than dry heat as in roasting and broiling. That means cooking in liquid so the heat will penetrate the tough muscle fibers of the meat. The chuck, rump, round, brisket, and plate are the beef cuts which need either pot-roasting—another name is braising—or stewing. The disadvantages of longer cooking time and the use of liquid in cooking meat can be offset by following the methods described under Stews and Pot Roasts for Epicures.


## SOME POINTERS ON MEAT COOKERY

### BASTING ROASTS

Basting is one of those moot questions on which good cooks can get together and argue by the hour. To baste or not to baste, and with what? One school of epicures counts it a crime to baste roast beef; the other says the secret of success is basting at 15-minute intervals. Veal, it is generally agreed, is improved by basting because it is so lean. Lamb is often basted.

As for what to baste with: Pan drippings of course. Sometimes you need more liquid, or fat in the case of veal. If you want herb flavor, you will be basting with herbs and wine or herbs and olive oil. Or use Hauser Broth, with or without herbs. For veal, try half butter and half Hauser Broth. You have plenty of latitude in what to baste with.

## HERBS FOR ROASTS

To impart herb flavors to roasts, you have your choice of rubbing the meat before cooking with olive oil flavored with herbs, or basting during the roasting with a liquor in which herbs have soaked. Garlic goes with all roasts, of course. For beef, try thyme and summer savory; for lamb, rosemary or spearmint either with or without the garlic.

## HERBS FOR STEAKS

Nothing can surpass a good steak quickly broiled and served immediately. But sometimes for variety try giving a steak a trace of herb flavor. First comes garlic. Rub the surface with a clove of garlic gashed so the juice can escape. Or insert thin slivers of garlic in the fat at the edge of the steak—not in the middle of the meat. Or soak crushed garlic cloves in olive oil for an hour, then rub the steak with the oil. Next time try minced thyme and rosemary in the olive oil instead of garlic. And the next time make it a bay leaf or a teaspoon of marjoram.

## CHOPS WITH HERBS

Chops, like steaks, can stand on their own feet. Quickly broiled, lightly salted, and served with a bit of butter melting on top, they can't be beat. But they can be varied by lending them the flavor of herbs. Bay leaf, garlic, marjoram, summer savory, thyme, sweet basil, parsley—try any one or a combination of two or three. Either let the herbs soak in olive oil, then brush the meat with the oil, or cream fresh minced herbs into the butter you spread over the broiled chops.

## STEWS AND POT ROASTS FOR EPICURES

1. Always sear the meat first in pure vegetable oil or shortening before the liquid is added. This improves the flavor, gives the stew or pot roast a more attractive color—and there's no denying that we Americans eat with the eye—and keeps in some of the vital juices which otherwise would escape into the liquid. (Of course you will eat every bit of the liquid, so you will get these juices, but the meat itself tastes better if you leave some of the flavor in it.)

2. Always use Hauser Broth instead of plain water for the cooking liquid. In this way you add to the meat the minerals and vitamins of vegetables. And also add onions, potatoes, carrots, turnips, or whatever you prefer to your stew and pot roast for extra nutritive value.

3. Never cook a stew or pot roast without parsley somewhere in the process—cooked in the stew the last half hour, sprinkled over the top, or simply whole sprigs decorating the dish if you can teach your family to eat the garnish instead of pushing it to the edge of the plate.

4. Use whole-wheat flour if you thicken the gravy, or substitute okra powder if you have to watch calories.

5. Be mindful of the glamour herbs impart to otherwise pedestrian dishes. Bay leaf, marjoram, thyme, summer savory, rosemary are all suitable for stews and pot roasts. Not all at once, of course, and not too much of any. Try them all at different times.

## BROILED STEAK

Preheat the oven for 10 minutes, wipe the steak dry, grease the broiling rack, and lay the steak on it. The top of the steak should be about 3 inches below the flame. Cook until the top is brown, turn with a pancake turner so as not to puncture the meat, and brown the other side.

For a rare steak 1½ inches thick, allow 6 to 8 minutes for each side. A 2-inch steak will take 8 or 9 minutes for each side. Increase the time for medium or well-done steak; but note that steak continues to cook by the heat already in it after it is removed from the broiler, so be careful not to overcook it. Have it a little bit rarer than you like when it is removed from the fire.

Sprinkle both sides with a bit of vegetable salt and spread with a little softened butter.

There are various schools of thought on steak. Some like to cut it in pieces before cooking so that all sides of each piece are seared. Others like to give the steak a good bath of olive oil before cooking; still others spread mustard and olive oil over the cooked steak just before cooking is finished. A more recent method is to coat the steak on both sides with wet vegetable salt, as much as half an inch thick, then put a paper napkin over it to hold the salt in place. The napkin burns away, leaving the caked salt against the meat; when the steak is cooked the salt is broken off and thrown away. This method has the advantage of preventing the meat from absorbing gaseous odors from a gas burner.

## BROILED HAMBURGERS

1 lb. chopped beef.
1 tbsp. minced onion if desired

1 tsp. vegetable salt
3 tbsp. wheat germ

Thoroughly mix all the ingredients and form the meat into flat cakes—thick or thin as you prefer. I like them about an inch thick. Panbroil them in a sizzling hot skillet with just a film of vegetable oil in it. Or broil them in a preheated oven as for Broiled Steak, allowing 4 minutes for each side for rare steak. Spread with softened butter and garnish with chopped parsley.

4 servings.

## STEAK MINUTE

Minute steak may be broiled, but it is generally panbroiled. Heat a heavy frying pan until sizzling hot. Sear the steaks quickly on both sides, lower the heat, and cook 2 minutes on each side. Remove to a hot platter, spread with softened butter, and sprinkle with vegetable salt and paprika. Garnish with parsley. Allow 1 steak, ¼ to ½ inch thick, for each serving.

## ELEGANT STEAK FOR PARTIES

Get a sirloin or porterhouse steak cut 1½ to 2 inches thick. Put a cup of French dressing in a bowl and add a bay leaf and a tablespoon of Worcestershire sauce to the dressing. Rub the steak all over with a gashed clove of garlic, put it in a shallow pan or a deep platter. Pour the dressing over it and let it marinate for at least an hour, turning it twice. Preheat the broiler for 10 minutes and put the steak under the flame with lots of dressing clinging to it. Sear quickly on both sides, then reduce the flame and broil more slowly.

Meanwhile sauté a pound of sliced fresh mushrooms in butter and take them out of the skillet. Put into the same butter slices of green pepper and pimento and sauté them. Put the steak on a platter, sprinkle with vegetable salt, cover with mushrooms, and garnish the top with the red and green slices of pimento and pepper.

This is a recipe where you have to work fast to have everything piping hot at the crucial moment, but it's well worth it for occasional times when you feel ambitious.

## STANDING RIB ROAST

Wipe the roast dry with a cloth, slap it hard with vegetable salt, and dredge it with whole-wheat flour. Place it fat side up in an uncovered roasting pan, or on a trivet or rack. If the top fat is thin, put a piece of suet over it and fasten it down with toothpicks.

Have the oven very hot—500°F.—before you put the roast in. Sear it for 20 to 30 minutes in the hot oven, then reduce the temperature to moderate (350°F.) for the rest of the time. Include the searing time in estimating the total roasting time according to the following table:

| Rare | Medium | Well Done |
|---|---|---|
| 20 min. per lb. for roasts under 5 lb. | 25 min. per lb. for roasts under 5 lb. | 35 min. per lb. for roasts under 5 lb. |
| 18 min. per lb. for roasts over 5 lb. | 22 min. per lb. for roasts over 5 lb. | 30 min. per lb. for roasts over 5 lb. |

If you have a meat thermometer, make a hole with a skewer through the fat side and insert the thermometer so the bulb will rest in the center of the fleshy part of the roast, but not touching the bone. The final reading will be 140° for rare, 160° for medium, and 170° for well done.

## ROAST BEEF GRAVY

The best, most delicate gravy is pan gravy, the juices in the pan after the roasting is done. Especially if you use herbs in your meat cookery! But if you insist upon a thick gravy, try okra powder to thicken without adding extra calories. If you use flour, make it whole-wheat flour and use it sparingly. Here is the method:

Remove all but 4 or 5 tablespoons of fat from the pan after placing the roast on a platter where it will keep warm. For each tablespoon of fat add a scant tablespoon of flour. Set the pan on top the stove and brown the fat in the flour. Add 1½ to 2 cups of Hauser Broth, stirring constantly, and cook until the gravy thickens. Add the broth cold, all at once, and your gravy will never lump.

## ROLLED ROAST OF BEEF

Have the bones removed from a rib roast and put them in the pan with the roast. Allow 10 minutes longer per pound than for Standing Rib Roast.

## BEEF STEW

2 lb. lean beef cut in 1-inch cubes
2 tbsp. pure vegetable shortening
1 large onion, chopped
Boiling Hauser Broth
3 stalks celery, leaves and all, chopped

8 small white onions
8 unpeeled carrots
8 small unpeeled potatoes
4 small turnips, cut in quarters
2 tbsp. whole-wheat flour

Cut the meat into cubes if the butcher hasn't already done it. Melt the shortening in a heavy iron kettle—a Dutch oven if you have one. Sprinkle the meat with vegetable salt and brown it in the fat with the chopped onion. Add the hot broth, enough so it almost but not quite covers the meat. Cover and simmer slowly over a low flame for 2 hours, or until the meat is almost done. Add the whole onions, carrots, potatoes, and quartered turnips. Continue simmering for another half hour. Remove the meat and vegetables to a platter. Thicken the liquid in the kettle with the 2 tablespoons of whole-wheat flour mixed to a smooth paste with a little cold Hauser Broth. Serve the gravy either over the stew or in a separate dish.

6 servings, 8 at a pinch.

## BEEF STROGANOFF

2 lb. lean beef cut in 1-inch cubes
⅓ cup seasoned whole-wheat flour
2 tbsp. vegetable shortening
1 large onion, sliced
½ lb. mushrooms, sliced
2 cups hot Hauser Broth

2 tbsp. chopped parsley
½ pt. sour cream or yogurt
1 tbsp. soy sauce
½ tsp. vegetable salt
Paprika to taste

Cut the meat into cubes if the butcher hasn't already done it. Dredge in seasoned whole-wheat flour. Melt the vegetable shortening in a heavy kettle or Dutch oven. Brown the meat with the onions and mushrooms. Add the Hauser Broth, cover tightly, and simmer slowly over a low flame until tender—about 2 hours. Remove the cover during the last part of the cooking and let the liquid cook down to about half the quantity. Five minutes before serving, add the parsley, pour in the sour cream or yogurt, and the soy sauce. Taste and season to suit with vegetable salt and paprika.

6 servings.

## HUNGARIAN GOULASH

2 lb. lean beef cut in 1-inch cubes
2 tbsp. pure vegetable shortening
4 onions, chopped
2 cloves garlic, minced
1 tsp. vegetable salt

1 tsp. paprika
1 bay leaf
½ tsp. caraway seeds
2 cups strained tomatoes
2 cups cubed unpeeled potatoes

Cut the meat in cubes if the butcher hasn't done it already—and, by the way, you may use half veal and half beef in this recipe if you prefer. Melt the shortening in a heavy iron kettle or Dutch oven and brown the meat with the chopped onion and garlic. Add the vegetable salt, paprika, bay leaf, and caraway seeds. Heat the tomatoes and pour them over the meat.

Cover tightly and simmer over a low flame about 2 hours, until the meat is tender. Add more tomatoes as needed. Add the potatoes a half hour before the meat is done. If desired, thicken the gravy with 2 tablespoons of whole-wheat flour mixed with a little cold water, or with okra powder.

### BEEF POT ROAST

5-lb. pot roast
½ cup seasoned whole-wheat flour
1 large onion, sliced
2 cups boiling Hauser Broth or
    tomato juice

1 bunch soup greens
1 tbsp. butter
1 tbsp. whole-wheat flour
Vegetable salt to taste
Paprika to taste

Dredge the meat with seasoned whole-wheat flour. Brown it in its own fat in a heavy iron kettle or Dutch oven. When a little fat collects in the bottom of the kettle, put in the onion slices and brown them. (If the meat hasn't enough fat, use a bit of vegetable oil or shortening.) Add the hot broth or tomato juice, toss in the soup greens, cover tightly, and simmer over low heat for 3 to 4 hours, or until tender. Turn the meat occasionally as it cooks. Remove the pot roast to a hot platter. Cream the butter and flour together and stir into the hot liquid. Cook, stirring constantly, until the gravy thickens slightly, and season to taste with vegetable salt and paprika. For variety try the Swedish method of adding ½ cup of sour cream to the gravy.

### SWEDISH MEAT BALLS

2 cups soft whole-wheat bread crumbs
¾ cup milk
2 tbsp. minced onion
4 tbsp. butter
1 lb. chopped beef
¼ tsp. nutmeg

1½ tsp. vegetable salt
¼ tsp. paprika
1 egg, slightly beaten
2 tbsp. whole-wheat flour
½ cup rich milk or thin cream

Soak the bread crumbs in the ¾ cup of milk for 10 minutes. Sauté the onion in half the butter until a golden brown. Add the onion to the meat along with the seasonings and the slightly beaten egg. Add the bread crumbs and put the whole mixture through the food chopper. Shape into small balls and sauté in a skillet in the remaining butter until the meat balls are light brown on all sides. Sprinkle with whole-wheat flour, coating each ball thoroughly. Cover and cook for 5 minutes, then add the milk or cream, cover again, and cook for another 5 minutes.

6 servings.

## VEAL

Veal is the flesh of the calf, which should be light in color with just a slight pinkish tinge. The grain is fine and the texture smooth in good veal, but not so firm as the texture of beef. Veal has very little fat, but what there is should be firm.

The best veal comes from milk-fed calves 6 to 8 weeks old. Many misconceptions have been prevalent about veal—that it is hard to digest, that it is poisonous if the calf is too young, and so forth. Recent experiments have proved the fallacy of these. Even veal a few days old has no injurious effects, although it is not recommended for the best flavor. Now nutritionists say that young veal is just as easily digested as beef, and it appears on diets for invalids for the first time.

Because veal lacks fat, more fat needs to be added during cooking than is the case with most other meats. It should always be thoroughly cooked. Pot-roasting, stewing, and roasting are the most suitable methods of cooking it.

*Cuts for Roasting:* Loins, ribs, and legs are the best cuts for roasting. The leg can be boned and stuffed. The boned rolled shoulder is also used for roasting, and the breast is sometimes stuffed and roasted.

*Cuts for Pot-roasting:* Breast, a chunk off the leg, the rib chops, loin chops, or shoulder chops are suitable for pot-roasting.

*Cuts for Stewing:* Any solid meat can be used for stewing, but the most popular are shoulder, breast, shank, and flank.

## ROAST VEAL

Wipe the meat with a cloth, rub with vegetable salt, and place it skin side up in an uncovered roaster. Sear in a hot oven (500°F.) for 30 minutes, or until the meat is browned. Reduce the heat to moderate (350°F.) for the rest of the time, allowing 25 to 30 minutes per pound. Include the searing time in estimating the time.

If a meat thermometer is used, insert it in the fleshy part of the roast so it does not touch the bone. The final reading should be 170°F. Veal needs basting while it roasts (see pp. 62-63).

## ROLLED ROAST OF VEAL

Have the bones removed from the shoulder or leg. Use the recipe above for Roast Veal, but allow 10 minutes longer per pound.

## ROAST STUFFED VEAL

Choose a shoulder or leg of veal and have it boned. Wipe the meat with a damp cloth and sew up the cuts on three sides, leaving the other side open for the stuffing. Rub it inside and out with vegetable salt. Make a suitable amount of Herb Stuffing or Savory Stuffing (see Index) and fill the cavity with the stuffing. Tie or sew the opening, dot with butter or meat drippings, and place in an uncovered roasting pan.

Roast in a hot oven (500°F.) for 15 minutes, or until the meat is browned. Reduce the heat to moderate (350°F.) for the rest of the time, allowing 35 minutes per pound. Baste every 15 minutes with your choice of basting liquids.

## MARION'S DELIGHT GOULASH

2 lb. veal cut in 1-inch cubes
2 tbsp. butter
2 tsp. paprika
3 medium-sized onions, coarsely chopped
1 clove garlic, chopped

1 qt. tomatoes
1 tbsp. natural brown sugar
1 tsp. vegetable salt
1 cup sour cream or yogurt

Cut the meat in cubes if the butcher hasn't already done it. Melt the butter in a large iron kettle or Dutch oven. Add the paprika, chopped onion, and garlic. Cook until tender but not dark. Add the veal and brown the pieces nicely. Then add the tomatoes, sugar, and salt. Simmer about 2 hours, or until the veal is tender. Just before serving add the sour cream or yogurt and stir well. Delicious served with wild rice or buttered noodles.

## VEGEBURGERS

½ lb. ground beef
1 cup ground raw carrots
1 cup ground unpeeled raw potatoes
2 tbsp. chopped onion
2 tbsp. chopped parsley

½ cup chopped celery
1 egg, slightly beaten
¼ cup top milk or light cream
¼ cup wheat germ
2 tsp. vegetable salt

Mix all the ingredients thoroughly. Form into 8 patties and place on a buttered shallow pan. Bake in a hot oven (425°F.) for 20 minutes. The patties should be quite moist.

## VEAL STEW

2 lb. veal cut in 2-inch cubes
2 tbsp. vegetable shortening
1 large onion, sliced
1 qt. boiling Hauser Broth
¼ cup chopped carrot
1 bay leaf
1 sprig thyme
2 sprigs parsley

2 tsp. vegetable salt
1 cup sliced mushrooms
12 small white onions
5 tbsp. butter
3 tbsp. whole-wheat flour
2 tbsp. lemon juice
2 egg yolks, slightly beaten
1 tbsp. chopped parsley

Cut the meat in pieces if the butcher hasn't already done it. Melt the shortening in a heavy iron kettle or Dutch oven. Brown the meat nicely, and with it the onion. Pour over it the hot broth. Add the chopped carrot, herbs, and vegetable salt. Simmer over a low flame, tightly covered, for about 2 hours, or until the meat is tender. Remove the veal and strain the stock. Cook the sliced mushrooms in a double boiler with a little of the stock for 15 minutes. Put the 12 small onions in a heavy covered saucepan with 2 tablespoons of the butter and stew for 20 to 30 minutes or until tender. Melt the remaining 3 tablespoons of butter, stir in the flour, and add 3 cups of the strained stock. Cook over medium heat, stirring constantly, until the gravy thickens and boils. Add the lemon juice to the slightly beaten egg yolks, stir in a little of the hot sauce, and return all to the hot mixture. Add the veal and chopped parsley and reheat. Serve on a platter with the onions and mushrooms.

6 servings.

## LAMB AND MUTTON

The younger the lamb, the more delicate the flavor and the tenderer the texture. Meat from lambs 3 to 5 months old is known as "spring lamb" and is in season from April through June. A small quantity of what is known as "hot-house lamb," bred under special conditions, is available from January through March, but is generally expensive. The flesh of both lamb and mutton should be fine-grained and smooth. The flesh of the yearling is a dark pink, and mutton is still darker. The fat of lamb should be white and firm, whereas that of mutton is pink and harder. The flavor is distinctive, so drippings from the cooked meat should not be combined with those of other meats for use in cooking. Lamb is generally served medium or well done in this country, but abroad the rare meat is preferred.

*Cuts for Roasting:* The legs, loin, and rack, which includes 10 ribs, are used for roasting. The leg may be boned. Shoulder, boned and rolled, is also used for roasting. The breast may be stuffed and roasted. For a large roast, the legs, loin, and sometimes the ribs are cut in one piece, known as the saddle.

*Cuts for Broiling:* The loin, ribs, and shoulders are cut into chops and used for broiling. Trimmed rib chops are known as "French chops." The shoulder and leg steaks cut into 1-inch cubes may be broiled on a skewer.

*Cuts for Stewing:* Shoulder, breast, neck, and shank are generally selected for stew.

## ROAST LAMB

Wipe the meat with a cloth. Rub into it the sauce for tenderizing meats given below, then treat with garlic or herbs as you prefer. When you are ready to start roasting it, put it in a roasting pan, skin side down in the case of a leg, and roast in a hot oven (500°F.) for 30 minutes. Turn down the heat and reduce the oven temperature to 350°F. and cook for another 2½ hours for a 5-lb. roast.

Baste during the last hour with any herb-flavored liquid you wish, keeping in mind the affinity between lamb and spearmint. A half cup of currant jelly mixed with a half cup of boiling Hauser Broth will give your roast an attractive glaze and an interesting flavor.

## FOR TENDERIZING MEATS

½ cup lemon juice
1 tbsp. chopped parsley
1 large onion, chopped
2 tbsp. chopped celery leaves

1 clove garlic, crushed
1 tsp. honey
1 tsp. vegetable salt

Mix all the ingredients and rub into roasts. If the meat is lean, add 3 tablespoons of vegetable oil. All tougher cuts of meat can be marinated in this mixture for several hours before cooking.

## BARBECUED LAMB

Wipe a leg or rolled shoulder of lamb with a cloth and slash deeply and frequently, at least ⅜ inch deep, on the skin side. Rub liberally with vegetable salt and sear, skin side up, in a hot oven (500°F.). Reduce the heat to 350°F. and baste at least every 10 minutes with Barbecue Sauce, using a pastry brush to apply the sauce.

## BARBECUE SAUCE

| | |
|---|---|
| 1 can tomato paste | 2 tbsp. natural brown sugar |
| 1½ cups warm Hauser Broth | ¼ cup finely chopped onion |
| ½ cup lemon juice | ½ clove garlic, finely chopped |
| 4 tsp. Worcestershire sauce | ½ tsp. salt |
| ½ tsp. vegetable salt | ½ tsp. chili powder |

Mix all the ingredients in a saucepan. Bring to a boil, reduce the heat, then simmer 20 minutes, stirring frequently.

2 cups enough for a 5-pound roast.

## BROILED LAMB CHOPS

Preheat the broiling oven for 10 minutes. Grease the broiler rack. Wipe the meat with a cloth, place on the rack, and broil 2 inches from the broiler flame. Unless directions for your range state otherwise, leave the door of the broiling oven open. Sear the chops on both sides under high heat, then reduce the heat and continue cooking, turning occasionally.

For single chops about ¾ inch thick, allow 10 to 12 minutes; for double chops from 1 to 1½ inches thick, 15 to 20 minutes.

Place on a hot platter and sprinkle both sides with vegetable salt and paprika. Spread with softened butter if desired.

## STUFFED LAMB CHOPS

Have your butcher cut chops double thick, 2 ribs to each chop, and split the lean meat in half, cutting right to the bone. Stuff the chops with the following stuffing and press the open edges together:

*Stuffing:* Sauté 1 teaspoon of chopped onion and 2 tablespoons of chopped celery 3 minutes in a tablespoon of butter. Add vegetable salt and paprika, 1 tablespoon minced mint leaves, and ½ cup of dry bread crumbs. Mix thoroughly.

Dip the stuffed chops in beaten egg and wheat germ and cook in a hot oven (425°F.) for 45 minutes, turning once.

## LAMB FRUIT GRILL

Broil chops as directed above. During the last 3 minutes of cooking place slices of canned pineapple or peeled orange alongside the chops on the broiler rack. Dot the fruit with butter and broil.

## BACON

Bacon is cured either with sugar and salt or with salt alone. It has either a sweet or a salty taste depending upon which method was used. The most desirable breakfast bacon is cut from the breast. Canadian bacon is from the loins. Bacon is the most desirable of the animal food products, especially when broiled crisp so all the grease is dried out. Bacon is the only part of the pig permitted in health cookery.

## BROILED BACON

Do not preheat the broiler for bacon. Broil a few minutes at a distance of 3 inches from the heat until the fat shows no white spots. Broiled bacon should be crisp—how crisp depends upon your taste—but not brittle.

CHAPTER 6

# Vitamin-Rich Organ Meats

TO THIS DAY IN some parts of Europe the bride still makes a broth for her future husband which is supposed to be out of this world. The chief contents are glandular meats such as liver, sweetbreads, heart, and tripe, all nicely chopped up and cooked in quarts of broth enriched with onions, leeks, celery roots, parsley, and other garden greens. It is a very thick soup and is never strained, for the peasants say that in order to get the "strength" of it, the groom has to eat the whole thing, plates and plates of it.

I don't know the origin of this bit of folklore, but I do know that in nature wild animals always eat the inner organs of their prey first. Only then do they start to eat the muscular meats. With the advent of food analysis it has become more and more evident that organ meats *are* veritable treasure hoards of vitamins and minerals and that they contain the first-class proteins. Brains, heart, and kidneys are rich in the vitamins of the B family, especially vitamin G. Liver and sweetbreads are rich in the vitamin A. Besides liver, try heart, kidneys, sweetbreads, and tripe.

Always remember to eat lots of fresh vegetables and fruits whenever you eat these organ meats, for they are on the acid side chemically speaking. They also contain a great deal of cholesterol, which is not desirable for older people. When you do prepare one of these dishes, remember your pooch. He likes all kinds of organ meats, especially liver and heart.

## LIVER

Liver has been the victim of ill treatment for years. Horse-and-buggy cookbooks used to tell you to soak all the good out of it, then cook the residue to the consistency of leather. No wonder liver was unpopular! Now we know that tender calves' liver, chicken and turkey liver need only be washed and cooked the barest minimum of time, just until they change color.

Beef liver, while tougher than calves' liver, still does not need soaking and scalding within an inch of its life. Lamb liver has come into use recently. Because it has a stronger flavor than beef or calves' liver, its flavor is improved if you scald it briefly before cooking.

## SAUTÉED LIVER

Roll slices of liver ½ to ¾ inch thick in seasoned flour. Melt butter or vegetable shortening in a heavy skillet. Sauté over medium heat about 5 minutes, turning to brown both sides. Add more butter as needed. Serve with onions or bacon in the time-honored manner. Or, if preferred, add sweet or sour cream to the pan after the liver is cooked and simmer just until the cream bubbles. Serve at once garnished with minced chives or parsley.

## LIVER PEASANT STYLE

Get 1 pound of fresh calves' liver sliced thin, then cut in strips about ½ inch wide. Melt a tablespoon of good butter in a heavy skillet. In it sauté 1 good-sized onion and 1 tablespoon of wheat germ. When the onion and wheat germ begin to turn brown, add the strips of liver and sauté for about 3 minutes. Then sprinkle with ½ teaspoon of vegetable salt. Just before removing the liver from the heat, put the cover on the skillet for a minute to further tenderize the liver.

This makes an elegant luncheon dish, especially when served with fried apples and a large green salad. It is my favorite liver recipe.

## BROILED LIVER

Have the liver sliced ½ to ¾ inch thick. Wash and dry thoroughly between paper towels. Brush the slices with melted butter or peanut oil and sprinkle with vegetable salt. Place on a buttered broiler pan or baking sheet and broil 3 inches from the heat until it just changes color. This will take about 3 minutes on each side. Place on a hot platter, dot with butter, and sprinkle with minced parsley or water cress.

## LIVER LOAF

| | |
|---|---|
| 1 lb. beef liver | 1 tbsp. minced celery leaves |
| 3 tbsp. butter | 2 tbsp. minced parsley |
| ½ cup minced onion | 1 tsp. wheat germ |
| ¼ cup diced celery | 1 tsp. vegetable salt |
| 4 tbsp. finely chopped green pepper | ¼ tsp. paprika |
| 1 lb. ground beef | 2 eggs |
| 1½ cups chopped carrots | |

Have the liver cut in ½-inch slices. Melt the butter in a heavy skillet and sauté the liver a few minutes. Remove the liver from the pan and put it through the fine blade of the food chopper. Add the onion, celery, and green pepper to the hot skillet, adding more butter if necessary, and sauté for 3 minutes, until the onion is golden brown. Combine all ingredients and mix thoroughly. Place in a buttered dish or casserole, cover, and bake 30 minutes in a moderate oven (375°F.). Uncover and bake another 15 minutes or more until the top is brown.

Not only your family but your pooch will go for this.

## MUSHROOM CHICKEN LIVERS

| | |
|---|---|
| ¾ lb. chicken livers | 2 tbsp. minced onion |
| ¼ cup butter | ½ tsp. vegetable salt |
| 2 cups sliced mushrooms | ⅛ tsp. paprika |

Wash, rinse, and cut the livers in pieces. Melt the butter in a heavy skillet and sauté the livers, mushrooms, and onion over low heat, stirring occasionally, for about 5 minutes. Add seasoning and serve on toast or boiled rice, or in the fold of an omelet.

## SWEETBREADS

Sweetbreads are perishable and should be prepared as soon as they come from the market. Then store in the refrigerator until ready to use.

## TO PREPARE SWEETBREADS

Place sweetbreads in cold salted water for half an hour. Simmer for 15 minutes in water to cover, adding 1 tablespoon of lemon juice and 1 teaspoon of vegetable salt for each quart of water. Or use Hauser Broth. The lemon helps to keep the sweetbreads white. When tender drain and plunge into cold water. Remove the tubes and membranes. Store in the refrigerator until ready to use.

## SAUTÉED SWEETBREADS

Split prepared sweetbreads and sprinkle with vegetable salt. Melt a little butter in a heavy skillet and sauté over medium heat until golden brown on both sides. Serve with lemon wedges and sprinkle with parsley.

## BROILED SWEETBREADS

Split prepared sweetbreads and preheat the oven. Dip the pieces of sweetbread in melted butter, sprinkle with vegetable salt, and place in a greased shallow baking pan. Broil 3 inches from the heat until golden brown on both sides—about 5 minutes for each side.

## CHICKEN AND SWEETBREADS À LA KING

| | |
|---|---|
| 1 cup diced cooked or canned chicken | ½ tsp. paprika |
| 1 pair prepared sweetbreads, diced | 1¾ cups milk |
| 4 tbsp. butter | 2 pimentos, minced |
| 1 cup sliced mushrooms | ¼ cup cream |
| 1 green pepper, minced | 2 egg yolks, slightly beaten |
| 3 tbsp. whole-wheat flour | 1 tbsp. lemon juice |
| ½ tsp. vegetable salt | |

Melt the butter in a heavy skillet and sauté the mushrooms, green pepper, and sweetbreads over medium heat for 5 minutes, stirring occasionally. Reduce the heat, stir in the flour and seasonings, and blend until smooth. Add the milk gradually, stirring constantly, until the mixture thickens and boils. Add the chicken and pimentos.

Beat the egg yolks slightly and add the cream, blending well. Stir in a little of the hot sauce, then return all to the skillet, stirring until well blended. Unless the dish is to be served immediately, turn it into the top of a double boiler to keep hot and blend the flavors. Add the lemon juice just before serving.

## CREAMED SWEETBREADS

2 pairs sweetbreads
¼ cup butter
1 tbsp. minced onion
1 cup sliced mushrooms
3 tbsp. whole-wheat flour
1 tsp. vegetable salt

⅛ tsp. paprika
2 cups milk
1 pimento, diced
1 tbsp. lemon juice
2 tbsp. minced parsley

Prepare the sweetbreads and dice. Melt the butter in a heavy skillet and sauté the onion and mushroom over low heat for a few minutes, stirring occasionally. Stir in the flour and seasonings and blend until smooth. Add the milk gradually, stirring constantly until the mixture thickens and boils. Stir in the sweetbreads, pimento, and lemon juice and reheat. Sprinkle with minced parsley.

## HEART

The heart must be cooked slowly over a long period of time, preferably in Hauser Broth or water left over from vegetable cookery. When the heart comes from the market, wash it thoroughly in cold water, changing the water several times. Remove the arteries, fat, and veins if the butcher has not already done it. Soak in sour milk or marinate for half an hour in French dressing to tenderize the heart. After this it can be cooked in vegetable water or Hauser Broth, or baked and braised.

### HEART COOKED IN BROTH

Cut lamb and veal hearts in half, beef hearts in small pieces. Put them in a heavy kettle with enough Hauser Broth to cover, and add a couple of whole cloves, a bay leaf, a few celery leaves, and some slices of onion. Cover and simmer over a low flame for about half an hour. Add 1 teaspoon of vegetable salt for each quart of broth and continue simmering until tender. It will take ¾ to 1 hour for veal or lamb heart and an hour to 1½ hours for beef heart. Trim off any remaining fat or gristle and serve hot or cold.

### BROILED HEART

Cook the heart in broth, then cut in ½-inch slices. Brush the slices with melted butter and place them on a shallow broiling pan. Broil 3 inches from the flame for about 3 minutes on each side.

## SAUTÉED HEART

Cook the heart in broth and cut in ½-inch slices. Melt a little butter in a heavy skillet and sauté the slices of heart about 3 minutes on each side.

## BRAISED HEART

Wash the heart and remove the arteries, veins, and fat. Soak in sour milk or marinate in French dressing for half an hour to an hour. Stuff with any well-seasoned stuffing and rub well with flour. Brown evenly in a heavy kettle, using as small an amount of vegetable shortening as possible. Slip a rack under the heart and add ¾ to 1 cup of Hauser Broth. Cover closely and simmer over very low heat until tender—2 hours for lamb or veal hearts and 3 hours for beef.

## BAKED STUFFED HEART

Wash the heart and remove the arteries, veins, and fat. Soak in sour milk or marinate in French dressing for half an hour to an hour. Cover with boiling water, reduce heat, and simmer slowly about 20 minutes. Dry and slit one side. Fill with any well-seasoned stuffing and fasten the edges together again. Place in a small roasting pan with 2 cups of canned tomatoes, 1 tablespoon of minced onion, a bay leaf, and ½ cup of chopped celery. Dot with butter, cover, and bake in a slow oven (300°F.) until tender— 2 hours for beef heart and 1½ hours for lamb and veal heart. Baste occasionally, and as the tomato juice cooks away, add Hauser Broth as needed. Bake uncovered during the last 15 minutes. Remove the bay leaf and serve the tomato sauce with the heart.

## KIDNEYS

Kidneys have one strange property—if they are cooked quickly they are tender, but if they are overcooked in the least it will take hours to make them tender again. For this reason they are good either broiled or sautéed, or cooked long in stews or meat pies.

Wash the kidneys thoroughly and remove the outer membrane. Split them through the center and cut out the fat and large tubules. A pair of scissors will make this job easier.

To eliminate excess acidity, we make an exception to the rule and soak beef kidneys in salted water for half an hour to an hour. Lamb or veal kidneys can be soaked or not as desired.

Lamb and veal kidneys may be broiled or sautéed; beef kidney is better adapted to braising or stewing.

## BROILED KIDNEYS

Drain, rinse, and dry kidneys. Brush with melted butter and broil 3 inches from the heat, turning to brown on both sides. Lamb kidneys take about 3 minutes on each side; veal kidneys 5 or 6 minutes. Test by cutting the largest part of the muscle. If the meat is still raw, continue to cook. When done, place on a hot platter, dot with butter, and garnish with minced parsley.

## SAUTÉED KIDNEYS

Drain, rinse, and dry kidneys and cut into thin slices. Melt a little butter in a heavy skillet and cook over medium heat 6 to 10 minutes for lamb kidneys, 10-12 minutes for veal. Stir occasionally to brown on both sides and add more butter as needed. Season to taste and serve sprinkled with minced parsley.

## KIDNEY STEW

| | |
|---|---|
| 1 beef, 3 veal, or 9 lamb kidneys | ¼ tsp. paprika |
| 4 tbsp. butter | 1 can vegetable soup |
| 3 medium onions, sliced thin | 1 tbsp. lemon juice |
| 1 tsp. vegetable salt | |

Prepare and soak the kidneys as directed above. Drain, dry, and slice thin. Melt the butter in a large skillet, add the kidneys and onions, and sauté over medium heat about 5 minutes, stirring occasionally. Add the seasonings and soup and simmer about 10 minutes until the kidneys are tender and the soup thoroughly heated. Stir in the lemon juice just before serving. Serve on toast or with boiled rice.

## BRAINS

Brains to be really appetizing should be parboiled as soon as they come from the market. Then store them in the refrigerator until ready to use. But first soak them in cold salted water for half an hour and remove all membranes.

## BRAINS COOKED WITH HERBS

Simmer in water to cover for 15 minutes, adding 1 tablespoon of lemon juice and 1 teaspoon of vegetable salt for each quart of water. The lemon will help to keep them white.

Better yet, use Hauser Broth for the simmering water; or, failing that, add a handful of chopped parsley and leeks to the water.

Don't boil them rapidly; it will make them tough. And don't overcook, for brains are very soft and you are likely to have nothing left. As soon as the brains are firm, remove them carefully from the water with a skimmer, plunge them into cold water, and store until you are ready to prepare them.

## HOW TO SERVE BRAINS ATTRACTIVELY

After the brains are prepared as above, they can be broiled, sautéed, used in salad alone or with chicken, served in a rich cream sauce or tomato sauce, or with mushrooms in a mushroom sauce.

## SAUTEED BRAINS

Dip the brains in egg and roll in wheat germ. Melt a little butter in a heavy skillet and sauté the brains over medium heat until they are golden brown on both sides. Serve with lemon wedges and sprinkle with loads of minced parsley.

## BROILED BRAINS

Brush prepared brains with melted butter and place in a buttered shallow baking pan. Broil 3 inches from the heat until delicately browned, which will take about 3 minutes for each side. Serve with lemon and sprinkle with minced parsley or chopped water cress.

## SCRAMBLED EGGS AND BRAINS

| | |
|---|---|
| 3 pairs calves' brains | ½ tsp. paprika |
| 4 eggs | 2 tbsp. butter |
| ½ cup milk | 1 tbsp. minced green pepper or onion |
| ½ tsp. soy sauce | 1 tbsp. minced parsley |
| 1 tsp. vegetable salt | |

Prepare the brains as directed above. Drain and dice. Beat the eggs with milk, soy sauce, salt, and paprika. Melt the butter in a heavy skillet and sauté the green pepper or onion about 2 minutes, until golden brown. Add the brains and sauté another minute. Then pour in the egg mixture and proceed as for scrambled eggs.

## TRIPE

Tripe is the walls of the stomach of a beef animal. Plain tripe comes from the first stomach, honeycomb tripe from the second. Fresh tripe is cooked before it is sold but always needs further cooking. Cured tripe takes less time to cook.

Cook the tripe in water to cover, simmering for about an hour or until tender. After that, brush it with melted butter and broil; or dice it and serve in a well-seasoned tomato sauce. This is another dish you can share with your pooch.

### CREOLE TRIPE

1½ lb. honeycomb tripe
2 tbsp. butter
2 tbsp. minced onion
1 green pepper, minced
½ cup chopped celery

1 tbsp. whole-wheat flour
Vegetable salt
Paprika
1 cup tomato paste
2 tbsp. minced parsley

Wash the tripe thoroughly and dice. Cover with cold water in a saucepan and bring to the boiling point. Drain, cover with fresh boiling water, and simmer covered until tender. This will take anywhere from 40 minutes to 2 or 3 hours, depending upon the age of the tripe.

Drain and save 1 cup of the water. Melt the butter in a heavy skillet and sauté the onion, green pepper, and celery about 3 minutes over low heat. Add the flour and seasonings and stir until well blended. Gradually stir in the tripe liquid and the tomato paste (or 2 cups of canned tomatoes if preferred). Stir constantly until the sauce is smooth and thick. Add the tripe, cover, and simmer over low heat about 10 minutes, just until the tripe is heated through. Add the minced parsley and serve on toast or boiled rice.

# CHAPTER 7

# Fish and Shellfish

YOU MAY NEVER learn to eat a squid nor greatly care for eel; but the creatures of the deep can still bring you adventures of the palate. Modern transportation and refrigeration bring to us the fruit of two great oceans, and our inland lakes and rivers. Crabs, scallops, smelts, shrimps, lobster—as well as the familiar flounder, shad, and cod—are now supplemented by more exotic fish—abalone, pompano, bonito. Quick-freezing makes many fish available out of season and far from the source of supply. Salted, smoked, and canned fish give additional variety.

Fish supply proteins, minerals, and vitamins. Fish liver is exceptionally rich in vitamins A and D. Salt-water fish are the most important source of iodine. Everyone should have fish once a week for that alone.

## FRESHNESS

Fish must be fresh; if not they can be indigestible, even poisonous. You can tell whether a whole fish is fresh by looking at its eyes. They should be bright and bulging. The gills should be fresh and bright, the flesh firm and elastic enough to spring back when pressed. In boned or filleted fish the general appearance and odor are all you have to go by. The fish should be firm, elastic, moist, and smell fresh.

Fish spoils quickly but will keep a short while if packed in ice or stored in the coldest part of an automatic refrigerator. When your fish comes from the market, wash it well if whole, wipe with a damp cloth if it is cut up. Sprinkle it lightly with vegetable salt, wrap in waxed paper to keep the odor from penetrating other food, and put it immediately into the refrigerator. Salt and smoked fish need not be kept in the refrigerator except in very warm weather.

## KINDS OF FISH

Fish are divided into two main classes—scaly fish and shellfish. The word "fish" in cookery usually applies only to scaly fish; shellfish are treated separately. Scaly fish are described as fresh-water or salt-water according to their origin, or as lean or fat according to the amount of fat they contain.

All fresh fish are adapted to all methods of cooking. There is a saying that lean fish are better suited for poaching, steaming, and sautéing; fat fish to broiling and baking; but there are too many exceptions to this rule to make it a good guide.

*Lean Fish:* The lean fish, which have white flesh, are: bass, bluefish, catfish, cod, flounder, haddock, smelt, brook trout, weakfish, halibut, king fish, perch, pickerel, hake, mullet, pike, pollock, red drum, red snapper, sheepshead, and whiting.

*Fat Fish:* Fat fish, with dark flesh, are: butterfish, alewives, barracuda, bonito, sea bass, blue runner, buffalo fish, chub, eel, sea herring, lake trout, lingcod, mackerel, pilchard, pompano, porgie, sablefish, salmon, scup, sardines, shad, sturgeon, swordfish, tuna, whitefish, and yellow tail.

## HOW TO COOK FISH

Fish is very tender and needs careful handling to keep its shape and texture. It should be cooked just until it flakes, never overcooked. Because it does not have the tough connective tissue of meat, fish cooks in a very short time. Overcooking will toughen the delicate proteins.

The taste of fish is so delicate that it needs seasonings to bring it out. For that reason fish is one of the best fields for using your knowledge of herbs and for fortifying with parsley and lemon juice. A sprinkling of parsley and a wedge of lemon served on the side is never amiss with fish.

*Sherry with Fish:* When you have removed sautéed fish from the pan, add 1 tablespoon of sherry per portion to the drippings. Heat slightly and pour over the dish. Or flavor creamed fish and shellfish with the sherry a minute or two before removing from the heat.

### BROILED FISH

Have whole fish split down the middle; have fillets or steaks of large fish cut ¾ to 1 inch thick. Wash the fish or wipe with a damp cloth. If desired, marinate for an hour in French dressing, then dry thoroughly before broiling.

Rub lean fish with butter or olive oil, but broil fat fish just as it is. Place skin side down on a well-buttered broiler pan if lean fish, a rack if fat. Sprinkle with lemon juice and broil 2 inches from the heat until brown. Turn and broil the other side. It will take 10-15 minutes to cook. Season with vegetable salt and serve with parsley, butter, and lemon.

### BROILED FISH WITH HERBS

Cream minced thyme, fennel, and parsley into a little butter and spread it over the fish before broiling. Other combinations of herbs will come to you also. This is better suited to lean fish than to fat.

### BAKED FISH

Split and clean small fish and place on a buttered baking pan. Or use fillets ¾-1 inch thick. Mix vegetable salt, paprika, and onion juice with butter or olive oil and brush over the fish. Bake skin side down in a hot oven (425°F.) 15-25 minutes, until the fish is browned and flakes with a fork. Garnish with lemon wedges and water cress and sprinkle with minced parsley.

### PLANKED FISH

Bake any fish as directed above, using a buttered heated plank or an oven-proof platter. When the fish is done, edge the plank with a border of mashed potatoes forced through a pastry tube. Brown the potatoes under a broiler. Arrange other vegetables on the plank as desired—mounds of spinach, French-fried eggplant, and broiled tomatoes. Serve with maître d'hôtel butter and wedges of lemon.

## FILLETS BAKED IN CREAM

2 lb. fish fillets
1 cup sweet or sour cream
1 tsp. vegetable salt

Paprika to taste
3 tbsp. butter
4 tbsp. minced onion or chives

Arrange the fillets in a buttered baking dish. Pour over them enough cream to cover. Sprinkle with salt and paprika and dot with butter. Sprinkle with chopped onion (and ¼ cup of grated cheese if desired) and bake in a hot oven (400°F.) 15-25 minutes or until tender.

## SAUTEED FISH

Wipe fillets or small fish with a damp cloth. Roll in seasoned flour or dip in beaten egg then roll in fine whole-wheat bread crumbs or wheat germ—some prefer corn meal. In a heavy skillet heat a few tablespoons of butter or vegetable shortening or a mixture of the two. Brown the fish over a medium fire, first on one side and then on the other. If the fish are thick, cover the pan for a few minutes to let the centers cook through, but remove the cover several minutes before you finish so the fish will be crisp. Take care not to crowd too many fish into the skillet. Results will be better if the pieces do not touch each other. Serve with tartar or Hollandaise sauce and garnish with parsley and lemon wedges.

## FRENCH-FRIED FISH

Prepare the fish as for Sautéed Fish, preferably with the bread-crumbs, wheat-germ, or corn-meal coating. Fry in deep hot fat—never less than 3 inches deep—putting in a few pieces at a time so the fat doesn't cool off too fast. Keep the fat at about 385°F., certainly not above 400°F. Don't put in so many pieces that they touch each other. Remove from the fat and drain on brown paper when the coating is crisp and brown.

## SHELLFISH

Richest of all fish in vitamins and minerals are the mollusks, the soft-structured shellfish such as clams, oysters, and scallops. Although they are classed as proteins, actually they supply more protective vitamins and minerals than they do proteins. Clams supply two-thirds as much vitamin C as orange juice; oysters and scallops also yield large amounts of this vitamin, and quantities of iron and iodine. As long as they are fresh and correctly cooked, mollusks are easily digested. They are low in calories and high in water, which makes them good balance wheels in an otherwise heavy meal.

Shrimp, crabs, and lobsters, the crustaceans, are also good protective foods, supplying vitamins C and G, and also iodine. Shrimp are especially valuable when fortified with peppers, onions, or pimentoes as in Shrimp Creole.

*Clams:* Hard-shelled clams, called quahogs, are quite tough and need to be chopped before eating. Soft-shelled clams, or steamers, have a tender meat somewhat like oysters.

A fresh clam shell is tightly closed, proving the clam is still alive. If a shell should happen to be open when you look at it, it should snap shut when you touch it if it's alive. Clams purchased at the market will be opened upon request. To prepare clams at home, let them stand in clean cold water for a while, then scrub with a brush under running water to remove the sand. Steam the shells open or cut them open with a knife, inserting a very sharp one between the shells to cut the muscle which holds the two halves together. Open the shell flat and cut the meat away from the shell.

A quart of shelled clams, or 2-3 cups of chopped clams, will serve 6.

*Crabs:* Crabs come both hard-shelled and soft-shelled. They may be the same crab—the soft-shells are crabs caught during the molting season when the old shell has been shed and the new one is still soft. Both kinds of crabs should be bought alive with large claws intact. The meat of hard-shelled crabs can be purchased already cooked at the market and also comes in cans.

*Lobster:* The familiar Atlantic lobster of the east coast is known for its huge claws. The Pacific-coast lobster has no claws. Lobster is generally bought alive, although in some markets it comes ready-cooked. Live lobster is bluish green, cooked lobster red. Quick-frozen lobster meat comes raw or cooked depending upon the brand. Canned lobster is cooked. The coral is found in female lobsters only.

*Oysters:* Oysters come in the shell or already shucked. Shucked oysters should be plump and shiny, the liquor around them fresh-smelling. Quick-frozen oysters come in packages ready for use. Oysters in the shell will be opened at the market if desired. To open them at home, scrub the shells with a brush under running water. Insert a sharp knife between the two halves of the shell and cut the muscle which holds them together. If the knife will not go in readily, hit the hinged side sharply until you make a hole.

*Shrimp:* Fresh shrimp have a grayish-green shell and firm flesh. Wash the shrimp and split the shell from front to back. Take out the meat in one piece and wash again. With the tip of a sharp knife remove the dark vein along the center of the shrimp's back. Shrimp may be shelled after cooking if preferred, but the odor of shrimp cooking in the shell is very unpleasant.

*Scallops:* In this country we eat only part of the scallop—the cube-shaped scallops we buy here are cut from the muscle which holds the two halves of the live animal's shell together. Two kinds are available —the small bay or cape scallops and the large sea scallops. Scallops should be odorless, clean, and cream-colored rather than white.

## STEAMED CLAMS

Put the scrubbed clams in a large kettle with half an inch of water in the bottom. Cover the kettle and steam until the shells open, which will take about 15 minutes. Overcooking will make the clams tough. Drain, saving the liquor. Serve with individual dishes of melted butter or hot lemon butter and serve the clam broth, seasoned with celery salt and minced parsley, in bouillon cups.

## SCALLOPED CLAMS

3 cups finely chopped clams
1 cup whole-wheat cracker crumbs
1 tbsp. butter
1 tbsp. whole-wheat flour
1 cup milk

½ tsp. poultry seasoning
½ tsp. vegetable salt
⅛ tsp. paprika
½ cup buttered crumbs

Arrange the clams and cracker crumbs in layers in a buttered baking dish. Melt the butter in a skillet, stir in the flour, and gradually add the.

milk, stirring constantly. Add the seasonings to this source and pour over the clams. Top with buttered crumbs and a dash of paprika. Bake in a moderate oven (375°F.) half an hour or until browned.

## DEVILED CRABS

2 cups cooked or canned crab meat
6 crab shells
¼ cup butter
2 tbsp. whole-wheat flour
½ tsp. vegetable salt
½ tsp. dry mustard
½ tsp. paprika
1 cup rich milk
2 tbsp. finely chopped parsley
1 tbsp. lemon juice
¾ cup buttered whole-wheat bread crumbs

Pick over the crabmeat to remove all bits of cartilage. Melt the ¼ cup of butter in a saucepan and stir in the flour, salt, mustard, and paprika. Add the milk slowly, stirring constantly over low heat until the sauce thickens and boils. Stir in the parsley, lemon juice, and crabmeat. Fill the crab shells with the mixture and top with bread crumbs and melted butter. Bake in a moderate oven (375°F.) about 10 minutes.

## BOILED LOBSTER

Plunge the lobster into a large kettle of boiling water. Cover and boil rapidly 20-25 minutes, or until the lobster turns bright red. Remove with tongs or 2 forks if you are serving it hot immediately. Otherwise let it cool in the water.

Cut off the small claws and keep them for garnish. Turn the lobster on its back and cut through the shell from head to tail. Remove and discard the stomach sac, which you will find near the head, and the black intestinal vein running from head to tail. Discard the spongy lung tissue but keep the green liver and the coral if there is any. Use a stainless steel or silver knife for cutting lobster—other metals discolor the meat.

Serve hot with melted butter or lemon butter; cold with mayonnaise. Crack the large claws and serve with the rest of the lobster meat, and provide a nutcracker for further work on the claws at the table. For each serving allow a whole small lobster or half a large one.

## LOBSTER THERMIDOR

2 boiled lobsters
4 mushrooms, sliced
4 tbsp. butter
1 tbsp. chopped parsley
1 cup cream sauce
½ cup sherry
2 tbsp. grated Parmesan cheese
Paprika to taste

Split the lobsters lengthwise. Remove the meat from the shell and claws and cut in small pieces. Sauté the mushrooms in butter, adding the lobster after 4 minutes. Slowly add the cream sauce—or, if none is prepared, add first 1 tablespoon of whole-wheat flour, then gradually 1 cup of milk. Add the parsley and sherry and cook for 2 minutes. Put the mixture back into the lobster shells, sprinkle with grated cheese, and dust lightly with paprika. Bake in a hot oven (400°F.) for 12 minutes, or until the cheese is browned.

## FRENCH-FRIED LOBSTER

Remove the meat from the shells of boiled lobsters. Sprinkle with vegetable salt, paprika, and lemon juice. Dip in seasoned flour, then in beaten egg, then in wheat germ. Fry in deep hot fat (385°F.) until browned. Serve with tartar sauce.

## OYSTER COCKTAIL

Scrub and open the shelled oysters as described on page 89. Keep the deep side of the shell down as you open them so as to keep in as much of the juice as you can, and open over a bowl to catch what drips out. Discard the other half of each shell and leave the oysters in the deep half. Serve on a bed of cracked ice around a small bowl of chili sauce or cocktail sauce. Garnish with wedges of lemon.

## OYSTERS CASINO

Prepare oysters on the half-shell as described for Oyster Cocktail. Sprinkle the oysters with chopped parsley, chopped chives, a few buttered bread crumbs, and a dash of paprika. Top each with a small piece of bacon and place under the broiler in a moderate oven (375°F.) until browned.

## OYSTERS ROCKEFELLER

| | |
|---|---|
| 1½ tbsp. grated white onion | ¼ tsp. vegetable salt |
| 1½ tbsp. finely chopped chives | ⅛ tsp. paprika |
| 1½ tbsp. finely chopped parsley | 5 tbsp. butter |
| 2 tbsp. finely chopped celery | 2 dozen oysters on the half-shell |
| 1 tsp. lemon juice | Buttered crumbs |

Combine the onion, chives, parsley, celery, lemon juice, and seasonings. Cream the butter and mix in the vegetables and seasonings. Place the oysters in a shallow baking pan and on top of each a spoonful of the onion and butter mixture. Sprinkle with buttered crumbs. Bake in a moderate oven (375°F.) 25-30 minutes, or until the crumbs are browned.

## SCALLOPED OYSTERS

⅔ cup melted butter
3 cups whole-wheat bread crumbs
1 tsp. grated onion
1 tsp. vegetable salt
⅛ tsp. paprika

¼ tsp. nutmeg
1½ pints oysters
⅓ cup oyster liquor
⅓ cup cream

Combine the melted butter, bread crumbs, onion, and seasonings. Drain the oysters, saving ⅓ cup of the juice. Put a layer of oysters in the bottom of a buttered baking dish. Top with a layer of buttered crumbs, then another layer of oysters. Pour oyster liquor and cream over the three layers, then top with the remaining crumbs. Sprinkle with paprika and bake in a moderate oven (375°F.) 25-30 minutes, or until the crumbs are browned.

## CREAMED SCALLOPS

Scallops are usually French-fried or creamed. For creamed scallops, add to 1 cup of cream sauce the following: ¼ teaspoon dry mustard, ½ teaspoon grated onion, 1½ tsp. finely chopped parsley, 1½ tsp. lemon juice, and ¾ pint of scallops, cut in small cubes. Heat and serve.

## CREOLE SHRIMP

2 or 3 tbsp. chopped onion
1 green pepper, chopped
2 tbsp. butter
2 tbsp. whole-wheat flour
2 cups condensed mushroom soup
½ tsp. vegetable salt

⅛ tsp. paprika
¼ tsp. thyme
1 small bay leaf
2 tbsp. chopped pimento
2 cups cooked or canned shrimp
3 tbsp. minced parsley

Melt the butter in a heavy skillet. Sauté the chopped onion and green pepper in the butter for a few minutes, then stir in the flour until smooth and well blended. Add the mushroom soup gradually, stirring constantly, and cook over low heat until the mixture thickens and boils. Add the seasonings and shrimps and cook about 5 minutes to heat the shrimps. Remove the bay leaf before serving. Serve on toast or boiled rice and garnish with the minced parsley.

## SALMON CASSEROLE

| | |
|---|---|
| 2 cups canned or cooked salmon | 3 tbsp. whole-wheat flour |
| 2 cups canned or cooked peas | 1½ cups liquid from salmon and |
| 1 tbsp. minced onion | peas and milk |
| 2 tbsp. minced parsley | 4 tbsp. whole-wheat bread crumbs |
| 5 tbsp. butter | |

Drain the salmon and peas, saving the liquor. Add enough milk to make 1½ cups. (Use all milk if the peas and salmon are home-cooked.) Melt 3 tablespoons of butter in a heavy skillet. Stir in the flour, blending well. Add the liquid gradually, stirring constantly, and cook over low heat until the mixture thickens and boils. Stir in the salmon, peas, and seasonings. Pour into a buttered casserole or shallow baking dish. Sprinkle with bread crumbs and dot with the remaining butter. Bake in a hot oven (450°F.) about 10 minutes, just until the crumbs are brown.

Tuna fish may be used instead of salmon.

## TUNA FISH À LA KING

| | |
|---|---|
| 1 can tuna fish | ¼ cup thin slices of pimento |
| 3 tbsp. butter | Vegetable salt to taste |
| ¼ cup green pepper cut in thin strips | Paprika |
| ½ cup sliced mushrooms | 1 egg yolk, slightly beaten |
| 2 tbsp. whole-wheat flour | 2 tbsp. sherry if desired |
| 1½ cups rich milk or thin cream | |

Open a can of tuna fish, preferably solid white meat. Wash under warm running water to remove the oil and the fish taste. Melt the butter in a skillet and sauté the green pepper and mushrooms until soft—about 5 minutes. Stir in the flour and when well blended slowly add the milk or cream. Stir over low heat until the milk thickens and bubbles. Add the pimento and tuna fish, broken into chunks, and season to taste with vegetable salt and paprika. Heat through. Slightly beat the egg yolk and stir into it a little of the hot sauce. When well mixed, stir it into the sauce. Add the sherry and serve at once on buttered whole-wheat toast or in patty shells.

An economical and delicious recipe which tastes exactly like chicken à la king.

CHAPTER 8

# Poultry and Game

FROM THE MILD domesticated capon to the gamey wild duck, there is a wide range of flavor and nourishment. Chicken is the favorite for the small dinner; for special occasions there is the noble brown turkey, guinea hen, goose, duck, quail, not to mention the game birds.

Poultry is slightly higher than meat in muscle protein and better serves those who have to watch their waistlines because it is comparatively low in fat except in the case of duck and goose.

## BROILED CHICKEN

Broiling is the preferred method of cooking chicken because the cooking time is shorter. Broilers are split down the back, and larger birds sometimes cut in four pieces.

Select young birds from 8-12 weeks old, weighing not more than 2½ pounds. Wash and dry. If you are using quick-frozen birds, defrost and let them warm to room temperature before broiling.

Brush with melted butter or softened vegetable shortening. Southerners like to wrap thin strips of bacon around the legs. Garlic fans should let a crushed clove of garlic permeate the melted butter before brushing the chicken. Or rub the broiler rack with garlic.

Preheat the broiler to 350°-375°F. Place the chicken skin side down. Be sure the chicken is 3 or 4 inches below the heating element, and leave the door of the broiling compartment ajar unless your stove gives instructions to the contrary. A 2-pound chicken will take from 35-45 minutes to broil thoroughly. Baste occasionally with pan drippings or with melted butter, and turn frequently to brown both sides. Sprinkle with vegetable salt before removing from the oven.

Serve immediately with its own juices on a hot platter and garnish with chopped parsley.

## BROILED TURKEY

Fat young turkeys about 3 months old can be broiled as a change from the traditional roast turkey. Split, or have them split, down the back and remove the breastbone. Divide the bird in half. Next, remove the leg bones by cutting the skin on the side next to the body and taking out the bones, disturbing the flesh as little as possible. Cut off the wings at the elbow joint and cut the skin on the rest of the wing on the side next to the body. Leave the backbone and ribs to help hold the turkey halves in shape.

Brush with melted butter and place skin side down on a broiling rack. Broil 60-75 minutes in a preheated broiling compartment, turning often to brown both sides and basting with melted butter.

Or the turkey halves may be stuffed before broiling. Prepare your favorite dressing, using about 3 cups of bread crumbs for a 4-pound turkey. Put a spoonful of stuffing into the boned legs and wings and sew or skewer neatly to the body. Broil as described above. When nearly done turn the turkey halves skin side down on the broiler and fill each cup-shaped hollow with stuffing, patting it into place. Return to the broiler to finish cooking the meat and brown the stuffing. Serve on a hot platter, skin side up, stuffing underneath.

## BROILED GAME BIRDS

Tender young birds, grouse, quail, pheasant, and wild duckling, are prepared and cooked much like chicken. If you buy them in the market the butcher will draw and split them, or ask him to bone them. If the birds come to you straight from a friend's game bag, best take them to your butcher and prevail upon him to dress and draw them for you.

Wash, dry, brush with melted butter, and broil in a preheated broiling compartment as for Broiled Chicken. Game birds are lean and require extra fat during cooking. Light-meat birds such as quail and partridge should be well done. The dark-meat birds may be served rare.

Length of broiling time will depend upon the size of the bird and whether you are serving it well done or rare. Quail will take 10-15 minutes; grouse 15-20 minutes; pheasant and partridge need 20-30 minutes.

Sprinkle with vegetable salt just before removing from the oven, and serve hot on toast with a tart jelly.

## BROILED WILD DUCK

Mallards and canvasbacks are good broiled. Clean the birds and split them down the back. Wash out the insides with a damp cloth. Rub inside and out with olive oil, sprinkle with vegetable salt, and place skin side down on a buttered broiling rack. Broil in a moderate oven (350°F.) for 20 minutes, or until tender, turning often. Teal and very small ducks can be left whole.

## BROILED SQUAB

Squab is young pigeon, domesticated of course, weighing ¾-1 pound. One squab will serve one person generously or two people more sparingly. Clean, wash, and dry as for any poultry. Split down the back and brush with melted butter and lemon juice. Broil as directed for Broiled Chicken, basting frequently. Allow 25-40 minutes for broiling. Serve on toast with a tart jelly.

## BROILED GUINEA

Use the squab guinea for broiling—young guineas weighing ¾-1¼ pounds. Split and broil as for Broiled Chicken, allowing 25-35 minutes. Baste frequently.

## BROILED DUCKLING

Broil plump young ducklings weighing 2-3 pounds. Split and broil as directed for Broiled Chicken, allowing 35-45 minutes.

## ROAST CHICKEN

Choose a young, well-fattened bird from 5-9 months old, weighing 3½-5 or 6 pounds (capons will weigh more). Singe and wash the chicken as directed, then sprinkle the inside lightly with vegetable salt. Prepare stuffing and fill the body and neck cavities. Stuff lightly, do not pack, for stuffing expands with cooking and may burst the skin if there is too much of it. If the body cavity has been cut lengthwise, draw the edges of the cut together with a darning needle and a heavy thread or with skewers. You will generally find, however, that the cavity has been cut crosswise, which means that the edges will not meet. Use a crust of bread tucked into the hole to keep the stuffing in. At the neck, tie a string around the skin to hold it tight if you are leaving the neck in. If you cut off the neck before cooking, simply fold the loose skin over and pin it to the back with a skewer.

Truss the bird to help it keep its shape while roasting. Place the bird breast down and tie the center of a piece of string around the tail. Pull the legs close to the tail and tie legs and tail together. Fold the wings back, like arms akimbo, and run a large skewer through both wings and the body to hold them in place. Cross the ends of the cord holding the legs and tie them to the skewer.

Brush the skin with melted butter or coat lightly with whole-wheat flour, as desired. Place the bird breast side down in a shallow baking pan with a rack in the bottom. Roast uncovered in a moderate oven (350°F.), allowing 30 minutes per pound for birds under 4 pounds; 22-25 minutes for birds over 4 pounds. If you use a meat thermometer, insert it in the thickest part of the thigh and roast to 185°F. Baste frequently or cover with a cloth dipped in melted fat.

About halfway through the cooking period turn the bird breast up, grasping it at head and foot with hands protected by clean cloths or paper toweling. The bird is done when a 2-tined fork will pierce the breast and thigh easily and the juice which runs out shows no trace of red.

Remove to a hot platter and take off the strings and skewers.

*Basting Poultry:* Baste roast poultry frequently with Hauser Broth. For new and subtle flavors, use 2 parts broth and 1 part sherry. Or dissolve a lump of butter in ¼ cup of hot broth; add vegetable salt to taste, 1 tablespoon of tomato paste, 1 tablespoon of olive oil, and ½ cup dry white wine.

## ROAST TURKEY

Roast as described for Roast Chicken, allowing 20-25 minutes per pound for birds under 10 pounds; 18-20 minutes for those from 10-16 pounds; and 15-18 minutes for those over 16 pounds. Start the turkey lying on one side; shift to the other side after a third of the cooking time has passed; then finish breast up.

## ROAST DUCK

Stuff and truss as directed for Roast Chicken, using a fruit stuffing since duck is very fat. Or omit the stuffing and fill the body cavity with quartered tart apples or celery stalks and leaves and a large onion cut in quarters.

Prick the skin all over with a fork to let the fat drain out. Roast in a moderate oven (350°F.), allowing 2-2½ hours for a 5-6 pound duck. Pour off the fat occasionally as it accumulates in the bottom of the pan. Do not use a buttered cloth with duck, and baste only occasionally if at all.

## DUCK WITH ORANGE

About an hour before Roast Duck is done, pour off all the fat in the pan and begin to baste with the following mixture:

1 cup orange juice                    ¼ cup shredded orange rind
½ cup natural brown sugar             2 tbsp. drippings

Baste frequently with this mixture during the remaining hour of roasting.

## ROAST GOOSE

Stuff and truss as described for Roast Chicken, using a fruit stuffing. Prick the skin all over with a sharp fork to let the fat drain out. Roast in a moderate oven (325°F.), allowing about 20 minutes per pound. Pour off the fat as it accumulates in the bottom of the pan. Goose need not be basted at all.

## ROAST GUINEA HEN

Select a guinea hen weighing 2½ to 3 pounds. Clean, stuff, and truss as described for Roast Chicken. Wild rice and mushroom stuffing is good with guinea, or you may omit stuffing and put an onion in the body cavity with 2 tablespoons of butter.

Guinea is dry, so it must be lavishly basted, or else lay 2 strips of bacon on top of the back—the bird will be breast down in the pan. Roast uncovered in a slow oven (300°F.), allowing 30 minutes per pound. After half an hour or so remove the strips of bacon and turn breast up.

Serve with broiled pineapple rings.

## SAUTÉED CHICKEN

Have the butcher cut a fryer into pieces for serving. Singe and wash each piece and coat with seasoned whole-wheat flour, wheat germ, or a mixture of 3 parts flour to 1 part corn meal. For a crisp, crunchy crust such as you find in some Southern fried chicken, add 1 teaspoon of baking powder to a cup of flour and leave the pieces of chicken dripping wet so they will coat heavily.

In a heavy skillet melt half butter and half vegetable shortening to a depth of an inch. Let the fat get moderately hot, then gently lower the pieces of chicken into it. Let them have plenty of room—don't crowd them. Brown quickly on one side, then turn and brown on the other. If you like a crisp crust, cover the skillet for the first half of the cooking time, then finish uncovered. For a tender crust reverse the process, browning the chicken in an uncovered pan and then covering to finish.

Sauté for ½ hour to an hour, depending on the size of the chicken. Pour off all but 4 tablespoons of the drippings, sprinkle a very little flour over the fat left in the pan, and blend thoroughly. Add 1½ cups of light cream —or more if desired—season with vegetable salt and paprika, and boil until thoroughly cooked and colored by the bits of crust left in the pan. Put the pieces of chicken on a platter, pour the gravy over them, and sprinkle with chopped parsley. Just before removing the gravy from the fire, add ¼ cup of sherry per cup of sauce if desired.

## FRENCH-FRIED CHICKEN

Coat the pieces of chicken with seasoned flour, dip in egg beaten up with a tablespoon of water, then coat with whole-wheat bread crumbs or wheat germ. Lower gently into deep hot fat—use vegetable oils or peanut oil—heated to 350°F. Cook 10-15 minutes until brown. Remove from the fat, drain on brown paper, and place on a rack in a shallow roasting pan. Cover and bake in a moderate oven (325°F.) about an hour.

## BRAISED CHICKEN

Select a plump fowl and have it cut into pieces for serving. Singe and wash, then wipe dry. Dredge with ½ cup of seasoned whole-wheat flour and save the flour which is left to thicken the gravy. Melt butter or vegetable shortening in a heavy skillet, just enough to brown the pieces of chicken. Start with 3 tablespoons and add more if necessary. Add ½ cup of sliced onions to the chicken if desired.

Remove to a heavy kettle which has a tight cover. Pour 1-2 cups of any of the following liquids over the chicken: Hauser Broth, milk, cream, sour cream, or red wine. Cover tightly and simmer over low heat 1½-2 hours, or until tender. Add more liquid as needed. Add vegetable salt to taste during the last few minutes of cooking.

If preferred, bake in a casserole instead of stewing on top of the stove.

## BRAISED DUCK

Duck may be braised like Braised Chicken, but drain off most of the fat before adding the liquid.

## BRAISED SQUAB OR PIGEONS

Squab may be cut in pieces and braised, or whole squab can be stuffed, trussed, and then braised. If you use older pigeons, cut them in pieces. Squab will take 45-60 minutes to cook; older pigeons longer.

## BRAISED GUINEA HEN

Prepare as directed for Braised Chicken, adding sliced mushrooms half an hour before the guinea is done.


## STEWED POULTRY

Fowl may be stewed either whole or in pieces, preferably whole to keep more flavor in the meat. Singe, wash, and groom the bird as though for roasting. Place on a rack in a heavy kettle. Half fill the kettle with Hauser Broth and add 1 tablespoon of lemon juice if the bird is an old one.

The bird may be stewed plain, or add vegetables and herbs to the stock— a carrot, an onion, a stalk of celery, a sprig of parsley, some cloves, bay leaf, thyme or marjoram, and so forth.

Cover and simmer gently over low heat until tender and the meat begins to loosen frcm the bones, adding more broth if necessary. Add 1½ teaspoons of vegetable salt during the last few minutes of cooking. Turn the bird occasionally.

A fowl will probably need 3-4 hours, an old turkey 5 hours or longer. Let the bird cool breast down in the stock.

Skim off the fat from the stock when cool and remove the chicken. Discard the skin and bones and slice or dice the meat. Strain the stock and use it for broth, gravy, sauces, and so forth.


## CHICKEN FRICASSEE

Chicken fricassee is essentially stewed chicken cut in pieces for serving, with the gravy thickened as for meat stews. But that is only the beginning, although some like their chicken fricassee plain. Others, however, appreciate the richness of cream, the tang of herbs with chicken. Try this:

Have the chicken cut in pieces for serving. Singe and wash each piece, then dry with paper toweling. Roll in seasoned whole-wheat flour. Melt 3 tablespoons of butter in a heavy kettle, or use olive oil, and brown the chicken. Cover with boiling Hauser Broth when the chicken is a rich brown. Add ½ bay leaf, 1 teaspoon summer savory, ½ cup chopped parsley, 1 small onion, chopped, or use 2 shallots if you can get them. Cover the pot tightly and simmer over low heat for an hour to an hour and a half, until the chicken is tender. Add 1 teaspoon of vegetable salt the last few minutes of cooking.

Remove the chicken from the water and put it where it will keep warm. Measure the liquor in the pot and add boiling broth if necessary to make 3 cups. Taste and see if you have enough salt. Melt 4 tablespoons of butter in a saucepan and stir in 3 tablespoons of whole-wheat flour, blending to a smooth paste. Gradually stir in 1 cup of stock from the pot, stirring constantly. When thick, add the rest of the stock and simmer for 10 minutes. Beat 2 egg yolks until thick and lemon-colored. Heat 1 cup of cream and add it gradually to the beaten egg yolks, stirring all the time. Remove the gravy from the fire and gradually blend the cream and egg mixture into it. Pour over the chicken and serve.

## CHICKEN À LA KING

Follow the recipe for Chicken and Sweetbreads à la King, using 2 cups of diced cold chicken and omitting sweetbreads.

## POULTRY STUFFINGS

Stuffings are all built upon a starchy base—whole-wheat or corn-bread crumbs, flaky boiled brown or wild rice, or well-seasoned mashed potatoes. Melted butter is added for richness, then herbs and vegetables for seasonings—savory, sweet marjoram, thyme, sage, celery, parsley, and onion are the favorites.

These are the basic ingredients. To them may be added such special ingredients as nuts, oysters, mushrooms, dried fruits, raisins, and tart apple cubes.

Some stuffings are fluffy and dry, moistened only with melted fat and juices from the bird as it cooks. Perhaps the majority of people prefer this kind because it is lighter. Others prefer a moist, more compact stuffing made with rice or potatoes or liquid added to the bread crumbs.

### HOW MUCH TO MAKE

Figure the amount of stuffing you will need from the dressed weight of the bird. For a bird weighing less than 10 pounds, use 1 cup less than the weight of the bird. That is, for a 5-pound bird, use 4 cups of crumbs. For a larger bird over 10 pounds, use 2 cups of crumbs less than the weight—10 cups for a 12-pound bird. Since rice swells a good deal, use 1 cup less of rice than you would of crumbs.

For dry stuffings use bread 2 or 3 days old. A 1-pound loaf will make about 4 cups of fluffy crumbs without crusts.

In the following recipes the weight of birds for which that amount is suitable are given in each case.

## TO MAKE BREAD CRUMBS

Cut the loaf of bread in two and fork out the inside, leaving the crusts. Pick the pieces of bread apart with the fingers, taking care not to crush it and make it soggy. For moist dressings you can use dry bread crumbs.

## HERB STUFFING
### (5-pound chicken)

1 small onion, chopped
1 clove garlic, if desired, chopped
4 tbsp. butter
½ cup minced celery, leaves and stalks

1 tbsp. summer savory
1 teaspoon thyme
4 cups whole-wheat bread crumbs
1 teaspoon vegetable salt
10 chestnuts or walnuts, chopped

Melt the butter in a heavy skillet. Add the onion and garlic and sauté 10 minutes over low heat. Stir in the celery, herbs, and salt. Put the bread crumbs into a bowl, add the vegetables and herbs and the chopped nuts, and mix well.

## SAVORY STUFFING
### (12-pound turkey)

¾ cup butter
2 cups chopped celery
½ cup chopped parsley
1 small onion, chopped
1 clove garlic, chopped, if desired

10 cups bread crumbs
2 tsp. summer savory
1 tsp. thyme
2 tsp. vegetable salt

Melt the butter in a heavy skillet. Brown the celery, parsley, and onion in it. Add the herbs and salt, mix well, and blend with the bread crumbs

## OYSTER STUFFING
### (12-pound turkey)

1½ pt. oysters
¾ cup butter
2 tbsp. chopped parsley
1 tbsp. chopped onion

10 cups bread crumbs
½ tsp. summer savory
¼ tsp. celery seed
2 tsp. vegetable salt

Heat the oysters gently in their own liquor, then drain. Melt the fat and brown the parsley and onion in it. Add with the oysters to the bread crumbs and mix well. Add the celery seed and salt.


## CELERY STUFFING

### (10-pound goose)

| | |
|---|---|
| ½ cup butter | 8 cups bread crumbs |
| 1 cup chopped parsley | 1 tsp. celery seed |
| 1 cup chopped onion | ½ tsp. summer savory |
| 4 cups chopped celery, leaves and stalks | 2 tsp. vegetable salt |

Melt the butter and brown the parsley and onion. Add to the raw celery, bread crumbs, and seasonings and mix well.


## CORN-BREAD STUFFING

### (5-pound chicken)

| | |
|---|---|
| 6 tbsp. butter | 4 cups corn-bread crumbs |
| ¾ cup chopped celery | ½ tsp. thyme |
| ¼ cup chopped parsley | 1 tsp. vegetable salt |
| 1 small onion, chopped | |

Melt the fat and brown the celery, parsley, and onion. Add to the corn-bread crumbs and seasonings and mix well.


## WILD RICE STUFFING

Prepare Fluffy Wild Rice (page 176) and season with your favorite garden herbs—chopped onion, celery, savory, and so forth. Add butter for richness and stuff the bird.


## WILD RICE AND MUSHROOM STUFFING

| | |
|---|---|
| 3 cups boiled wild rice | 1 tbsp. grated onion |
| ½ lb. mushrooms, sliced | ½ tsp. vegetable salt |
| ½ cup butter | Paprika to taste |

Melt the butter and sauté the sliced mushrooms until soft. Combine all the ingredients and toss together lightly.

## ORANGE STUFFING
### (5-pound duck)

3 cups dry bread cubes, toasted
½ cup hot Hauser Broth
1 tsp. grated orange rind
1 cup diced orange pulp
2 cups diced celery
3 tbsp. minced parsley

4 tbsp. melted butter
1 egg, slightly beaten
½ tsp. vegetable salt
¼ tsp. paprika
½ tsp. poultry seasoning

Combine the ingredients and mix lightly. If desired, sauté the celery in butter for 3 minutes before combining.

## ANNA LEE'S POULTRY DRESSING
### (5-pound chicken)

2 cups shredded carrots
2 apples, shredded
1 cup shredded celery
1 large onion, shredded
1 cup shredded summer squash
½ cup raisins, chopped fine

1 cup chopped nutmeats
2 green peppers, chopped
Vegetable salt to taste
Bit of garlic
2 eggs, well beaten

Combine all ingredients. Very delicious and particularly good for reducing diets.

# CHAPTER 9

# Eggs and Cheese

EGGS ARE AS important in the diet as milk. They contain first-class protein and are rich in all vitamins except vitamin C. Four or five eggs per week is recommended for everyone, although old people should perhaps have less because of the high cholesterol content of eggs.

Parsley, milk, pimento, cheese, etc., give variety to egg dishes and increase the protective food value as well.

## HOW YOU CAN TELL A FRESH EGG

One egg is much like another from the outside. There is little for you to judge by until you open it. However, there is one point—if the shells are shiny instead of dull, it means that the thin mucilaginous coating on the outside of the shell has been rubbed off, and therefore the egg has been deteriorating more rapidly than usual because the shell is porous when the coating is removed. But for the most part you will have to trust the grading system, by which eggs are separated into grades according to size and quality, and your grocer's integrity. If you can, see that your grocer keeps his eggs in the refrigerator. Not enough of them do, but if enough of you ladies insist on it, the day will come when eggs sitting on the open counter will be as outmoded as the open cracker barrel of the horse-drawn-carriage days.

When you get your eggs home, put them in the refrigerator at once. The longer eggs stand at room temperature, the faster they deteriorate. If they are dirty, wipe them with a soft cloth or rub lightly with a brush. Do not wash them unless just before you use them, for washing removes that fragile protective coating on the shell.

When you break an egg you can tell whether it is fresh by the thickness of the egg white. In a good fresh egg, the white is very thick and the yolk stands up above the white instead of settling down. In a stale egg the white is runny and the yolk flattens out tiredly. When a recipe calls for more than one egg, it is wise to break each one separately into a saucer and examine it for freshness before you add it to the others.

## COOKING EGGS

"She doesn't know enough to boil an egg," you hear, as though cooking eggs were the simplest thing in cookery. Well, it is if you know that high heat toughens eggs. A delicate, tender, well-cooked egg can be produced only if you cook it at low heat.

## SOFT-COOKED (BOILED) EGGS

Eggs cooked in the shell are still generally called "boiled eggs," either soft-boiled or hard-boiled. Properly speaking, however, eggs should never be boiled, only simmered. The water should completely cover the eggs and should not boil once the eggs have been put into it.

Bring water to a boil in a saucepan large enough to accommodate the number of eggs you plan to cook. Lower the eggs carefully into the water on a spoon and reduce the heat so that the water doesn't bubble. Let the water simmer 3-5 minutes, according to how hard you like your eggs. Remove them immediately when the time is up.

It is best to let eggs stand at room temperature for a little while before cooking them. Your timing will be more accurate and you run less risk of having the shells crack when the hot water touches them.

## HARD-COOKED (BOILED) EGGS

Simmer the eggs in water to cover as described above, allowing 15-20 minutes. Stir the eggs carefully with a spoon once or twice during cooking to keep the yolk in the center. Too-hot water or too-long cooking may give that unattractive greenish rim you sometimes see around the yolk of a hard-boiled egg.

## EGGS À LA MODE

Butter generously a slice of whole-wheat toast for each person to be served. On it place one or two hot soft-cooked eggs removed from the shell without breaking. Cover each portion with ⅓ cup of well-seasoned hot stewed tomatoes. Serve on a hot platter and garnish each with a sprig of fresh water cress or parsley. More tomato may be served from a separate dish if desired.

## POACHED EGGS

If the eggs are not perfectly fresh, pick some other way of cooking them. Poaching, for good results, demands a perfectly fresh egg.

Fill a shallow pan or skillet two-thirds full of water. Add ½ teaspoon of vegetable salt for each 2 cups of water. Bring the water to the boil and reduce the heat. Break each egg into a cup and slip it into the water. Don't try to cook more eggs than can sit comfortably in the water without touching each other. When all the eggs are in the water, cover the pan and simmer gently for 3-5 minutes; longer if you like the yolk firm. Lift the eggs from the water with a draining spoon and serve immediately on buttered whole-wheat toast.

Eggs may also be poached in Hauser Broth, in milk, or in condensed tomato soup.

## SHIRRED EGGS

Butter a shirring dish for each person to be served. In each dish put 1 tablespoon of raw celery juice (or any other desired vegetable juice) and 1 tablespoon of heavy cream. Break an egg into each dish and sprinkle with vegetable salt. Set the dishes into a pan of hot water and bake in a moderate oven (350°F.) until the egg is sufficiently set—about 10 minutes. Garnish with chopped parsley or paprika.

## SCRAMBLED EGGS

Break fresh eggs into a bowl. Add a generous tablespoonful of cream for each egg, and sprinkle with vegetable salt to taste. Beat until blended with a rotary egg beater. Melt butter in a heavy skillet and pour in the eggs. Cook over low heat, stirring up the cooked layer of egg along the bottom of the pan as it forms. When the eggs are done, either firm or a little wet as your taste requires, remove immediately from the heat and from the skillet and serve.

Before cooking the egg mixture, you can add grated onion, finely chopped chives, minced parsley, or sautéed chopped fresh mushrooms.

## FRENCH OMELET

French omelet is made with the same mixture as scrambled eggs. The difference is in the way of cooking. Instead of stirring up the eggs as they cook, lift the edge of the bottom gently with a spatula and tip the skillet to let the uncooked top run under the bottom and be cooked in its turn. When the bottom is brown and the omelet is firm all through, fold it in half and serve. Cheese, vegetables, chopped leftover meat or chicken can be spread over the top of the omelet before you fold it.

## APPLE OMELET

4 eggs, well-beaten
1 cup shredded raw apple
¼ cup tomato juice

2 tbsp. thick cream
½ tsp. vegetable salt

Beat the eggs until light, then beat in the other ingredients. Pour into a well-oiled baking dish and bake in a moderate oven (375°F.) about 15 minutes, until browned.

## EGG OMELET WITH SQUASH

2 eggs
2 tbsp. vegetable oil
2 cups cubed summer squash
1½ cups cubed tomato

½ green pepper, coarsely chopped
⅜ tsp. vegetable salt
2 tbsp. vegetable oil or butter

Soft-cook the eggs. While they are cooking, heat the vegetable oil in a covered casserole or skillet. Add the prepared vegetables and stew slowly until the squash is sufficiently tender—about 15 minutes. Add the vegetable salt. Shell and chop the eggs and add to the vegetable mixture. Garnish with a sprinkling of chopped chives.

## RAGOUT OF EGGS

⅓ cup vegetable oil
1 onion, chopped
½ eggplant, cubed
½ clove garlic, minced
½ pimento, diced

1 large ripe tomato
⅛ tsp. powdered sage
⅜ tsp. vegetable salt
3 hard-cooked eggs cut in 16ths
3 tbsp. minced parsley

Put half the oil in a heavy skillet and brown the onion and eggplant in it. Add the rest of the oil, the other vegetables, and the sage. Cover and simmer gently about 10 minutes, until the eggplant is cooked through. Add the salt and the pieces of egg and heat the eggs through. Stir in the parsley just before dishing up. Serve with toast points.

## EGG CHOP SUEY

3 tbsp. vegetable oil
2 medium-sized onions cut in thin
    wedges
5 large stalks celery cut in 1-inch
    pieces

1 large green pepper cut in squares
1 4-egg omelet, well browned on
    both sides and cut into cubes
2/3 can tomato soup
1/4 tsp. vegetable salt

Heat the oil in a covered skillet. Sauté the onion and celery in the oil for 15 to 20 minutes, adding a little water if necessary to keep them from burning. Five minutes before they are soft, add the green pepper. When the vegetables are done, add the omelet and tomato soup and vegetable salt. Stir over low heat until heated through. Serve in a ring of hot mashed summer squash or other cooked vegetable, well seasoned.

Preparation: 15 to 20 minutes.

4 servings.

## CHINESE EGGS

3 eggs
1½ cups shredded raw vegetables

¾ tbsp. butter and vegetable oil mixed
¾ tsp. vegetable salt

Beat the eggs and shredded vegetables together until the mixture is thick and the egg evenly distributed through the vegetables. Take a third of the mixture and press against the curving sides of a teacup or ladle so that the vegetables will lie flat when the mixture is carefully poured into the frying pan. Heat the fat in the skillet and pour in the mixture to make 3 thin flat cakes. Brown on one side, salt, and turn over, then brown the other side—about 10 minutes in all.

Any quick-cooking tender vegetables may be used alone or in combination. One part cucumber to 2 parts spinach is good; or summer squash or eggplant and onion with green pepper, or a mixture of leafy greens.

Preparation: 5 to 10 minutes.

3 servings.

## EGGS ON VEGETABLE TOAST

For each person to be served, cut a slice of eggplant ¾ inch thick. Moisten in milk or egg diluted with milk and dust with whole-wheat flour. Place in a buttered baking dish, allowing 1 tablespoon of butter for each slice. Bake in a hot oven (400°F.) until the bottom is browned, about 15 minutes. Turn the slices over and in the center of each scoop out a hollow large enough to hold an egg yolk. Sprinkle with vegetable salt and break an egg into each hollow. Return to the oven and bake until the egg is set—about 5 minutes. Sprinkle with paprika and serve with a garnish of any desired green.

## CHEESE

Some 400 varieties of cheese, stemming from all parts of the world, would suggest that cheese is a popular food. Every people has produced a distinctive variety of this food derived from their own customs and preference. Cheeses of all kinds are made from the coagulated curd of milk, hence they are high in protein and in fat. Their food value depends upon what kind of milk they are made of—whole milk, skimmed milk, or cream. Cheese made from whole milk is rich in vitamin A. Cottage cheese, made from skim milk, is low in fat.

Keep in mind that cheese is a concentrated food. It should be used as a substitute for meat or combined with foods which need added nutritive value. When used for dessert, it should always follow a light meal, never a heavy one.

Of the many varieties, the American or Cheddar cheeses are best for cooking. Cheddar cheese melts easily without forming strings, has a sharp flavor which can compete with the flavors of other ingredients in a dish, and is relatively inexpensive.

## MAKE YOUR OWN COTTAGE CHEESE

Cottage cheese is made by heating sour milk until the curds coagulate and separate from the watery part, the whey. You can either let the milk turn sour by itself, heat it over low heat to lukewarm, and drain through cheesecloth, or sour the milk by adding lemon juice. Put fresh milk in a saucepan, heat it gently to lukewarm, stirring with a wooden spoon, and then put into it 2 teaspoons of lemon juice per cup of milk. Stir well and when the milk is thoroughly curdled, strain it through cheesecloth, pressing out the whey with a wooden spoon to drain the cheese thoroughly. Flavor with a little vegetable salt and vitaminize it by adding chopped chives and lemon. Keep in the refrigerator.

## MAKE YOUR OWN CREAM CHEESE

Take a bottle of fresh cream and let it sour, which will take about 2 days at room temperature. Pour the contents into a cheesecloth bag and let it drain. When solid, put it in the icebox and chill it, forming it into a flat cake or into balls. Delicious for desserts or cake fillings.

## SOYA CHEESE STICKS

½ cup sifted whole-wheat flour
1 tsp. baking powder
1 tsp. vegetable salt
¾ cup soft bread crumbs
3 tbsp. milk

¼ cup soya grits mixed with ¼ cup milk
Pinch of paprika
½ cup grated cheese

Sift together the flour, baking powder, and salt. Combine all ingredients and blend thoroughly (¼ cup soya flour may be used in place of grits, in which case omit the ¼ cup of milk).

Roll the dough very thin on a lightly floured board. Cut into narrow strips. Bake in a greased pan in a moderate oven (350°F.) for about 20 minutes, or until lightly browned.

## CHEESE SOUFFLÉ

4 tbsp. butter
3 tbsp. whole-wheat flour
⅔ cup milk, scalded

1 cup grated yellow cheese
5 eggs, separated
½ tsp. vegetable salt

Melt the butter in the top of a double boiler. Blend in the flour and gradually stir in the scalded milk. Cook over hot water, stirring constantly, until thick and smooth. Add the grated cheese and remove from the heat. Beat the egg yolks until thick and lemon-colored and add to the cheese mixture with the vegetable salt. Let the mixture cool to lukewarm, then beat the egg whites until stiff but not dry. Have your baking dish ready and well buttered, your oven heated. Fold the egg whites swiftly into the cheese mixture and pour into the baking dish. Bake in a moderate oven (350°F.) 30-40 minutes, until the center is firm. Serve at once. Delicious with a man-sized green salad.

## CORN AND CHEESE SOUFFLÉ

3 tbsp. butter
2 tbsp. minced green pepper
3 tbsp. whole-wheat flour
1⅓ cups thin cream
⅔ cup grated yellow cheese

⅔ cup corn, grated raw or chopped canned
1 tsp. vegetable salt
2 eggs, separated

Melt the butter in a saucepan. Sauté the pepper until soft, then add the flour. Stir until well blended. Add the cream gradually, stirring until thick and smooth. Add the cheese and stir until melted. Remove from the heat and add the corn and salt. Beat the egg yolks until thick and lemon-colored and add slowly to the cheese mixture. Let the mixture cool and beat the egg whites stiff but not dry. Fold into the cheese mixture, then pour into a buttered baking dish. Place in a hot oven (400°F.) for a few minutes, then turn the heat down to 325°F. Bake until the center is firm—about 30 minutes. Serve immediately.

Preparation: 25 to 30 minutes.

4 servings.

## CHEESE RICE ROLL

| | |
|---|---|
| 1 cup cottage cheese | 1 tbsp. lemon juice |
| 1 cup cooked brown rice | ½ tsp. grated lemon rind |
| ¼ cup chopped nutmeats | 1 tsp. paprika |
| 2 tbsp. buttered whole-wheat crumbs | 1 egg, well beaten |
| 2 tbsp. heavy cream | Whole-wheat cracker crumbs |
| 1 tsp. vegetable salt | |

Mix the cottage cheese and rice thoroughly. Add the remaining ingredients and mix until the mixture holds together, using more bread crumbs if it is too soft to roll. Form into a roll about 3 inches in diameter and cover the roll with cracker crumbs. Place in a buttered baking pan and bake in a moderate oven (350°F.) about 25 minutes until browned. Serve with tomato sauce and garnish with sprigs of parsley.

Preparation: 20 to 25 minutes.

4 servings.

## CREOLE TOAST

For each person to be served, cut 2 or 3 slices of ripe tomato. Put each slice on the buttered side of a square of bread cut slightly larger than the tomato slice. Put these into a very hot oven (400°F.) for 5 or 10 minutes. Then add to each slice a sprinkling of minced onion, minced green pepper, a dash of vegetable salt, and paprika. On top put a thick layer of grated American cheese and return to the oven to bake until the cheese and bread are browned.

Drained canned tomato pulp may be used in place of tomato slices.

## CREAM-CHEESE ICING FOR CAKES

1 3-oz package cream cheese      ⅛ tsp. vegetable salt
¼ cup fruit juice or heavy cream      2½ cups natural brown sugar

Soften the cream cheese with a fork and work in the fruit juice or the cream. Add the vegetable salt as you work, then gradually stir in the sugar until the consistency of the icing is right for spreading. Beat until creamy and spread over the cake.

## CHAPTER 10

# *Meat Substitutes*

WHEN WE SPEAK of the protein requirement to keep the body firm, we refer to first-class or complete proteins—proteins which by themselves contain all the amino acids necessary for both growth and maintenance of the body. Second-class or incomplete proteins are those which can maintain life but do not promote growth.

Most of the first-class protein foods are animal foods, but the vegetable kingdom does give us a few foods which can supply the same kind of proteins as meat. Soybeans, nuts, wheat germ, and cottonseed flour supply first-class proteins.

It is possible for those who prefer not to eat meat to supply the body with enough protein by eating generously of walnuts, soybeans, almonds, peanuts, and cottonseed flour. If generous quantities of eggs and fermented milk are added to these foods, a balanced diet can be provided.

### BLANCHING NUTS

Cover the nutmeats with boiling water and let stand until the skins wrinkle—about 3 minutes. Drain and plunge into cold water. Rub with the fingers or the dull side of a knife to remove the skins. Dry thoroughly on absorbent paper or in a warm oven (250°F.).

### SALTED NUTS

Shell the nuts and blanch if necessary. Dry thoroughly. Allow about 1 teaspoon of vegetable oil or melted butter to 1 cup of nuts. Stir the nuts in the oil and spread in a single layer on a baking sheet. Place in a moderate oven (350°F.) about 10 minutes, or until lightly browned, Stir frequently. Remove, drain on absorbent paper, and sprinkle with vegetable salt.

## TOASTED NUTS

Spread the nutmeats in a shallow pan and heat in a slow oven (250°F.) 15 to 20 minutes, or until slightly browned. Stir occasionally.

Another method is to brown the nuts in a little butter in a skillet over low heat, stirring or shaking them so they brown evenly.

## TOASTED BRAZIL NUTS

Pour boiling water over Brazil nuts. Let stand several hours or overnight. Slice with a sharp knife and spread out on a shallow pan. Toast as described above.

## ROASTED SOYBEANS

Cover ½ cup of dried soybeans with 1½ cups of water and let soak overnight. Next morning put the soaked beans into a towel and dry thoroughly. Put the beans in a heavy heated skillet and stir until they are crisp and a golden brown (between 20 and 30 minutes). Just before removing beans from the skillet, add 1 tablespoon of butter or olive oil and sprinkle with ½ teaspoon of vegetable salt.

Toasted soybeans prepared in the above manner without the butter and salt can be put through the food grinder or chopped up finely. They make an excellent substitute for the more expensive nutmeats and are utterly delicious when used with cereals, sprinkled over cakes, or in omelets.

## BOILED CHESTNUTS

Slit the skin of the chestnuts with two crossing gashes. Place in a heavy skillet with a little vegetable oil. Cover and shake over low heat until the skins loosen. Shell and place in boiling salted water to cover. Boil 15 to 20 minutes, or until tender. Slice, or mash or put through a ricer. Season to taste and serve as a vegetable with butter or use in stuffing.

NOTE: The chestnuts may be gashed and then boiled in the shells. This method takes longer.

## PURÉED CHESTNUTS

Boil the chestnuts until very tender. Force through a strainer or ricer. Season to taste with salt and add a little cream or butter. Good with poultry or game.

## MOCK MEAT LOAF

1 cup minced onion
3 tbsp. minced celery, leaves and all
2/3 cup finely chopped walnuts
2/3 cup drained cooked tomatoes
1 tbsp. grated raw beet

3/4 tsp. vegetable salt, crushed thyme, or nutmeg as desired
1 egg, slightly beaten
3/4 shredded wheat biscuit crumbled fine

Combine the ingredients in the order listed. Mix well after adding the egg, then add the crumbled shredded wheat and mix in lightly. Pack into a buttered and floured loaf tin and bake in a moderate oven (350°F.) until firm enough to be turned out—about 45 minutes. Serve with gravy and garnish with sprigs of parsley.

Preparation: 15-20 minutes.

4 servings.

## ROAST-PEANUT LOAF

1 cup ground roasted peanuts
1 cup cooked brown rice
1 cup ground raw carrots
1/2 cup whole-wheat bread crumbs

1 cup tomatoes
1 tbsp. chopped parsley or chives
1/2 tsp. vegetable salt

Mix all the ingredients thoroughly. Pack in a buttered loaf pan and bake in a moderate oven (350°F.) for 45 minutes. Serve with Spanish sauce.

## CORN AND NUT LOAF

1 cup grated raw corn or chopped canned corn
1/2 cup finely chopped nutmeats
2 tbsp. chopped green onions
2 tbsp. minced parsley and celery leaves, mixed

1/2 cup stale whole-wheat bread crumbs
1/2 tsp. vegetable salt
1/4 cup cream
1 egg, well beaten
1 tbsp. melted butter

Combine all the ingredients and mix thoroughly. Pack into a buttered and floured loaf pan. Bake in a moderate oven (350°F.) until firm enough to be turned out—about 30 minutes. Serve with a green-pepper sauce and garnish with a sprig of parsley.

Preparation: 15-20 minutes.

4 servings.

## SAVORY NUT LOAF

¾ cup finely chopped nutmeats
1 cup finely chopped celery
⅓ cup chopped parsley
1¼ cups drained cooked tomato
  pulp
½ cup finely shredded onion

1 egg, slightly beaten
1 tsp. vegetable salt
½ tsp. crushed summer savory
1 cup dry whole-wheat bread
  crumbs
2 tbsp. vegetable oil

Mix the nutmeats, celery, parsley, tomato, and onion with the beaten egg. Add the remaining ingredients and mix thoroughly. Pack into a buttered and floured loaf pan and bake in a moderate oven (350°F.) until firm enough to be turned out—about 35 minutes. Serve with lemon butter, parsley butter, or tomato sauce

Preparation: 20-25 minutes.

5 servings.

## SUMMER NUT LOAF

9 oz. cream cheese (3 packages) or
  creamed cottage cheese
2 large stalks celery, sliced fine
¾ cup blanched almonds, chopped
  fine

2 tsp. grated onion
½ green pepper, minced
½ pimento (or sweet red pepper),
  minced
1 tsp. vegetable salt

Mix all ingredients thoroughly. Press firmly into a buttered loaf pan and chill. Slice before serving.

Preparation: 10-15 minutes.

3 servings.

## CHEESE AND NUT LOAF

1½ cups tomato soup
1 tbsp. vegetable salt
2 tbsp. minced onion
2 tbsp. butter
1 tbsp. grated yellow cheese

1¼ cups dry whole-wheat bread
  crumbs
¾ cup ground nutmeats
1 cup minced celery
2 eggs, well beaten

To the tomato soup add all the ingredients except the eggs. Beat the eggs until thick and lemon-colored and mix with the other ingredients. Bake in a buttered loaf pan in a slow oven (300°F.) 45 minutes. Serve with any good sauce.

## EGGPLANT AU GRATIN

1 small eggplant
2 tbsp. olive oil
4 or 5 tomatoes, cut up

1 oz. grated yellow cheese
Whole-wheat bread crumbs
Vegetable salt to taste

Peel the eggplant and slice in fairly thin slices. Sauté the slices a few minutes in the olive oil with the tomatoes. Butter a pie dish, sprinkle the bottom with bread crumbs, and fill with layers of eggplant and tomatoes, with bread crumbs and grated cheese between the layers. Bake in a moderate oven (350°F.) for 15 minutes.

## ASPARAGUS LOAF

2 cups cooked asparagus cut in
½-inch pieces
1 onion, shredded
4 tbsp. grated yellow cheese
1 tsp. vegetable salt

2 eggs, well beaten
½ cup fine whole-wheat cracker
crumbs
2 tbsp. melted butter
1 cup hot milk

Combine the ingredients in the order listed. Mix thoroughly after adding the eggs and again after adding the milk. Transfer carefully to a loaf pan prepared with 2 teaspoons of vegetable oil and a thick layer (2 or 3 tablespoons) of whole-wheat crumbs sprinkled on the bottom. Bake in a moderate oven (350°F.) about 20 minutes. Loosen the sides by running a knife all around, and invert the pan over a platter. Turn out the loaf and serve with parsley butter or any desired sauce.

Preparation: 20-25 minutes.

3 servings.

## SCRAMBLED CORN

3 tbsp. chopped green onion tops
3 tbsp. butter
¾ cup corn cut from cob (or whole-
grain canned corn, drained)

2 tbsp. milk
3 eggs, slightly beaten
¾ tsp. vegetable salt

Sauté the onion tops in the butter for a minute. Mix together the other ingredients and pour into the skillet. Cook over low heat, stirring from the bottom as for scrambled eggs, until the egg is set. Remove from the heat and stir until the mixture reaches the desired consistency.

Preparation: 5 minutes.

3 servings.

## EGGPLANT SOUFFLÉ

| | |
|---|---|
| 1 cup milk | 2 tsp. vegetable salt |
| 2 tbsp. whole corn meal | 2 eggs, separated |
| 1 cup mashed cooked eggplant | |

Heat the milk in the double boiler. Slowly scatter the corn meal in the milk to prevent lumps. Stir for a few minutes, then let cook at least an hour to thicken. Stir occasionally. Add the eggplant and seasonings and mix well. Beat the egg yolks until thick and lemon-colored and slowly add to the eggplant mixture. Let the mixture cool a little, but not set. Then add the egg whites beaten stiff but not dry. Turn into a buttered baking dish. Place in a hot oven (400°F.) for 15 minutes, then turn the heat down to 325°F. Bake 30 to 40 minutes, until the center is firm.

Preparation: 1 hour and 10 minutes.

4 servings.

## PINE-NUT STEAK

| | |
|---|---|
| ¾ cup finely shredded carrots | ½ tsp. dried sage |
| ½ cup ground or crushed pine nuts | ¼ tsp. celery seed |
| 2 eggs, well beaten | 1 tsp. vegetable salt |
| ½ cup dry whole-wheat bread crumbs | 2 tsp. melted butter |

Add the carrots and nuts to the well-beaten eggs and mix thoroughly. Add the remaining ingredients and mix well. Turn out onto a small greased dripping pan and spread in a sheet, or drop by heaping serving-spoonfuls onto a buttered pan for individual steaks. Bake in a moderate oven (350°F.) until nearly firm—15-20 minutes. Finish cooking under the broiler to brown on top. Garnish with any fresh greens and serve with lemon butter.

Preparation: 20-25 minutes.

3 servings.

## VEGETABLE CASSEROLE

| | |
|---|---|
| ¾ cup thinly sliced celery | ¼ cup finely chopped nuts |
| ¾ cup finely shredded raw beet | ¼ tsp. vegetable salt |
| ¾ cup finely shredded raw carrot | ¼ cup cream |
| 2 tbsp. vegetable or olive oil | 1 tbsp. butter |
| ⅜ cup minced onion | |

Start cooking the celery, beets, and carrots in a covered casserole with a little Hauser Broth until they begin to soften. Add the minced onion and chopped nuts, the vegetable salt and the oil. Mix well. Cook covered in a moderate oven (350°F.), or gently on top the stove, for about 15 minutes. Pour the cream over the vegetables and dot them with butter, then cook uncovered for another 5 minutes.

Preparation: 15-20 minutes.

3 servings.

## SQUASH PATTIES

1 lb. white squash
½ cup whole-wheat bread crumbs
½ cup grated nutmeats
2 eggs
1 small onion, grated

1 small green pepper, grated
¼ lb. butter
1 tsp. vegetable salt
1 tbsp. natural brown sugar

Short-cook the squash and mash fine. Mix the remaining ingredients into the squash in the order listed. Drop by spoonfuls onto a hot greased griddle.

## NUT RICE ROAST

1 cup cooked brown rice
⅓ cup drained cooked tomatoes (pulp)
1 small onion, chopped fine
½ tsp. vegetable salt

½ cup finely chopped nutmeats (Filberts or black walnuts are good)
Butter for basting

Combine all ingredients and mix thoroughly. Turn out onto a buttered pan and pat into loaf shape. Bake in a moderate oven (375°F.) until browned, basting several times with a mixture of butter and Hauser Broth in equal parts. Bake about 35 minutes. Serve with a tomato sauce and garnish with sprigs of parsley or chopped green onion tops.

Preparation: 15-20 minutes.

3 servings.

## BAKED SPANISH RICE

¼ cup finely chopped nutmeats
2 cups hot Hauser Broth
¼ cup brown rice
1 cup drained cooked tomato pulp
3 tbsp. minced green pepper

1 large onion, minced
¾ tsp. vegetable salt
½ tsp. paprika
1 tbsp. butter

Place the chopped nuts in a casserole and gradually stir in the hot broth, mixing thoroughly to make a milk. Add the rice, vegetables, and seasonings. Mix thoroughly, then cover. Place over heat and bring to the boiling point, then transfer to a hot oven (400°F.) and bake until the rice is done—about 35 minutes. Five minutes before the rice is done, remove the cover, sprinkle the top generously with paprika, and dot with butter. Return to the oven uncovered to dry out the top and brown it.

Preparation: 15-20 minutes.

4 servings.

## STUFFED ONIONS

6 medium-sized onions
3 tbsp. minced celery, leaves and stalks
2 tbsp. vegetable oil
½ cup ground walnuts

½ cup drained cooked tomato pulp
¾ tsp. vegetable salt
Pinch of crushed thyme
⅔ cup tomato juice

Remove the center of each onion, leaving a shell 2 or 3 rings thick. Mince the centers, which should make about 1 cupful. Wilt the onion and the minced celery in the vegetable oil. Add the ground nuts, tomato pulp, and seasonings, and simmer until heated through. Put the mixture in a casserole, pour in the tomato juice, and simmer on top the stove until the onion shells are cooked. Serve in the casserole, garnished with parsley.

Preparation: 20-25 minutes.

3 servings.

## STUFFED PEPPERS

6 medium-sized sweet green peppers
½ tsp. vegetable salt
1½ tbsp. melted butter
¼ cup chopped celery
¼ cup finely chopped green pepper, including tops and seeds cut off

1 onion, shredded fine
½ cup chopped walnuts or pecans
⅔ cup dry rye-bread crumbs
1 cup milk
½ cup buttered whole-wheat bread crumbs

Wash the peppers and cut off the stem end. Remove the veins and seeds and sprinkle the inside with vegetable salt. Combine all the ingredients and stir over heat until well blended. Fill the peppers with the mixture, then fit them snugly into a baking dish with 1 inch of hot Hauser Broth. Bake covered in a moderate oven (350°F.) about 30 minutes. For the last 5 or 10 minutes of cooking, sprinkle the peppers with buttered crumbs and bake uncovered to let the crumbs brown. Serve in the dish garnished with sprigs of parsley.

Preparation: 25-30 minutes.

4 to 6 servings.

## SCALLOPED SPINACH

½ cup chopped parsley, packed tight    2 tbsp. ground nuts
2 cups cut raw spinach    2 eggs
1 large onion, minced    ½ cup buttered whole-wheat bread
1 tsp. vegetable salt    crumbs

Put the parsley and spinach through the medium knife of the food grinder and save the juice. To the pulp add the onion and seasonings. Dilute the spinach juice with enough water to make 1 cup and gradually stir in the nuts to make a cream. Add to the eggs and beat lightly, then combine the two mixtures. Turn into a buttered baking dish and top with buttered crumbs. Cover and bake in a moderate oven (350°F.) about 30 minutes. Remove the cover during the last 5 minutes to let the crumbs brown.

Preparation: 20-25 minutes.

3 servings.

## BAKED FILBERTS WITH VEGETABLES

½ cup diced celery    1 tsp. vegetable salt
½ cup sliced onion    ¼ tsp. garlic seasoning
1 cup filberts    Pinch of summer savory
1 cup finely shredded winter squash    1 cup Hauser Broth
2 canned pimentos, minced    2 tbsp. butter

Put the celery, onion, and filberts through the medium knife of a food grinder. Add the squash, pimentos, and seasonings. Add the Hauser Broth and mix all together thoroughly. Turn into a buttered baking dish, dot with the butter, and cover. Bake in a moderate oven (350°F.) until the vegetables are cooked, about 25 minutes. Serve in a baking dish garnished with chopped parsley.

Preparation: 15-20 minutes.

4 servings.

## BAKED STUFFED MUSHROOMS

6 large mushroom caps    1 tbsp. minced parsley
1½ tsp. butter    2 tbsp. vegetable oil
Garlic seasoning to taste    1 tbsp. cheese, finely grated, or 2
Vegetable salt to taste    tbsp. chili sauce
½ cup minced mushrooms (includ-    1 cup Hauser Broth
     ing stems of 6 caps)    Crumbs for topping—2 parts whole-
4 tbsp. minced onion    wheat crumbs to 1 part cheese

Place the 6 mushroom caps in a buttered casserole and bake in a hot oven (400°F.) for a few minutes. Then into each cap put ¼ teaspoon of butter and a sprinkling of garlic seasoning and vegetable salt. Return to the oven and cook while the stuffing is prepared.

*Stuffing:* Mix together the minced mushrooms, onions, and parsley. Sauté in the oil for 5 minutes. Add the cheese or chili sauce and ½ cup of the broth. Boil up. Fill the mushroom caps with the mixture and sprinkle over each some crumbs mixed with cheese. Pour the remaining ½ cup of broth into the casserole and return to the oven. Bake about 25 minutes. Serve in the casserole or on hot buttered toast with dish gravy.

Preparation: 20-25 minutes.

3 servings.

## MUSHROOM-EGG DELIGHT

| | |
|---|---|
| 4 hard-cooked eggs | 2 cups cream |
| ½ lb. mushrooms | ½ cup ripe olives cut from the pits |
| 2 tbsp. butter | Whole-wheat bread crumbs |

Shell and slice the eggs. Sauté the mushrooms in the butter for 5 minutes. Butter a glass casserole generously and put a layer of cream in the bottom. Cover this with toasted whole-wheat bread crumbs, then a layer of sliced eggs, more cream, a layer of mushrooms, a layer of olives, and finish with a layer of bread crumbs. Lay strips of pimento across the dish and set in the oven to heat through. Brown and serve.

## EGGPLANT WITH RICE

Peel and slice a small eggplant. Sauté the slices in butter with a chopped garlic clove. Transfer to a buttered baking dish with 1 cup of cooked brown rice and grated yellow cheese to taste. Pour tomato sauce generously over the dish and bake in a moderate oven (350°F.) for 15 minutes.

## STUFFED EGGPLANT

| | |
|---|---|
| 2 medium-sized eggplants | 1 small onion, minced |
| Vegetable salt to taste | 1 tbsp. chopped parsley |
| 1 oz. olive oil | 1 tsp. whole-wheat flour |
| ½ lb. spinach, chopped | ½ cup Hauser Broth |

Peel the eggplants and cut them in half lengthwise. Lay the halves side by side in a buttered baking dish and sprinkle them with vegetable salt. Heat the olive oil in a skillet and lightly sauté the chopped spinach, onion, and parsley until golden brown. Blend in the flour.

Scoop out the centers of the eggplants and chop the pulp. Add it to the spinach mixture, then fill the hollows of the eggplant halves with the stuffing. Sprinkle them with whole-wheat crumbs and pour the Hauser Broth over them. Cover and bake in a moderate oven (350°F.) for 20-25 minutes.

## SPINACH ROLL

| | |
|---|---|
| 1 large onion | ½ tsp. nutmeg |
| ⅓ lb. raw spinach | ½ cup whole-wheat bread crumbs |
| 1 cup chopped nuts | ½ tsp. vegetable salt |
| 2 eggs, well beaten | |

Put the onion, spinach, and nutmeats through the medium knife of a food grinder and save the juice for the sauce. Mix the eggs and nutmeg with the spinach pulp. Lightly mix in the bread crumbs, then form into a roll. Roll in a half-and-half mixture of chopped nuts and cracker crumbs. Place in a buttered shallow baking pan and bake in a moderate oven (375°F.) for 35 minutes. Baste two or three times during baking with a half-and-half mixture of butter and Hauser Broth. Serve with chopped parsley sauce made from the vegetable juices.

Preparation: 15-20 minutes.

3 servings.

## GOLDEN CARROT LOAF

| | |
|---|---|
| ¾ cup grated raw carrot, packed | 2 tbsp. chopped parsley |
| 1 small onion, minced | 2 tbsp. whole-wheat bread crumbs |
| 1 stalk celery (with some leaves), sliced thin across the grain | 2 tbsp. cream |
| ½ cup chopped nutmeats (Brazil nuts are good) | 2 eggs slightly beaten |
| | 1½ tsp. vegetable salt |
| | Buttered whole-wheat bread crumbs |

Mix thoroughly all the ingredients except the buttered crumbs. Butter a loaf pan well and cover the bottom thickly with the bread crumbs. Pack in the loaf mixture and dot the top with the butter. Cover and bake in a moderate oven (350°F.) for 30 minutes. Uncover the last 5 minutes of baking to dry out the loaf a little. Remove from the oven, loosen the sides by running a knife around, and invert over a platter. Turn out the loaf and serve with tomato sauce.

Preparation: 20-25 minutes.

3 servings.

## CELERY LOAF

½ cup sliced celery
½ small onion
⅜ cup nutmeats
¾ cup tomato soup or juice
½ tbsp. grated yellow cheese
1 tsp. vegetable salt

1 tbsp. melted butter
⅔ cup whole-wheat bread crumbs
   or crumbled shredded wheat
   biscuit
2 eggs, well beaten

Put the celery, onion, and nutmeats through the medium knife of a food grinder. Add all the ingredients except the eggs and mix well. Add the beaten eggs and mix in lightly. Pack into a loaf pan prepared with 2 teaspoons of vegetable oil and a thick layer of crumbs (2 or 3 tablespoons) evenly sprinkled on the bottom. Bake in a moderate oven (375°F.) about 35 minutes, until thick enough to be turned out. Remove from the oven and loosen the sides with a knife. Invert the pan over a platter and turn out the loaf. Garnish with wedges of ripe tomato and a generous sprinkling of chopped parsley.

Preparation: 20-25 minutes.

3 servings

## VEGETABLE LOAF

1½ cups vegetable pulp from Hauser
   Broth, pressed dry
½ cup cooked brown rice
¼ cup chopped parsley
¼ cup finely shredded onion
½ clove garlic, minced
2 eggs, well beaten

1½ tsp. vegetable salt
½ tsp. paprika
1 tbsp. melted butter
¼ cup dry whole-wheat bread
   crumbs
⅔ cup tomato juice

Combine the vegetables, rice, and the beaten eggs. Add the seasonings, melted butter, and bread crumbs and mix well. Put 2 teaspoons of vegetable oil in a loaf pan and sprinkle over the oil a thick layer (2 or 3 tablespoons) of bread crumbs. Pack in the loaf mixture, then pour the tomato juice over it. Bake in a moderate oven (375°F.) until brown on the bottom—about 30 minutes. Loosen the loaf at the sides with a knife and invert the pan over a platter. Turn out the loaf and garnish with chopped parsley or water cress.

Preparation: 15-20 minutes.

4 servings.

## VEGETABLE SALISBURY STEAKS

2 medium-sized onions
¼ lb. fresh mushrooms
2 tbsp. finely chopped parsley and celery tops mixed
2 tbsp. vegetable oil
1 tbsp. finely grated raw beet
1 cup finely chopped walnuts

⅔ cup cooked tomato pulp, drained
1 tbsp. grated yellow cheese
¾ tsp. vegetable salt
1½ shredded wheat biscuits, crumbled fine

Put the onions and mushrooms through the medium knife of the food grinder. Mix with the chopped parsley and celery in a covered saucepan and sauté in the vegetable oil until soft—about 10 minutes. Remove from the heat and add the remaining ingredients. Mix well before adding the shredded wheat, then add enough to make a mixture which will hold its shape. Drop by heaping tablespoonfuls onto a hot greased skillet and flatten into cakes. Brown one side, turn, and brown the other side. Serve with tomato sauce or brown gravy and parsley.

Preparation: 20-30 minutes.

8 steaks.

## CHICK PEA AND VEGETABLE STEW (GARBANZO)

¼ cup chick peas
1 cup cubed carrot
¾ cup sliced celery (cut across the grain)
½ cup sliced onion (wedge-shaped pieces)

¼ cup diced yellow turnip
2 tbsp. vegetable oil
1½ tsp. vegetable salt
1 tbsp. whole-wheat flour
1 tbsp. butter

Put the chick peas to soak for a few hours in a covered casserole with hot Hauser Broth to cover. At the required time, bring the peas to a boil and boil slowly for half an hour. Then add the vegetables, vegetable oil, and enough hot broth to half cover. Boil slowly, stirring occasionally, until the vegetables are nearly done—about 15 minutes. Add the vegetable salt.

Brown the butter and flour together, then gradually add 5 or 6 tablespoonfuls of liquid from the stew, stirring constantly, and blend until smooth over low heat. Pour the thickening into the stew, bring to the boil again, and let boil, stirring occasionally, until all the vegetables are done, which will take only a few minutes. Serve with a generous sprinkling of chopped parsley.

Preparation: About 3 hours.

3 servings.

## BAKED BEANS

1 cup dried beans—navy, kidney,
   lima, grabanzos, or lentils
5 tbsp. vegetable oil
2 tbsp. blackstrap molasses

3 cups hot Hauser Broth
1 onion, sliced
1 tsp. vegetable salt
Juice of ½ lemon

Wash the beans and soak overnight in 2 cups of cold water. Next morning put the beans in a baking dish and add the oil and molasses. Pour the hot broth over the beans and cover the dish. Bake in a slow oven (300°-325°F.) for 3-5 hours. Stir occasionally and add more broth as needed to keep the beans covered with liquid until they are almost done. Then add the onion, vegetable salt, and lemon juice and return to the oven uncovered. Allow the top to brown and the beans to finish cooking. Serve in the baking dish and garnish with parsley or water cress.

4 servings.

*Special Suggestions:*
  1. Lima beans are delicious seasoned with a bit of garlic.
  2. Lentils need twice the amount of lemon juice.
  3. Stewed tomatoes are a delicious accompaniment for all baked beans.

## LENTIL LOAF

½ cup finely shredded onion
1 clove garlic, minced
1 cup finely shredded raw beet
Rind of 1 small lemon, finely shredded
¼ cup chopped parsley

1½ cups cooked lentils, seasoned
1 tsp. vegetable salt
¼ tsp. crushed thyme
2 eggs, well beaten
2 tbsp. melted butter

Combine the ingredients in the order listed and mix thoroughly. Pack into a loaf pan well buttered and floured. Bake in a moderate oven (350°F.) about 30 minutes, until it is brown on the bottom and firm enough to be turned out of the pan. Serve with lemon butter.

Preparation: 25-30 minutes.

4 servings.

## LIMA BEAN ROAST

1½ cups cooked lima beans
1 3-oz. package cream cheese
2 canned pimentos, minced
1 tbsp. minced celery leaves

2 tbsp. minced parsley
⅜ tsp. vegetable salt
¾ cup dry whole-wheat
   bread crumbs

Mash together the lima beans, cheese, and pimentos. Add the other ingredients and mix thoroughly, using enough crumbs to make a mixture which can be molded. Turn onto a buttered shallow pan and pat into the shape of a loaf. Bake in a moderate oven (350°F.) about 30 minutes, until brown. Baste several times during basting with a mixture of butter and hot Hauser Broth in equal parts. Serve garnished with slices of ripe tomato marinated in French dressing.

Preparation: 15-20 minutes.

3 servings.

## BEAN ROAST

1½ cups cooked dried beans
1 onion, minced
¼ cup chopped parsley and green celery tips, mixed
2 eggs, well beaten

¾ cup whole-wheat bread crumbs
½ tsp. vegetable salt
2 tsp. melted butter
Paprika

Combine the beans, onion, and parsley with the well-beaten eggs. Mix in the remaining ingredients and turn onto a buttered shallow baking pan. Pat into loaf shape and sprinkle well with paprika. Bake in a moderate oven (350°F.) 15-20 minutes, until browned. Serve with green pepper sauce and garnish with sprigs of parsley.

Preparation: 15-20 minutes.

3 servings.

## LIMA-BEAN PUDDING

⅓ cup dried sweet corn or ¾ cup canned corn, dry pack
1 cup warm milk
¾ cup cooked dried lima beans
1 egg
1 tbsp. grated onion

¼ tsp. garlic seasoning
1½ tsp. vegetable salt
1 tsp. natural brown sugar (or more to taste)
1 tbsp. melted butter
¼ tsp. paprika

Grind the dried corn with the fine knife of the food grinder. Put to soak in the milk for at least half an hour. If canned corn is used, you will need only ⅓ cup of milk and soaking is not necessary. Add the lima beans, egg, and seasonings to the corn. Turn into a buttered baking dish and sprinkle with paprika. Bake in a moderate oven (350°F.) for ⁻0-40 minutes.

Preparation: 30-35 minutes.

3 servings.

## PEA LOAF

2 cups cooked fresh or canned peas
1 onion, chopped
¼ cup finely chopped walnut meats
¾ cup dry whole-wheat bread crumbs
2 eggs, slightly beaten

4 tbsp. melted butter
¾ cup milk
1 tbsp. natural brown sugar
1 tsp. vegetable salt

Mash or purée the peas—they will make about ½ cup of pulp. Add the remaining ingredients and mix thoroughly. Butter a baking dish or small loaf pan and sprinkle well with dry crumbs, then turn the pea mixture into it. Let stand for 15 minutes, then cover and bake in a moderate oven (350°F.) for 40 minutes. Turn out onto a hot serving dish and garnish.

Preparation: 15-20 minutes.

4 servings.

## BEAN PATTIES

2 cups cooked navy or other beans
1 onion, chopped
½ green pepper, minced
½ cup chopped parsley, packed
1 cup canned tomato pulp

2 eggs, well beaten
4 tbsp. melted butter
1 tsp. vegetable salt
1 cup whole-wheat bread crumbs

Mash the beans or press them through a sieve. Mix in the other ingredients to make a mixture dry enough to shape. Form into round cakes and place on an oiled shallow baking pan. Brush the top of each cake with milk several times during the baking. Bake 15 minutes in a hot oven (450°F.) Serve with tomato sauce or any other desired.

Preparation: 20-25 minutes.

8 patties.

## VEGETARIAN MEAT LOAF

1 cup cooked red beans
½ green pepper, finely chopped
½ cup finely chopped walnut meats
1 cup dry whole-wheat or rye bread
    crumbs

2 tbsp. vegetable oil
2 tbsp. cream
¼ tsp. celery seed
1 tsp. vegetable salt
1 egg, slightly beaten

Combine the ingredients in the order given and mix thoroughly. Turn onto a buttered shallow baking pan and pat into the shape of a loaf. Bake in a moderate oven (350°F.) about 30 minutes. Serve with a tomato sauce.

Preparation: 15-20 minutes.

4 servings.

### SPANISH BEANS

| | |
|---|---|
| 1½ cups baked red beans, with liquid | 1½ cups drained cooked tomato pulp |
| ½ cup raw brown rice | ½ medium-sized green pepper cut in strips lengthwise |
| 10 small whole onions | |
| 2 tbsp. vegetable oil or olive oil | 1 tsp. vegetable salt |

Put the ingredients into a covered casserole in the order given. Boil gently on top of the stove for 25 minutes or bake in a moderate oven (350°F.) about 45 minutes, until the rice is done. Garnish with sprigs of parsley and serve with grated cheese.

Preparation: 10-15 minutes.

5 servings.

### BEAN CROQUETTES

| | |
|---|---|
| 1½ cups baked beans | ¾ tsp. curry powder |
| 1 onion, shredded fin | 1½ tbsp. vegetable salt |
| ⅜ cup tomato juice | 1½ tbsp. melted butter |
| 1 tbsp. chili sauce | 1½ cups dry whole-wheat bread crumbs |

Mash the beans or press them through a sieve. Add the remaining ingredients, except crumbs, and mix thoroughly. Then add the crumbs, using only enough to make a mixture firm enough to mold. Divide into heaping servingspoonfuls and mold into the desired shape. Roll in whole-wheat flour or crumbs. Dip in either the white or yolk of 1 egg, thoroughly blended with 1 tablespoon of water. Roll in whole-wheat cracker crumbs and place on a buttered baking pan. Bake in a hot oven (425°F.) about 15 minutes, until browned. Turn once during baking if necessary to brown both sides. Serve with a vegetable cream sauce or as an accompaniment for a raw-vegetable salad.

Preparation: 20-30 minutes.
8 croquettes.

## MUSHROOM CHOP SUEY

4 cups diced celery
3 cups diced onions
½ cup boiling Hauser Broth
2 tsp. vegetable salt
1 lb. mushrooms, diced

4 tbsp. salad oil
2 tbsp. whole-wheat or soya flour
¼ lb. bean sprouts
¼ lb. toasted blanched almonds

Simmer the celery and onions over low heat for 10 minutes, having added the hot water to start the steam. Drain off the liquor and dissolve the vegetable salt in it. Brown the diced mushrooms in the oil, sift the flour over them, and brown the flour. Pour the bouillon liquor over the mushrooms and stir until it thickens. Then add the bean sprouts and cook 2 minutes. Add the cooked onions and celery. Heat through and serve, garnished with shreds of green onion and hot toasted almonds.

## MUSHROOM AND CHEESE SOUFFLÉ

2 tbsp. butter or vegetable shortening
3 tbsp. whole-wheat flour
1 cup thick cream or mushroom soup

⅓ cup grated yellow cheese
½ tsp. vegetable salt
2 eggs, separated

Melt the shortening in a saucepan, add the flour, and stir until well blended. Gradually add the cream or soup, stirring constantly, and cook over low heat until the boiling point is reached. Add the cheese and stir until melted, then remove from the fire and stir in the minced parsley and the vegetable salt. Beat the egg yolks until thick and lemon-colored. Stir in a little of the hot sauce, and when the yolks are thoroughly blended, add to the cheese mixture. Let the mixture cool, then beat the egg whites until stiff but not dry. Fold them into the cheese. Pour into a buttered baking dish and bake in a moderate oven (325°F.) about 45 minutes, until the center is firm.

Preparation: 20-25 minutes.

3 servings.

## MUSHROOMS AND CELERY

¼ lb. mushrooms
1 cup thinly sliced celery, cut across
    the grain
½ cup whole-wheat or rye crumbs

½ tsp. vegetable salt
⅜ cup thin cream
1 tsp. butter

Clean the mushrooms by brushing the tops and stems under running water. Cut in slices ¼ inch thick and put a layer in the bottom of a buttered baking dish. On top put a layer of celery slices, then a layer of crumbs. Repeat. Sprinkle the top layer of crumbs with salt and pour the cream over all. Dot generously with butter. Cover the casserole and bake in a hot oven (400°F.) 30-40 minutes, until the vegetables are done. Remove the cover during the last few minutes of cooking to let the crumbs brown. Garnish with a sprinkling of chopped parsley.

Preparation: 15-20 minutes.

3 servings.

## SCALLOPED MUSHROOMS AND EGGS

⅛ lb. mushrooms
1 tbsp. butter
1½ cups medium light sauce
1 tbsp. minced parsley
3 tbsp. minced celery
2 tsp. minced onion

2 tbsp. minced green pepper
1 small pimento, diced
1½ tsp. vegetable salt
Pinch of brown sugar
3 hard-cooked eggs, diced
Whole-wheat crumbs

Break or cut the mushrooms fine and sauté for 5 minutes in the butter. Prepare the light sauce and add to it the mushrooms, prepared vegetables, salt, and sugar. Then stir in the diced eggs. Transfer the mixture to a buttered baking dish, sprinkle thickly with whole-wheat crumbs, and dot with bits of butter. Place the dish in a pan of hot water and bake in a hot oven (400°F.) about 15 minutes, until heated through and browned on top.

Preparation: 20-25 minutes.

4 servings.

## MUSHROOM-EGGPLANT TIMBALE

⅔ lb. mushrooms, chopped fine
¼ cup vegetable or olive oil
2 cups diced eggplant
½ cup minced onion
¼ cup minced parsley
2 eggs

½ cup milk
1 tsp. vegetable salt
¼ tsp. powdered sage
1 tbsp. finely grated cheese (Parmesan preferred)

Sauté the mushrooms in the oil for about 8 minutes. Remove and keep out 1 cupful. Spread the remainder in the bottom of a buttered baking dish. Cook the eggplant, onion, and parsley in the hot pan, with a little Hauser Broth added, till soft—about 8 minutes. Beat the eggs in the milk. Add the 1 cup of mushrooms, the vegetables, and the seasonings. Mix thoroughly and pour over the mushrooms in the baking dish, then sprinkle the top with cheese. Place the dish in a pan of hot water and bake in a moderate oven (350°F.) 30-40 minutes, until firm.

Preparation: 20-25 minutes.

4 servings.

## BAKED MUSHROOMS

Gently brush the caps of the mushrooms under running water to remove the grit. Avoid wetting the gills. Break out the stems. Cut stale whole-wheat bread in squares to fit the mushroom caps and lay 1 cap on each square, stem side up, allowing 2 or 3 to each person. Place in a buttered baking dish or on a tin. Put in a hot oven for a few minutes. Then to each cap add a sprinkling of vegetable salt and a lump of butter and return to the oven. Bake in a hot oven (400° F.) about 15 minutes, until the mushrooms are tender and the bread has dried out and browned.

# CHAPTER 11

# *Sauces and Relishes*

DO YOU KNOW that the word "sauce" comes from the Latin word meaning "to salt"? Right there in its derivation is the key to what a sauce should be—something to season a dish, to add zest and piquancy—*not* a blanket to disguise it.

It's almost impossible for me to talk about sauces without saying something about the French. They are justly famous for their imagination in blending flavors, and you cannot go too far in emulating them. But there is another side to the picture. The whole philosophy of cooking in France is based on two things which do not apply to us. First, their cookery presupposes that a woman spends her whole time in the kitchen. Second, the masses of the French people have never had the opportunities we have to get really first-class foods at prices within their range. For that reason many of the French sauces are designed to disguise second-rate ingredients. But to us good eating is based on foods of the first quality, and our sauces merely enhance the flavor.

A sauce can be made a vehicle for all sorts of delicious herbs and seasonings. The number of these vehicles, or bases, is really very simple; the variety lies in the seasonings. The base can be butter or cream; or milk, broth, or fruit juice either thickened or unthickened. The butter sauces and cream sauces—that is, sauces made of pure cream, sweet or sour—are the simplest, and hence the best. Of the thickened sauces, Hollandaise is the most delicate because it is thickened with egg. The flour-thickened sauces, most often used—and abused—in this country, belong to three families: light sauce, dark sauce, and mixed sauce. They will, I hope, have little or no place in your cuisine, especially if you have to watch your waistline. But in case you have to stretch a leftover or give body to a croquette, you will find them tucked away in the middle of this chapter. Even these sauces we make with whole-wheat flour and mineral-rich broths or milk. If you happen to be in the money you can always thicken your sauces with a few egg yolks. They give added protein value and a delicious flavor.

*Herbs in Sauces:* Sauces is another of the places where herbs will make all the difference. Look over the herbs on pages 285-289 and consider adding to the sauce any which go with the dish you are serving. For instance, the herbs which go with vegetables can be added to your vegetable sauce; those which go with meat to your meat sauce; and so forth. With a small pinch of the right herbs you can change an ordinary dish to a festive one. Herbs have been given to us by good old Mother Nature to prevent monotony—the saddest thing that can befall any household.

## WHAT SAUCES TO USE

*Sauces for Meats and Poultry:* Gravy is the first and simplest sauce for meat and poultry—preferably dish or platter gravy, which is the pure juice from the meat. For roasts and broiled meats, dish gravy is the best of all possible sauces. It can be made utterly delicious by putting carrots and onions around the roast. Onions especially have a natural oil which helps to thicken your gravy without the addition of flour. Braised meats and stews usually have thickening added to give body.

When there isn't much gravy, or you want a change, the butter and cream sauces are best.

*Sauces for Vegetables:* Vegetables buried in a pasty concoction euphemistically known as "white sauce" belong to the horse-and-buggy days. A good white sauce has its place in cookery, as a base for soufflés; but don't let it mask the rare and delicate flavor of good vegetables. For them the simplest dressings are the best. Here are three ways to dress vegetables:

1. Simply add butter as you serve.

2. Add sweet cream *after* you turn out the flame but before you dish up the vegetable. Or make it sour cream if you like an exotic "foreign touch," especially on greens.

3. When you want a "dressier" sauce, serve Drawn Butter or Hollandaise Sauce. Hollandaise is particularly good with the cabbage family—broccoli, cauliflower, Brussels sprouts. Try it also on string beans, asparagus, etc.

*Sauces for Fish:* Since fish does not provide its own gravy, it seems to cry out for a sauce. Butter and lemon juice, cream and cucumber are combinations appropriate for fish. If you use a thickened sauce, substitute fish stock for half the milk.

## BUTTER SAUCES

More than any other one word, "butter" suggests richness and good eating. Yet on the other hand our plainest eating is "bread and butter." And so for dressing vegetables and meats the simplest sauce, the one which will enhance the flavor of the dish without masking it, is a butter sauce—which means simply melted or creamed butter with herbs and seasonings added. Drawn Butter is the basic melted-butter sauce, Maître d'Hôtel Butter the basic creamed butter sauce. Other sauces can be made with either; it is a matter of choice except perhaps with Horse-Radish Butter, which is best with the butter creamed, not melted.

### MAÎTRE D'HÔTEL BUTTER

⅓ cup butter
2 tbsp. finely chopped parsley
2 tbsp. lemon juice

⅛ tsp. vegetable salt
Dash of paprika

Cream the butter. Add the parsley, then gradually blend in the lemon juice, salt, and paprika.

## PARSLEY BUTTER

To 1/3 cup of creamed butter, add 2 tablespoons of finely minced parsley.

## LEMON-CHIVE BUTTER

To 1/3 cup of creamed butter, add 2 tablespoons of lemon juice and 2 of finely chopped chives.

## WATER-CRESS BUTTER

To 1/3 cup of creamed butter, add 2 tablespoons of finely chopped water cress.

## VITAMIN-C BUTTER

To 1/3 cup of creamed butter, add 2 tablespoons of finely chopped bean sprouts.

## MINT BUTTER

To 1/3 cup of creamed butter, add 2 tablespoons of finely chopped mint leaves.

## LEMON BUTTER

To 1/3 cup of creamed butter, add 2 tablespoons of lemon juice.

## HORSE-RADISH BUTTER

To 1/3 cup of creamed butter, add 2 tablespoons of horse-radish.

## MUSTARD BUTTER

To 1/3 cup of creamed butter, add 1 1/2 tablespoons of prepared mustard.

## BUTTER SAUCES FOR SANDWICHES

These butters make excellent spreads for thin whole-wheat or rye-bread sandwiches.

## GOOD HERB BUTTER

| | |
|---|---|
| 1/4 lb. fresh butter | 1 tbsp. finely chopped chives |
| 1 tbsp. finely chopped water cress | 1/4 tsp. vegetable salt |
| 1 tbsp. finely chopped parsley | |

Cream the butter at room temperature and blend in the different greens, a tablespoonful at a time. When well mixed, place in refrigerator and let harden. Delicious when a lump is served on steaks, chops, or on flat-tasting vegetables and broths.

## DRAWN BUTTER

⅓ cup butter
1 tbsp. chopped parsley

1 tbsp. lemon juice
Pinch of vegetable salt

Melt the butter and add the other ingredients. Letting the butter get brown—not black—gives an unbelievably delicious flavor.

## CREAM SAUCES FOR FISH

The butter sauces are as good for fish as for meats and vegetables. But for variety serve a whipped-cream sauce occasionally with fish and shell-fish. Whip ½ cup of heavy cream and fold in any one of the following combinations:

1. ¾ cup chopped and drained cucumber, 2 tablespoons lemon juice, ¼ teaspoon vegetable salt, dash of paprika.

2. 3 tablespoons horse-radish, 1 teaspoon lemon juice, ¼ teaspoon vegetable salt. Thick sour cream can be used instead of whipped cream.

3. 1½ tablespoons prepared mustard, 2 teaspoons horse-radish. This is also good with cold cuts.

## HOLLANDAISE SAUCE

2 egg yolks
1 tbsp. lemon juice
½ cup unsalted butter

⅓ cup boiling water or Hauser Broth
Pinch of vegetable salt
¼ tsp. garlic powder

Beat the egg yolks slightly in the top of a double boiler. Have the water in the bottom of the boiler hot but *not boiling*. Add the lemon juice and about half the butter to the egg yolks and place over the hot water. Stir until the butter is melted. Gradually add the rest of the butter, stirring continuously, then the boiling water or broth, stirring slowly. Cook until thick.

Hollandaise sauce will curdle if it is cooked at too high a temperature, if it cooks too long, or if it stands too long before serving. If you cannot make it at the last minute, it is better to let it cool, then reheat it for 5 minutes over hot, not boiling, water.

If the sauce curdles add very slowly, beating with a rotary egg beater, 1 tablespoon of boiling water or heavy cream.

## NEVER-FAIL HOLLANDAISE FOR SKINNIES

2 egg yolks

½ tsp. vegetable salt

Dash of paprika

½ cup melted butter

1 tbsp. lemon juice

Beat the egg yolks until thick. Beat in the salt and paprika and 3 table-spoons of the melted butter a drop at a time. Then beat in the rest of the butter alternately with the lemon juice.

## LIGHT SAUCE

A smooth creamy texture is the end to be desired in all flour-thickened sauces. And the way to get it is by thoroughly blending the flour and fat before adding the liquid, then adding the liquid gradually with unremitting stirring.

There are various ways of taking precautions, each of them favorites with some cooks. Take your pick or try them all until you find the one you like. To lessen the risk of lumps, some say take the pan off the heat while adding the liquid. Others say have the liquid hot before adding. Another school recommends an asbestos mat under the saucepan or using the top of a double boiler. This lengthens the process considerably, however, and there is no reason why a smooth sauce can't be made over direct heat—low, of course—if you are faithful to your stirring.

The ingredients listed below are those for a thin sauce. This is the consistency sometimes used for cream soups and for more elaborate sauces. For creamed or scalloped dishes or as a base for savory sauces, use medium light sauce. Thick light sauce is used only for binding the ingredients of croquettes and cutlets.

The light sauce itself is only the beginning. Before you use it to dress a dish, add the ingredients listed under Variations. However, always remember to make all sauces tasty with as little thickening as possible.

2 tbsp. butter

1 tbsp. whole-wheat flour

½ tsp. vegetable salt

⅛ tsp. paprika

1 cup milk

Melt the butter in a saucepan over low heat. Add the flour, salt, and paprika and stir until thoroughly blended. Gradually stir in the milk and cook, stirring constantly, until thick and smooth. Let the sauce boil before you take it off the flame or it will taste of raw flour.

*Medium Light Sauce:* With 1 cup of milk use 2 tablespoons of butter and 2 tablespoons of flour.

*Thick Light Sauce:* With 1 cup of milk use 4 tablespoons of butter and 4 tablespoons of flour. This thick sauce should never be used unless you look like a starved Indian.

## VARIATIONS OF LIGHT SAUCE

*Cream Sauce:* Use 1 cup of light cream instead of milk.

*Sour-Cream Sauce:* Use 1 cup of thick sour cream instead of milk; add 1½ tablespoons of lemon juice when done.

*Yogurt Sauce:* Use 1 cup of thick yogurt and 1 teaspoon of lemon juice.

*Cheese Sauce:* Just before removing from the flame, add 1 cup of grated cheese. Season with ½ teaspoon of soy sauce and ½ teaspoon of prepared mustard. Good with eggs, macaroni, and rice.

*Deviled Sauce:* Add ½ teaspoon of grated onion to Cheese Sauce.

*Brown Almond Sauce:* Brown ¼ cup of chopped blanched almonds in the butter before adding the flour. Another good fish sauce.

*Mushroom Sauce:* Sauté 1 cup of sliced mushrooms and 1 teaspoon of grated onion in the butter before adding the flour. Cook the mushroom stems in water for 10 minutes and use ½ cup of the liquor for ½ cup of milk.

*Egg Sauce:* After the sauce is done, add 2 chopped hard-cooked eggs, ½ teaspoon of soy sauce, 1 tablespoon of minced parsley, and ½ teaspoon of onion juice. Serve with fish.

## DARK SAUCE

Dark sauce is made by the same method as light sauce. The difference is that the butter is browned before the liquid is added, and the liquid is always Hauser Broth or leftover vegetable water.

2 tbsp. butter
1 tbsp. whole-wheat flour
1 tbsp. grated onion
1 tbsp. grated carrot
Small piece of bay leaf

Sprig of thyme or parsley
Vegetable salt to taste
Paprika
1 cup Hauser Broth

Melt the butter in a saucepan and add the vegetables and herbs. Cook over low heat until the butter is browned. Stir in the flour until well blended. Add the broth, stirring constantly, and cook until the mixture thickens and boils. Season with salt and paprika.

## VARIATIONS OF DARK SAUCE

Dark sauce is primarily a meat sauce, and various additions to it will suggest themselves, according to the kind of meat you are dressing. Here are a few:

*Onion Sauce:* Use 3 tablespoons of butter instead of 2; substitute ½ cup of sliced onions for grated onion. Remove the bay leaf and thyme, but do not strain this sauce. Serve with braised or leftover meats.

*Dill Sauce:* To the hot sauce add 1 tablespoon of lemon juice and chopped dill to taste. Serve with lamb or veal. A great favorite with Scandinavians.

*Olive Sauce:* To the hot strained sauce add ¼ cup of chopped black olives. Serve with tongue.

*Orange Sauce:* Add 1 tablespoon of grated orange rind with the onion and carrot. Substitute ½ cup of orange juice for half the broth. Serve with roast duck or goose.

*Jelly Sauce:* To the hot sauce add ¼ cup of currant jelly. Stir until the jelly dissolves and add lemon juice to taste or 1 tablespoon of sherry. Good for Sunday-night cold cuts.

*Chestnut Sauce:* To the strained sauce add 1 cup of shelled cooked chestnuts, coarsely chopped.

*Raisin Sauce:* To the broth add 2 tablespoons of natural brown sugar, 1 tablespoon of lemon juice, and ½ cup of seedless raisins after the sauce begins to thicken. Remove the bay leaf and thyme but do not strain.

## MIXED SAUCE

This is a light sauce made with chicken or veal stock in place of milk. It is served with croquettes, fish, or poultry. Use fish stock in making it to serve with fish.

| | |
|---|---|
| 2 tbsp. butter | Dash of paprika |
| 2 tbsp. whole-wheat flour | Grating of nutmeg |
| ¼ tsp. vegetable salt | 1 cup seasoned chicken or veal stock |

Melt the butter over low heat and combine as described for Light Sauce.

## VARIATIONS OF MIXED SAUCE

*Sauce Allemande:* When the sauce is thick, stir a little of it into 1 well-beaten egg yolk. Stir the mixture into the sauce and cook over very low heat for 2 minutes. After removing from the heat, add 1 teaspoon of lemon juice and 2 tablespoons of cream. To serve with fish, use sour cream instead of sweet.

*Sauce Supreme:* Substitute ½ cup of mushroom stock for meat stock. Slightly beat an egg yolk and add to it ¼ cup of heavy cream. When the sauce has thickened, stir in the egg and cream and heat over hot water.

## DELICIOUS TARTAR SAUCE

| | |
|---|---|
| 8 black olives | 1 hard-cooked egg, chopped fine |
| ½ bunch water cress, chopped fine | 1 dill pickle, chopped fine |
| 2 tbsp. finely chopped parsley | 2 cups mayonnaise |

Mix the chopped ingredients into the mayonnaise. This sauce is delicious with shrimps, oysters, scallops, or any breaded fish. In case your conscience troubles you, use chopped cucumber in place of the dill pickle.

## MUSTARD SAUCE

| | |
|---|---|
| ½ cup natural brown sugar | ½ cup mild prepared mustard |
| ½ cup hot Hauser Broth | ¼ tbsp. whole-wheat flour |
| 3 egg yolks, slightly beaten | |

Mix all the ingredients and cook them in the top of a double boiler. Serve this sauce cold. It's delicious with cold cuts.

## SWEDISH DILL SAUCE

| | |
|---|---|
| 3 tbsp. butter | 3 tbsp. natural brown sugar |
| 3 tbsp. whole-wheat flour | 4 tbsp. finely chopped dill |
| 2½ cups hot Hauser Broth | ½ tbsp. vegetable salt |
| ½ cup lemon juice | 2 egg yolks, well beaten |

Melt the butter in a saucepan or the top of a double boiler. Blend in the flour until smooth. Slowly add the hot broth and cook until thick and smooth. Stir in the lemon juice, sugar, dill, and salt. Just before serving, beat in the egg yolks. Don't let the sauce boil after the eggs have been added.

Very delicious with lamb.

## MY FAVORITE CURRY SAUCE

| | |
|---|---|
| 2 tbsp. fresh butter | 2 egg yolks |
| 2 tsp. curry powder | ½ pt. cream |
| ½ cup Hauser Broth or gravy | ½ tsp. vegetable salt |

Melt the butter, but do not brown it, in a skillet. Blend in the curry powder until smooth. Add the broth or gravy and let simmer a few minutes.

Beat the egg yolks and mix them with the cream. Reduce the heat so the egg and cream mixture will not boil and pour it into the skillet. Don't let the sauce boil again after the eggs have been added.

This is a basic curry sauce given me years ago by my brother-in-law, Dr. Gordon Gysin, who lived in India. It has been a favorite in our family for years. You will be amazed how many different curry dishes, every one delicious, you can prepare with this sauce, and all on a moment's notice.

*Chicken Curry:* Cook chicken in the usual manner; stew or sauté. When tender and ready to serve, pour Curry Sauce over the chicken and simmer for not more than 5 minutes.

*Lamb Curry:* Cook young lamb in the usual manner. When tender pour over Curry Sauce and let simmer for 5 minutes.

*Sea-Food Curry:* Put shrimps, crab meat, or lobster into the hot curry sauce before the egg yolk and cream are added. When the fish is thoroughly heated, pour in the egg yolk and cream and simmer for 3 more minutes.

*Egg Curry:* Take 6 hard-cooked fresh eggs. Cut them into quarters. Drop these into the hot curry sauce until thoroughly heated. Sprinkle with a bit of paprika and serve hot.

*Avocado Curry:* Take 2 or 3 not-too-ripe avocadoes; peel and cut into thick slices. Put in hot curry sauce and simmer until thoroughly heated.

*Leftover Meat Curry:* Any leftover meat can be made more delicious by heating it and pouring hot curry sauce over it.

*Lentil Curry:* Cook large lentils in vegetable broth. When tender pour hot curry sauce over them and serve at once.

All curries taste best when served with dry cooked rice. Curry, salad bowl, and broiled grapefruit make a good meal.

## SAUCES FOR MEAT SUBSTITUTES

### FINES HERBES SAUCE

1½ tsp. butter
2 tsp. grated onion
Sliver of garlic
1 tbsp. chopped parsley
1 tbsp. whole-wheat flour
2 cups tomato juice

¼ cup Hauser Broth
½ tbsp. powdered sage
1 tbsp. vegetable salt
1 bay leaf
1 tsp. lemon juice

Melt the butter in a saucepan. Add the onion, garlic, and parsley, and sauté until golden brown. Blend in the flour and cook for a moment, then add the sage, bay leaf, and vegetable salt. Gradually add the tomato juice and broth and cook over low heat, stirring constantly, until the mixture thickens. As soon as it reaches a boil, remove from the fire and add the salt and lemon juice. This is the favorite sauce in one of Beverly Hills' most exclusive restaurants.

Preparation: 5-10 minutes.

2½ cups.

### MUSHROOM SAUCE

| | |
|---|---|
| 1 tbsp. butter | ¼ bunch parsley, chopped |
| ½ green pepper, minced | ½ can tomato soup |
| 5 mushrooms, minced | ½ tsp. vegetable salt |
| 1 onion, minced | ½ cup Hauser Broth |
| ½ clove garlic, minced | |

Melt the butter in a heavy skillet. Add the minced vegetables and sauté. When they are soft, add the tomato soup, vegetable salt, and Hauser Broth. Let come to a boil.

### TOMATO SAUCE

| | |
|---|---|
| 2 tbsp. butter | 1 cup Hauser Broth |
| 1 clove garlic, minced | 1 tsp. celery seed |
| 1½ tbsp. whole-wheat flour | 1 tsp. vegetable salt |
| 1½ cups tomato soup | |

Melt the butter in a heavy skillet. Add the minced garlic and brown lightly. Stir in the flour and blend thoroughly. Gradually add the tomato soup and Hauser Broth and stir constantly until the mixture thickens and boils for 5 minutes. Add the seasonings.

### SPANISH SAUCE

| | |
|---|---|
| 2 tbsp. butter | 2 cups canned tomatoes |
| 1 large onion, chopped | 1 tsp. vegetable salt |
| ½ clove garlic, chopped | ¼ cup chopped stuffed olives |
| 1 green pepper, chopped | |

Melt the butter in a skillet. Sauté the onion, pepper, and garlic until browned. Add the tomatoes and vegetable salt and stew about 20 minutes.

## SYRUPS AND DESSERT SAUCES

### LEMON-HONEY SAUCE

¼ cup honey  
¾ cup water

½ tsp. grated lemon rind

Mix all ingredients and bring to the boiling point. Boil gently a few minutes to blend the flavors. Chill. Use with fresh fruit, alone or in combination. Or as a syrup for stewing fruits, in which case adjust the amount of lemon peel to taste. Orange peel may be added if desired.

Preparation: 1 or 2 minutes.

1 cup.

### DEVONSHIRE CREAM SAUCE

1 cup cream  
1 egg yolk, well beaten

Pinch of vegetable salt

Scald the cream in the top of a double boiler. Pour slowly over the beaten egg yolk, stirring constantly. Return to the double boiler and cook until thick, stirring occasionally. Serve hot or cold with puddings. It is especially good with a tart fruit dessert.

Preparation: 5-10 minutes.

1 cup.

### HARD SAUCE

⅓ cup fresh butter  
¾ cup natural brown sugar  
1 egg yolk, beaten

1 tsp. vanilla or lemon extract, or  
2 tbsp. brandy or sherry

Cream the butter until soft, gradually add the sugar, and cream together until light and fluffy. Beat in the egg yolk and flavoring, turn into the dish in which you will serve it, and set in the refrigerator to harden.

For a fluffy hard sauce, beat in ¼ cup of heavy cream, whipped, after you add the flavoring, and omit the egg yolk. For a fruit hard sauce, leave out the egg yolk and flavoring and beat in instead ½ cup of crushed strawberries, raspberries, or cranberry sauce.

## HAWAIIAN SUGAR BUTTER

Use equal parts of soft butter and natural brown sugar and blend thoroughly. This sauce takes the place of either syrup or honey on waffles and pancakes and makes a pleasant surprise for children's sandwiches and so forth.

## HONEY BUTTER

Blend ½ cup of honey and 1 teaspoon lemon juice into ⅔ cup fresh butter. Keep on ice. Delicious for pancakes or puddings.

## STRAWBERRY SYRUP

¼ cup water                          ½ cup cut-up strawberries
⅓ cup honey

Scald the water and honey in the top of a double boiler. Stir in the strawberries and let cool. Other fruit sauces can be made the same way.

## CARAMEL SAUCE

1 tbsp. butter                          ¼ cup boiling water
½ cup natural brown sugar

Melt the butter in a heavy skillet and add the sugar. Cook over moderate heat until the sugar is melted. Reduce the heat and continue cooking, stirring until the mixture boils and gives off smoky fumes. Then stir in the boiling water by the spoonful. If lumps form, return to the heat and stir until melted. Use hot or cold.

This sauce may be thinned with more water if desired.

Preparation: 8-10 minutes.

⅓ cup.

## MAPLE CREAM SAUCE

½ cup maple syrup                          Pinch of vegetable salt
1 egg yolk                          ½ cup heavy cream

Heat the syrup in the top of a double boiler. Beat the egg yolk well, slowly stir in the hot syrup, then return to the double boiler. Cook over boiling water, stirring constantly, until the mixture thickens—about 6 minutes. Cool. Whip the cream and fold into the sauce with the salt.

The grated rind of lemon may be added to taste. Or chill and mix with 1 cup of any diced fruit or berries just before serving.

Delicious as a sauce for brown rice.

## SHERRY WITH DESSERTS

Use ¼ cup of sherry to each cup of caramel, custard, or hard sauce. Or pour it over the dessert by itself, about ¼ cup per serving. In baked grapefruit, cookies, fruit cake, and custards use 2 tablespoons of sherry per cup of other liquid ingredients.

## RELISHES AND GARNISHES

Americans, even more than other peoples, eat with their eyes. Half the pleasure in a dish is its appearance, and garnishes are the decorations which put the finishing touches on appearance. But the simpler the garnish and the more functional, as we say nowadays, the better. Radish roses and lemon-rind baskets tied with parsley ribbons belong with antimacassars—we have better things to do with our time. Fresh, crisp sprigs of parsley—in their natural shapes!—water cress, tender tips of celery, carrot sticks, and raw cauliflowerets are the standbys among garnishes. For fish, of course, there is the wedge of lemon— sometimes thin slices of tomato. The main thing is to give a color accent to the dish.

Relishes serve a double purpose—they add piquancy to the flavor of the dish they accompany and serve also as a garnish if they are full of color. Cranberry and beet relishes always strike a vivid note. In the paler cucumber, onion, or apple relishes we use pimento or red or green sweet peppers for color accent.

## RAW CRANBERRY RELISH

| | |
|---|---|
| 1 golden orange | 2 cups cranberries |
| 1 red-skinned apple | ⅔ cup honey (or to taste) |

Remove the peel from one-third of the orange and the core from the apple. Cut the fruit into chunks the right size for grinding. With the medium knife on the food grinder put the cranberries and the orange and apple through the grinder alternately—first a few berries, then some orange and apple. Mix honey to taste with the ground fruit and let stand to blend the flavors. It should stand at least overnight. A delicious relish which keeps well in the refrigerator.

Use as a garnish on fruit cup or on fruit or vegetable salad; or mix with mayonnaise for a dressing with a raw cabbage or spinach salad.

This relish may also be used as a dessert, either topped with whipped cream or mixed with whipped cream and garnished with chopped nuts.

### HORSE-RADISH RELISH

Combine equal parts of currant jelly and freshly grated horse-radish. Delicious for Sunday-night cold cuts.

### BEET AND HORSE-RADISH RELISH

| | |
|---|---|
| 1 cup chopped cooked beets | ¼ cup natural brown sugar |
| ½ cup grated horse-radish | 3 tbsp. lemon juice |

Combine the ingredients, cover, and let stand overnight. Serve with meat and fish.

### RAW CRANBERRY RELISHES

These are especially good with poultry. They should be allowed to stand at least several hours before serving—preferably longer. A day or two in the refrigerator blends and mellows the flavors.

### CRANBERRY AND HORSE-RADISH RELISH

| | |
|---|---|
| 1 lb. cranberries | ⅓ cup grated horse-radish |
| ½ cup natural brown sugar | 1 tsp. lemon juice |

Put the cranberries through the medium knife of the food grinder. Add the other ingredients and mix thoroughly.

### CRANBERRY AND PINEAPPLE RELISH

Put 1 pound of cranberries through the medium knife of the food grinder. Add 1 cup drained crushed pineapple, honey to taste, and 1 tsp. lemon juice.

## CUCUMBER RELISH

1 medium cucumber
2 tbsp. chopped pimento
1 tsp. grated onion
½ tsp. vegetable salt

Dash of paprika
2 tbsp. mayonnaise
2 tbsp. lemon juice

Grate the cucumber with a coarse grater. Wrap in a piece of cheesecloth and wring dry. Put in a bowl and add the other ingredients. Chill thoroughly and drain before serving. Serve with fish or veal.

## RAW-APPLE RELISH

3 tart apples
1 sweet green pepper
1 sweet red pepper
1 small onion

2 stalks celery
1½ tsp. vegetable salt
¾ cup natural brown sugar
⅓ cup lemon juice

Chop the apples, peppers, onions, and celery. Add the remaining ingredients and mix thoroughly. Cover and chill thoroughly. Serve with poultry.

## ONION RELISH

½ cup lemon juice
1 tbsp. natural brown sugar
¾ cup chopped fresh mint leaves

1 cup thinly sliced onion
1 pimento cut in strips

Put the lemon juice and sugar in a saucepan. Add the mint leaves and heat gently for half an hour. Add the onions and pimento—if necessary more lemon juice to cover the onions. Chill until the onions are crisp before serving.

CHAPTER 12

# *Fruits and Fruit Desserts*

THE BIBLE PAYS tribute to the fragrance and beauty of pome-granates; the ancient Egyptians knew the soft bloom of grapes; the Chinese bit into the sweet yellow flesh of peaches a thousand years before the Christian era began; and Homer sang of pears in the days of Helen. In those far-off days fruit was a rarity; now we know that it is a necessity. We have orange or grapefruit every day as a matter of course; apples, bananas, and pears to eat out of hand. Fruits make the best and most delicious desserts, especially after a heavy meal. Serve them fresh, sweetened with uncooked honey. Sometime try the French way of combining fruit with cheese—a slice of cheese on a slice of apple, or cheese served with radishes.

For a delightful change from fresh raw fruits try stewing them in the French manner or baking them as in the recipes in this section. And remember that when you eat fruit, you are absorbing those necessary minerals and vitamins.

*How to Store Fruit:* All fruit should be purchased in small quantities, as fresh as possible. But when you have to keep fruits for a day or so, store them in a cool dry place, not in the refrigerator, spread out so the individual pieces do not touch each other. Never pile up soft fruits—spread them out flat on a plate. Handle fruit as little as possible and leave wrapped fruit in its wrappers until you are ready to use it.

Chill fruit in the refrigerator only just before serving, but bananas should never be chilled. Fruit juices, you remember (see page 214), should be squeezed at the last moment. Cut-up fruits should be cut as late as possible to prevent loss of vitamins.

*To Prevent Discoloration:* Fruits which turn dark upon exposure to air—apples, peaches, etc.—can be kept their own fresh color by dipping in a tart fruit juice such as orange, grapefruit, or pineapple juice.

### FRENCH STEWED FRUIT

Use any soft fruits or berries. Place in a saucepan and cover with cold water. Sweeten to taste with honey—orange-blossom honey is delicious for this. Bring to the boil and remove immediately from the heat. This method takes only a few minutes and does not destroy the natural color or flavor of the fruit.

The secret of a really delicious *compôte des fruits*—a mixture of stewed fruits as prepared in Paris—is to cook each fruit separately. Do not mix them until you are ready to serve them.

On a famous beauty farm in Maine French stewed fruits were served several times a week during my Elimination Diet [1] and were extremely popular with the spoiled rich ladies.

[1] See my *Diet Does It*, New York: Coward-McCann, 1944.

### STEWED DRIED FRUITS

Wash the fruit, cover it with *warm* water, and add honey to taste. *Do not cook*, but let soak overnight. Fruit prepared this way will look and taste like fresh fruit. A few drops of lemon or orange juice give additional flavor.

### ALMOND APPLES

| | |
|---|---|
| 4 red-skinned cooking apples | Shredded lemon or orange peel to taste |
| 2½ cups boiling water | 20 blanched almonds |
| 1 cup honey | |

Pare the apples without removing the stems and save the peelings. Have the water boiling in a pan shaped so the apples can float—a bowl-shaped vessel is best. Drop the apples into the water and boil gently, turning the apples often, until they are nearly soft. Remove the apples and add the peelings. Cook them for about 10 minutes and strain, pressing out all the juice. Discard the peels and save the apple liquor—there should be about 2 cups. Add the honey and the orange or lemon peel. Bring to the boil again, add the apples, and simmer until transparent. Do not let the water boil. Then transfer the apples to a baking pan and stick 5 almonds into the outer edge of the stem end of each apple. Cover the bottom of the pan with apple liquor and bake in a moderate oven (375°F) until the almonds are a rich brown—10 to 15 minutes. Baste frequently with the syrup while baking. Serve cold with cream.

Preparation: 10 to 15 minutes.

4 servings.

### LEMON APPLE SLICES

2 large apples                                          2 tbsp. honey
Juice of ½ lemon                                        2 tsp. butter

Cut the apples in slices about ⅜ inch thick. Arrange the slices in a buttered baking dish large enough so that you need only 3 or 4 layers. Add the lemon juice and honey and dot with the butter. Bake in a moderate oven (350°F.) about 30 minutes, until the slices are tender. Serve hot or cold with sweetened whipped cream.

Preparation: 5 to 10 minutes.

3 servings.

### MAPLE APPLE CUPS

2 large apples                                          ⅓ cup water
½ cup maple syrup                                       1 tbsp. butter

Halve the apples crosswise and remove the core with the tip of a spoon. Mix the syrup and water in a baking pan and place the apples in it, cut side down. Bring to the boiling point on top of the stove, then place in a moderate oven (350°F.) for 15 minutes. Turn the apples over, fill the hollows with syrup from the pan, and put a quarter of the butter on each half. Return to the oven and bake until cooked through—another 15 or 20 minutes.

If the syrup thickens too much, add a little more water. Serve cold with the syrup and a spoonful of chopped walnuts in each hollow.

Preparation: 4 or 5 minutes.

4 servings.

## HONEY APPLES

Core apples and put them in a baking pan, adding a little water. Put a piece of butter in the center of each, fill with honey, and top with a dash of cinnamon. Bake in a moderate oven (350°F.), basting occasionally with the juice formed in the pan, until the apples are tender but not mushy—about 35 minutes. Delicious when cooked this way.

## FIVE-MINUTE APPLESAUCE

Melt some butter in a heavy skillet, as carefully as you would for scrambled eggs. When the butter is hot but still golden, not browned, throw in shredded unpeeled apples. Heat them through, turn them over once, and you will have an applesauce fit for kings and gods. For additional flavor, add honey to taste.

## BAKED BANANAS

Peel 6 large ripe bananas, split in half, and place in a shallow baking dish. Mix 1 tablespoon of melted butter, 1/3 cup of natural brown sugar, and 2 tablespoons of lemon or lime juice. Pour over the bananas and keep on basting. Bake 20 minutes in a slow oven (300°F.). For extra flavor and elegance, sprinkle with shredded coconut.

## PALM BEACH BANANAS

Whole-wheat pie crust (p. 197)     Lemon or lime juice
6 large ripe bananas               2 tbsp. natural brown sugar

Prepare whole-wheat pie crust and roll it out very thin. Peel the bananas, sprinkle with lemon or lime juice, and roll in the sugar. Cut the pie crust in squares large enough to wrap up a banana and still leave some crust at the ends. Moisten the edges of the crust with cold water and pinch together with a fork. Place on a pie plate or cookie sheet and bake 10 minutes in a hot oven (425°F.). Serve with whipped cream or spiced hot milk.

## BROILED GRAPEFRUIT

Select firm grapefruits and cut in half. Cut the sections free from the membrane surrounding them, but do not remove the center. To each half add 1 teaspoon of honey or natural brown sugar and 1/2 teaspoon of butter unless you are on a reducing diet, of course. Place in a shallow baking pan with a little water in it and broil slowly for about 30 minutes, or until heated through and bubbling.

## FAVORITE DESSERT

Fresh raspberries, strawberries, blackberries, loganberries—in fact, all berries—taste like gifts from the gods when sprinkled with honey and shredded coconut.

My favorite dessert is a large bowl full of fresh berries sprinkled with orange-blossom honey, and for special occasions the berries are arranged in layers; between each layer of berries is a layer of shredded coconut.

## BAKED MERINGUE PEACHES

4 slices whole-wheat cake
Fruit juice to moisten
2 large ripe peaches

1 egg white
2½ tbsp. honey

Cut the slices of cake in rounds slightly larger than the peaches. Butter the top side of each round and set them in the fruit juice, sweetened to taste. When moistened with juice, transfer to a buttered baking pan. Peel and halve the peaches and put a half on each round of cake. Beat the egg white stiff but not dry. Add the honey by degrees, beating after each addition. Fill the hollow of each peach and cover the cut surface with meringue. Bake in a moderate oven (325°F.) until the meringue is browned —about 2 minutes.

Preparation: 10-15 minutes.

4 servings.

## CRANBERRY SOYA PUDDING

2 eggs, separated
½ cup honey
¾ cup sifted soya flour
½ tsp. baking powder
2 tbsp. thinly sliced citron

3 tbsp. chopped toasted almonds
¼ cup currants
⅜ cup chopped seeded raisins
⅜ cup cranberries
¼ tsp. almond extract

Beat the egg yolks until thick and lemon-colored. Beat in the honey bit by bit. Sift the flour and baking powder together three times and stir into the egg yolks. Add the citron, nuts, and fruit rolled in flour, then the almond extract. Mix well. Beat the egg whites until stiff but not dry and fold into the other mixture. Fill a buttered mold two-thirds full (tin cans may be used instead). Cover and steam until the center is cooked through—1¾ to 2 hours. Serve hot with lemon sauce.

*Directions for Steaming:* Put an inch of water in the bottom of a steamer. Place the pudding mold on a rack and cover the steamer. Use medium or high heat until steam escapes, then reduce the heat to low. Steaming should be steady but light.

If you don't have a steamer, use a covered roasting pan or kettle with a rack on the bottom. In this case the water should half cover the mold. Have the water boiling when the molds are put in and add more as needed.

## DATE PUDDING

½ tsp. cream of tartar
½ cup natural brown sugar
½ cup chopped dates
⅛ tsp. vanilla

1 egg yolk
2 egg whites
Pinch of vegetable salt
2 tbsp. chopped nuts

Mix the cream of tartar and the sugar in a bowl, then thoroughly mix in the chopped dates. Beat in the vanilla and egg yolk. Beat the egg whites with the salt until stiff but not dry and fold into the date mixture. Transfer to a buttered baking dish and sprinkle with chopped nuts. Bake in a moderate oven (350°F.) until the center is firm—about 20 minutes. Serve hot or cold with cream or custard sauce.

Preparation: 15-20 minutes.

4 servings.

## DELMONICO PUDDING

3 cooking apples
⅛ lb. blanched almonds, finely ground
5 tbsp. natural brown sugar

2 tbsp. butter
1 peach
Grated rind of ¼ lemon

Slice the apples thin and remove the core. They should make over 2 cups. Butter a baking dish and arrange about a third of the apples in the bottom. Add 1 tablespoon of water. Sprinkle 1 tablespoon of almonds and 1 tablespoon of sugar over the top, then dot with a teaspoon of butter. Arrange a second layer of apples, this time mixed with the sliced skinned peach. Top with almonds, sugar, and butter as before; then a third layer of apples topped with almonds, sugar, and butter. Grate the lemon rind over the top of all. Bake covered in a moderate oven (350°F.) for about ½ hour, then remove the cover and finish baking until the apples are done and the top browned—another half hour. Serve warm as a relish with cold meats. For dessert, serve cold with cream and garnish with finely crumbled dried macaroons.

Preparation: 15-20 minutes.

6 servings.

## FRUIT-JUICE AGAR DESSERT

1 tbsp. flaked agar-agar            1⅔ cup sweetened flavored liquid—
⅓ cup lukewarm water                   fruit juice, coffee, etc.

Soak the agar-agar in the water for 20 minutes. Bring to the boiling point and cook gently until clear—about 10 minutes. Remove from the heat and add the fruit juice. (There should be 2 cups of liquid in all. If the agar water has boiled down, add hot water to make up the measure.) Strain into a mold rinsed in cold water. Chill until set. Serve with custard sauce or whipped cream sweetened with honey.

## FRUIT JELLY

Any fruit juice can be used as a base for fruit jelly except fresh pineapple. Prepare as for Fruit-Juice Agar Dessert, or use 1 tablespoon of granulated gelatine soaked in ½ cup of cold water to 1¾ cups liquid. Combine diced fruit with the jelly up to an equal quantity.

## LEMON JELLY

1 tbsp. flaked agar-agar soaked in ⅓        6 tbsp. lemon juice
   cup lukewarm water, or 2 tbsp.           ⅝ cup honey (or to taste)
   granulated gelatine soaked in ½          Grated rind of 1 lemon
   cup cold water                           1 cup water

Combine as for Fruit-Juice Agar Dessert.

## PINEAPPLE JELLY

Fresh pineapple contains an enzyme which makes gelatine liquefy, hence it must be scalded before using. This is not necessary with canned pineapple.

1 tbsp. flaked agar-agar soaked in ⅓        1¼ cups unsweetened pineapple
   cup lukewarm water or 2 tbsp.               juice
   granulated gelatine soaked in ½         2⅔ tbsp. lemon juice
   cup cold water                            3 tbsp. honey (or to taste)

Combine as for Fruit-Juice Agar Dessert.

## BAVARIAN CREAM

1⅓ tbsp. flaked agar-agar soaked in        1 cup fruit juice (or water and
   ⅓ cup lukewarm water or 2                   flavoring) sweetened to taste
   tbsp. granulated gelatine soaked       ⅔ cup heavy cream
   in ½ cup cold water

Prepare as for Fruit-Juice Agar Dessert. Let the gelatine mixture cool until it just begins to set. Whip the cream and fold it into the stiffening gelatine mixture. Pour into a mold rinsed with cold water and chill until set. Serve with fruit juice for the sauce.

## PINEAPPLE BAVARIAN CREAM

1⅓ tbsp. agar-agar soaked in ⅓ cup lukewarm water or 2 tbsp. granulated gelatine soaked in ½ cup cold water

2 tsp. lemon juice

1⅔ cups canned crushed pineapple

⅓ cup honey (or to taste)

⅔ cup heavy cream

Prepare as for Bavarian Cream.

## ALMOND BLANC MANGE

1 tbsp. flaked agar-agar

2 cups soya milk

⅓ cup honey

½ cup heavy cream

⅛ tsp. vegetable salt

¼ tsp. almond extract

¼ tsp. vanilla

Soak the agar-agar in ½ cup of the soya milk for 20 minutes. Set over boiling water until melted—about 10 minutes. Add the remaining ingredients and mix thoroughly. Pour into a mold rinsed in cold water. Chill until set, then turn out onto a serving dish. Serve with cream.

Preparation: 20 to 25 minutes.

4 servings.

## LEMON MERINGUE PUDDING

1 tsp. flaked agar-agar

⅔ cup soya milk

4 eggs

Grated rind of 1 lemon

6 tbsp. lemon juice

2 tsp. butter

½ cup honey

Soak the agar-agar in the soya milk for 20 minutes. Cook in the top of a double boiler over hot water until dissolved—about 15 minutes. Beat two whole eggs and two egg yolks to an even consistency. Add slowly to the hot milk, stirring constantly. Cook, stirring, until the mixture thickens and coats a spoon inserted in it—about 6 minutes. Stir in the lemon rind and juice, the butter, and the honey. Turn into a shallow pudding dish and cool. When stiff, spread with a meringue made from the remaining

2 egg whites, beaten stiff but not dry with 2 tablespoons of honey. Place under a broiler flame until the meringue is delicately browned. Serve cold.

Preparation: 25-30 minutes.

4 servings.

### BAKED RHUBARB WITH FRUIT

¼ lb. rhubarb                          ⅙ cup water
⅜ cup seeded raisins, chopped fine     ½ cup quartered strawberries

Cut the rhubarb, unpeeled, into 1-inch pieces. Pour boiling water over it and let stand 10 minutes, then drain. This is to reduce the oxalic-acid content of the rhubarb. Put the rhubarb in a buttered baking dish, add the raisins and the ⅙ cup of water. Cover and bake in a moderate oven (350°F.) until tender—about 25 minutes. Remove from the oven and add the strawberries while the rhubarb is still piping hot. Replace the cover and cool before serving. Serve with a mixture of thick buttermilk and heavy cream.

If preferred, cook in a double boiler instead of baking.

Preparation: 15-20 minutes.

3 servings.

### PUMPKIN CUP

1 cup grated raw pumpkin               1 egg
¼ cup honey or natural brown sugar     ½ cup soya milk
½ tsp. vegetable salt                  3 tbsp. heavy cream
1⅓ tbsp. molasses                      Grated rind of ⅔ lemon
⅔ tsp. cinnamon                        1 or 2 walnuts, chopped
⅜ tsp. ginger

Mix all ingredients thoroughly except the walnuts. Pour into buttered individual custard cups and top with a sprinkling of chopped nuts. Bake in a moderate oven (325°F.) until set. Serve cold, garnished with whipped cream.

Preparation: 10-15 minutes.

3 servings.

### ONE-TWO-THREE DESSERT

Soak in warm water overnight a handful of dried apricots, a handful of raisins, and a handful of prunes with 1 tablespoon of honey. This makes an excellent iron-rich breakfast dish as well as dessert.

## SUNSHINE FRUIT CAKE

½ lb. dried apricots
½ lb. seedless raisins
1 lb. dates
1 lb. dried figs

1 lb. shredded coconut
1 lb. walnut meats
1 tsp. vegetable salt

Mix all the ingredients in a bowl and then put them through the medium knife of a food chopper. Knead the mass well to mix thoroughly, then pack tightly in a buttered square pan or mold. Cover the dish with a plate or something slightly smaller than the dish. Put a weight on top and set in the refrigerator. Leave for 2 or 3 days until the loaf is very firm. Cut in thin slices and serve as cake, or use in place of candy.

Use pure sun-dried fruits for this "sunshine candy" which both children and adults will like.

## COCONUT DATE PUDDING

½ cup pitted dates
½ cup finely shredded fresh coconut
1 egg

1 cup water
⅛ tsp. vegetable salt
Grated orange rind

Cut the dates lengthwise in quarters. Arrange half of them on the bottom of a buttered baking dish. Spread half the shredded coconut on top, make another layer of dates, then a layer of coconut. Beat the egg into the water and pour over the dish. Sprinkle with salt, cover, and bake in a slow oven (300°F.) until the dates are very soft—about 50 minutes. Sprinkle the top with a bit of grated orange rind, cool, and serve with whipped cream.

Preparation: 10-15 minutes.

4 servings.

## DRIED FRUIT AND NUT PUDDING

½ cup fruit purée
⅜ cup ground nuts
2 egg whites

1½ tbsp. honey
⅓ tsp. vegetable salt
Lemon juice and rind to taste

Make the purée from dried fruits soaked overnight in warm water. Mix the ground nuts with the fruit. Beat the egg white with the salt until stiff but not dry. Beat in the honey by degrees and fold in the fruit mixture. Butter the top of a 1-quart double boiler and turn the pudding into it.

Cook over boiling water until the center is set—about 1 hour. Turn out of the pan and serve hot or cold with cream or the sweetened juice of fruit. Prunes and Brazil nuts, apricots and pecans are two good combinations.

If preferred, turn the pudding into a buttered baking dish, set the dish in a pan of hot water, and bake in a slow oven (300°F.) for 45 minutes.

## CARROT CUSTARD

1 cup finely grated raw carrot
2 eggs, slightly beaten
4 tbsp. honey
2 cups milk

Grated rind of 1 lemon
½ tsp. vegetable salt
2 tbsp. melted butter
Sprinkling of cinnamon

Combine the ingredients in the order given. Mix thoroughly and pour into a buttered baking dish or individual custard cups. Sprinkle the top with cinnamon. Set the mold in a pan containing hot water. The water should cover the mold or cups up to the level of the custard. Bake in a moderate oven (375°F.) until the custard is set—about half an hour. To test the custard, insert a silver knife in the middle of it. If the knife comes out clean, the custard is done.

Preparation: 10-15 minutes.

4 servings.

## CARROT PLUM PUDDING

¾ cup chopped raw carrots
½ cup seeded raisins
¾ cup broken nutmeats
2 tbsp. thinly sliced citron
½ cup currants
½ cup natural brown sugar
¼ cup vegetable oil

½ cup soya flour
¾ tsp. baking powder
½ tsp. vegetable salt
½ tsp. cinnamon
¼ tsp. nutmeg
Rind of ½ lemon

Put the carrots, raisins, and nutmeats through the medium knife of a food grinder. Add the citron, currants, sugar, and vegetable oil. Mix well. Sift the soya flour and baking powder together three times and add. Grate in the lemon rind and mix all together thoroughly. Fill a buttered pudding mold two-thirds full, cover, and steam until the center is cooked through—about 2 hours. Serve hot with hard sauce or custard sauce.

This pudding improves if it is allowed to ripen a few days, then reheated.

Preparation: 25-30 minutes.

4 servings.

## APRICOT SOUFFLÉ

¾ cup apricot purée                   5 tbsp. natural brown sugar
5 egg whites                          Pinch of salt

To make the apricot purée, soak ½ to ¾ pound of sun-dried apricots in warm water overnight. Fresh apricots will not give the same delicate flavor. Press through a sieve or fruit press to purée.

Beat the egg whites until stiff but not dry, beating in the sugar and salt toward the end. Fold into the apricot purée, pile lightly in a buttered baking dish, and bake in a slow oven (300°F.) until the center is firm— about 45 minutes.

## OTHER SOUFFLÉS

Following the recipe for Apricot Soufflé, try other fruit soufflés. Bananas, fresh peaches, crushed pineapple, cranberries, prunes, a combination of dates and applesauce, and fresh strawberries are a few suggestions.

## OREGON PRUNE WHIP

Soak large sweet-sour Oregon prunes in half water and half orange juice for 24 hours. Remove the pits. Sweeten to taste with honey. Mash and fold into whipped cream, 1 cup of whipped cream to 2 cups of prunes. Top with finely chopped pecans or walnuts.

This is also an excellent filling for continental pie shells.

## PASADENA APRICOT WHIP

Wash dried apricots thoroughly. Soak for 24 hours in water or orange juice until the apricots are large and plump. Sweeten to taste with orange-blossom honey and fold into whipped cream, 2 cups of apricots to 1 cup of whipped cream. This is also superb when frozen.

## APPLE FOAM

2 tart apples                         2 egg whites
½ tsp. grated lemon or orange rind    2 tbsp. honey

Shred the unpeeled apples on a fine shredder. Add the rind. Beat the egg whites until stiff but not dry, then slowly beat in the honey. Fold in the shredded apple. Pile lightly in individual glasses, chill thoroughly, and serve with a bright garnish such as cranberry relish or currant jelly.

Preparation: 10-15 minutes.

4 servings.

## BROILED FRUIT WITH MEAT

Fruits, of course, are most nutritious when served raw. However, on special occasions, when your rich relatives come to dinner or for variety's sake, try some of these broiled fruits.

Use apple rings, orange sections, peach halves, pineapple sticks or rings. Prepare as directed below, then place on a greased broiler rack 3 to 4 inches from the heat. Broil until delicately browned.

*Broiled Oranges:* Dip large orange sections or slices into French dressing before broiling. Serve with duck.

*Broiled Peaches:* Put 1 tsp. butter in the cavity of each fresh or canned peach half. Sprinkle with brown sugar and, if desired, a dash of curry powder.

*Broiled Pears:* Fill the cavities of cooked pear halves with mayonnaise and sprinkle with paprika. Especially good with spring lamb.

*Broiled Pineapple:* Sprinkle pineapple sticks or rings, fresh or canned, with brown sugar and dot with butter. Serve with fried chicken.

*Broiled Apples:* Dip apple rings, cut ¾ inch thick, in melted butter and then in a mixture of sugar and cinnamon. Turn to brown on both sides. Serve around meats.

# CHAPTER 13

# Milk Desserts--Custards, Ice Creams, and Puddings

HERE ARE THE OLD standbys with which mothers induce children to eat their quota of milk:

## BAKED CUSTARD

| | |
|---|---|
| 4 eggs | 3 cups milk |
| 1/3 cup natural brown sugar | Sprinkling of nutmeg |
| 1/2 tsp. vegetable salt | |

Beat the eggs slightly, stir in the sugar and salt, and add the milk. Stir until the sugar is completely dissolved, then pour into a buttered baking dish or individual custard cups. Set the mold in a pan containing hot water up to the level of the custard. Bake in a moderate oven (375°F) until the custard is set—about half an hour. To test the custard, insert a silver knife into the middle of it. If the knife comes out clean, the custard is done.

Preparation: 10 minutes.

6 servings.

## CARAMEL SOYA CUSTARD

| | |
|---|---|
| 1/3 cup caramel sauce | 6 tbsp. natural brown sugar |
| 2 cups soya milk | Pinch of vegetable salt |
| 2 eggs | 1/2 tsp. vanilla |

Butter individual custard cups and put 1 tablespoon of caramel sauce in the bottom of each. Beat the eggs slightly, add the sugar and salt, milk, and the rest of the caramel. Stir until the sugar is dissolved. Pour gently into the custard cups, set the cups in a pan of hot water up to the level of the custard, and bake in a moderate oven (375°F.) until the custard is set—about 30 minutes. When a silver knife inserted in the middle of the custard comes out clean, the custard is done. Chill, turn out each cup into a dessert dish, and garnish with whipped cream.

Preparation: 5-10 minutes.

4 servings.

## RICE PUDDING

| | |
|---|---|
| 2 tbsp. uncooked brown rice | ⅛ tsp. nutmeg |
| 2 cups soya milk | ¼ tsp. vegetable salt |
| ¼ cup natural brown sugar | 2 tsp. butter |

Wash and pick over the rice. Scald the soya milk, add the rice, then the other ingredients. Turn into a buttered baking dish and bake in a moderate oven (350°F.) 1½ hours, stirring occasionally as a brown crust forms. During the last half hour do not stir. Serve with heavy cream, or add the cream to the pudding at the last stirring.

Preparation: about 10 minutes.

3 servings.

## HONEY RICE PUDDING

| | |
|---|---|
| 3 tbsp. uncooked brown rice | ½ tsp. vegetable salt |
| 1 qt. rich milk | 2 tbsp. seedless raisins |
| 2 tbsp. honey | |

Wash and pick over the rice. Put it in a buttered casserole—it should barely cover the bottom of the dish. Mix the milk, honey, and salt and pour over the rice. Last sprinkle in the raisins. Bake in a moderate oven (350°F.) for 1½ hours, or until set. Chopped dates in place of raisins make a welcome change.

## RICE AND RAISIN PUDDING

Prepare Boiled Rice (page 174), adding 1 cup of raisins when you turn off the heat. Let stand an hour over hot water and serve with cream. This makes either a dessert or a breakfast food.

## RICE AND DATE PUDDING

Prepare Boiled Rice (page 174), adding 1 cup of chopped dates when you turn off the heat. Let stand an hour over hot water and serve with cream.

## FROZEN DESSERTS

The smooth, creamy texture which marks a good ice cream comes from the churning of the dasher. Since most of us freeze ice cream in an automatic refrigerator these days, special ingredients have to be used to counteract the formation of ice crystals. The gelatine-base method of making ice cream gives a smoother consistency.

Nearly all ice creams are improved by standing an hour or more in the refrigerator after they are frozen.

## DIRECTIONS FOR FREEZING IN A REFRIGERATOR

Set the control for fast freezing. Pour the mixture into a tray and place the tray on the bottom of the freezing compartment or on a shelf with a freezing coil. Freeze until firm throughout.

If egg white or whipped cream is called for, beat it at this time. Heavy cream should be whipped only until it will just hold its shape, never until stiff.

Remove the frozen mixture from the tray to a chilled bowl and break it up with a wooden spoon. Beat with an electric mixer or a rotary egg beater until the mass is free from hard lumps but still crumbly. Don't beat so long that liquid forms. Fold in the whipped cream or egg white with a turn or two of the beater or the spoon. Return the mixture at once to the tray and put it back in the refrigerator to finish freezing. Wet the bottom of the tray to insure good contact and thus hasten freezing.

Set the control halfway between fast freezing and normal operating to hold the ice cream until time to serve.

## VANILLA ICE CREAM

Beat 1 quart of light cream to a stiff froth. Sweeten with honey to taste and flavor with 2 teaspoons of vanilla. Freeze according to directions.

## VANILLA ICE CREAM WITH GELATINE

2½ cups milk
½ cup natural brown sugar
1½ tsp. gelatine

2 tsp. vanilla
1 cup heavy cream, whipped

Scald the milk with the sugar and sprinkle the gelatine over the top. Stir until the gelatine is dissolved and cool. Add the vanilla and pour into refrigerator trays to freeze. Add the whipped cream when you take out the mixture after its first freezing, as directed.

## OTHER FLAVORS OF ICE CREAM

Use either of the recipes above for Vanilla Ice Cream and make the following changes:

*Peach Ice Cream:* Reduce vanilla to 1 tsp., add ½ tsp. almond extract and 2 cups crushed peaches sweetened with ½ cup natural brown sugar or honey.

*Strawberry or Raspberry Ice Cream:* When ready to freeze, add 2 cups crushed berries sweetened as necessary, according to the kind of berries.

*Pineapple Ice Cream:* Use 1 tbsp. lemon juice instead of vanilla and add 2 cups well-drained crushed pineapple or grated fresh pineapple.

*Black Walnut Ice Cream:* Reduce the vanilla to 1½ tsp. and add ¾ tsp. almond extract. Before freezing add 1 cup finely chopped black walnuts.

*Pistachio Ice Cream:* Reduce vanilla to 1½ tsp. and add ¾ tsp. almond extract or rose flavoring. Add 1 cup finely chopped blanched pistachio nuts. Tint green with vegetable coloring, remembering that the color will be lighter when the cream is frozen.

## JIFFY ICE CREAM

| | |
|---|---|
| 1 pt. ripe strawberries or raspberries | Juice of ½ lime |
| ⅓ cup water | ½ cup heavy cream, whipped |
| 2 tbsp. honey | Pinch of vegetable salt |

Mash the berries thoroughly. Combine the water, honey, lime juice, and salt. Mix thoroughly and add to the berries. Fold in the whipped cream and freeze according to directions.

## AVOCADO ICE CREAM

| | |
|---|---|
| ½ large avocado | ½ cup heavy cream |
| 2 tbsp. honey | ¼ cup chopped walnuts |
| Juice of 1 orange | ¼ cup chopped dates |
| ½ tsp. vegetable salt | Grated lemon and orange rind |

Mash the avocado pulp, add the honey, and beat smooth. Add the orange juice and salt. Whip the cream and fold in with the nuts, dates, and rind. Freeze according to directions.

## FRUIT ICE CREAM

1 tsp. powdered agar-agar
½ cup boiling water
¾ cup natural brown sugar
1 tbsp. lemon juice

2 cups fruit pulp
1 cup thin cream
½ cup cookie crumbs
1 cup whipped cream

Dissolve the agar-agar in the boiling water. Add the sugar, lemon juice, and fruit pulp, then the thin cream and cookie crumbs. Freeze until stiff, then fold in the whipped cream as directed under Directions for Freezing.

## VANILLA ICE CREAM WITH CONDENSED MILK

⅔ cup condensed milk
⅔ cup milk
1 tsp. vanilla (or more to taste)

Pinch of vegetable salt
1 cup heavy cream, whipped

Combine the condensed milk, milk, vanilla, and salt. Put in the freezing tray and freeze. Add the cream whipped until it will just hold its shape when the mixture is taken out after the first freezing, as described in Directions for Freezing.

## SOYA ICE CREAM

1½ tsp. flaked agar-agar
1 cup soya milk, scalded
¼ cup honey

⅛ tsp. vegetable salt
¾ tsp. vanilla
¾ cup heavy cream

Soak the agar-agar in the warmed milk for 20 minutes, then dissolve over boiling water—about 10 minutes. Remove from the heat, add the honey and salt, and let cool. When the agar solution begins to stiffen, whip the heavy cream and add with the vanilla. Freeze until firm, stirring well once when partly frozen.

## ICES AND SHERBETS

An ice is a mixture of fruit juices, sugar, and flavoring; a sherbet is an ice with egg whites, milk, cream, or gelatine added. Milk sherbets are smoother than ice cream and add fewer calories.

## DIRECTIONS FOR FREEZING

To freeze ices and sherbets in a refrigerator, set the control for fast freezing. Combine the fruit juices and chilled syrup according to directions.

Mix well and pour into the freezing tray. Freeze until firm, remove from the tray and break up with a wooden spoon in a chilled bowl. Beat with an electric mixer or a rotary egg beater until free from hard lumps but still a thick mush.

If you are making an ice, return to the freezing tray and freeze until firm. For a sherbet, beat the egg whites until stiff and add at this time before returning to the freezing tray.

## LEMON ICE

3 cups water
¾ cup honey
1¼ cups natural brown sugar

1 tbsp. grated lemon rind
⅔ cup lemon juice

Combine the water, honey, sugar, and lemon rind in a saucepan. Place over low heat and stir until the sugar is dissolved. Bring to a boil and boil 5 minutes without stirring. Cool, add lemon juice, strain, and freeze.

## OTHER ICES

To make ices with other flavors, make the following changes in a recipe for Lemon Ice:

*Lime Ice:* Use grated lime rind and lime juice instead of lemon.

*Orange Ice:* Reduce the water to 2 cups and use 1½ cups of orange juice and ¼ cup of lemon juice.

*Strawberry Ice:* Reduce the water to 2 cups and the lemon juice to 1 tbsp. Mash 1 quart of ripe strawberries, strain through a cheesecloth, and add the juice to the cooled syrup. There should be 1½ cups of juice.

*Raspberry Ice:* Follow directions for Strawberry Ice.

*Pineapple Ice:* Reduce the water to 1½ cups and the lemon juice to ¼ cup. Add 1½ cups pineapple juice and pulp to the cooled syrup.

## SHERBETS

Use any of the above recipes for ices, and add 2 stiffly beaten egg whites when the ice is broken up after the first freezing.

## MILK SHERBETS

Use any of the above recipes for ices, using milk instead of water. Scald the milk with the sugar and honey in the top of a double boiler. Cool, add remaining ingredients, and proceed as directed for ices.

## BUTTERMILK SHERBET

½ cup fruit juice or crushed pulp
¼ cup honey (or to taste)
1 cup buttermilk

1 tbsp. lemon juice
1 egg white
Pinch of vegetable salt

Mix together the fruit and honey. Add the buttermilk and lemon juice and mix thoroughly. Transfer to a freezing tray and freeze until firm, stirring well once if the ingredients separate. Beat the egg white until stiff and fold in as directed under Directions for Freezing.

*Pineapple Buttermilk Sherbet:* Use ½ cup unsweetened canned crushed pineapple.

*Grapejuice Buttermilk Sherbet:* Use unsweetened grape juice and reduce the amount of honey.

*Orange Buttermilk Sherbet:* Use freshly squeezed orange juice and pulp, substituting the grated rind of ¼ lemon instead of lemon juice and reducing the amount of honey.

# CHAPTER 14

## *Cereals in the Modern Manner*

GRAIN, ONCE THE STAFF of life, has become the Cinderella among foods. Partly because of the emphasis on meat as a body-builder and fruits, vegetables, and salads as weight-reducers—both of which are excellent aims in themselves—cereals and grains have come to be despised. As a matter of fact, the denatured cereals produced by refining deserve this low esteem. Probably no other food has been so cruelly robbed of its food elements as cereals.

If, however, cereals are eaten as nature meant them to be—entire—they are good sources both of energy and of protection. Nature in her wisdom gave the starchy grains a generous helping of vitamin $B_1$, which helps to transform starch into energy. But man, ever since he learned to make milling machinery, has been doing his best to ruin this natural balance—to reduce cereals to pure starch and refine away everything else. The bran which contains cellulose, the germ which hoards most of the vitamins, and a good part of the protein of grains are thrown away—and we eat what's left. Whole-grain cereals which have not been despoiled by refining are a good source of energy, a fine source of the vitamin B complex, and contribute some protein. So you need not give up that comforting hot cereal which sticks to your ribs through the long morning, nor the bland, crunchy cold cereals which comfort the less hearty eater. Keep right on enjoying them—but make sure they are made of entire grain, with all their nutty flavor intact.

## COOKED CEREALS

A blend of cereals supplying rich nourishment with excellent flavor was my goal when I worked out the Best Cereal below. Thousands of my American students testify that it's the best cereal they ever tasted. Swedes, Englishmen, Irishmen, and Dutchmen all praise it. So get a large jar with an airtight cover and hie yourself to the nearest place where they sell freshly milled whole-grain cereals. Buy grains to make the following mixture:

## THE BEST COOKED CEREAL

½ cup natural whole barley
½ cup natural whole rye
½ cup natural brown rice

¼ cup whole millet
¼ cup wheat germ
¼ cup whole flaxseed

Take 1 cup of this cereal blend and stir it into 3 cups of boiling water. Add 1 teaspoon of vegetable salt and let simmer for five minutes. Turn off the heat, cover the pot, and let stand overnight. Next morning simply reheat and serve with rich milk and honey. One cup of cereal will make 4 generous servings.

## DELICIOUS CEREAL THE LAZY WAY

Do you get off to work in a great hurry in the morning? Try this way of making hot cereal:

Stir ½ cup of the cereal mixture described above into 2 cups of boiling water. You need lots of water this way. Let simmer a minute or two, then pour into a wide-mouthed preheated thermos bottle. Close tightly and lay the thermos on its side so the cereal won't pack in the bottom. Sleep calmly, and next morning wake up to steaming hot cereal prepared by a genie in the night, ready to be eaten with rich milk and honey.

## A CEREAL YOUNGSTERS GO FOR

Get some nice plump cracked whole-wheat kernels, steel-cut oats, or brown rice. Stir ½ cup of any one of them into 2 cups of boiling water. Pour into a preheated thermos bottle—a wide-mouthed one. Next morning the kernels will be puffed up and fat. Sprinkle with raisins and serve with rich milk and honey.

## OTHER COOKED CEREALS

The two methods described for the Best Cooked Cereal can, of course, be applied to unmixed grains or to other mixtures. Whole wheat, whole rye, whole barley, whole oats or any other cereal can be prepared quickly and deliciously.

## READY-MADE CEREALS

There must be at least "57 varieties" of prepared cereals on the market. But look at the labels and use only those made of entire grain. You will probably have to go to a specialty shop or the health food stores to get them. All cereals are best when served with rich milk, honey, and some fresh or dried fruit.

## THE BIRCHER-MUESLI BREAKFAST

One of the most famous breakfasts in all the world is served at 7 o'clock in the morning in a wonderful sanatorium on top of a hill in Zurich. This is the Bircher-Muesli breakfast formulated by Dr. Bircher-Benner, who told me that when he made this breakfast he was trying to make a food as perfect as possible by putting into it everything mothers' milk contains. Thousands of Swiss thrive upon it, and people from all over the world come to the hill in Zurich to eat it in the morning and again at 6 o'clock at night; for Dr. Bircher-Benner believes that the big meal should be taken at noon.

I have tried to popularize the Bircher-Muesli Breakfast in this country, and many of my students enjoy it. Certainly it is a whole and natural food, superior to the tortured, denatured foods shot from guns and otherwise divorced from nature—milled, smashed, rolled until nothing is left but pure starch.

Below is the original formula as served in Switzerland. The Swiss Breakfast following that is my adaptation of it for Americans. Note that I have included wheat germ, a super-food which should be added to all your cereals.

## APPLE BIRCHER-MUESLI

1 tbsp. whole oats
2 tbsp. water
Juice of ½ lemon

1 tbsp. rich cream
2 apples
Honey to taste

Soak the whole oats in the water overnight. In the morning add the lemon juice and cream and mix well. Wash the apples but do not peel them. Shred them into the oats and stir. Serve at once.

By using the whole apple, skin and all, you increase the minerals in the Muesli and make it a really 100 per cent natural breakfast.

## SWISS BREAKFAST

1 tbsp. fresh wheat germ
1 tsp. whole oats
4 tbsp. water
1 tsp. lemon juice

1 unpeeled apple
Honey to taste
Cream or top milk
Chopped nuts if desired

Soak the wheat germ and whole oats in the water overnight. Put it in the icebox. Next morning add the lemon juice, honey, and cream and mix well. Shred the unpeeled apple into this and serve at once. Scatter a handful of chopped nuts on top if you like—it makes the cereal more nutritious.

There are as many variations of the Swiss Breakfast as there are fruits on the market. Fresh berries, grapes, peaches, bananas, or any other favorite fruit can be mashed or shredded into the cereal.

## MILLET

A new cereal to us—but long known to the Russians as *kasha*—is millet. It was introduced into this country some years ago but never caught on. No wonder, when they gave it the name "hog millet." But now it can be had, though you may have to go to a specialty store to get it.

Millet promises well for its protein quality, its high content of lecithin, a necessary constituent of every living cell. It is nonfattening and high in minerals and vitamins.

## KASHA

1 cup millet
5 cups water

1 tsp. vegetable salt

Wash the millet well and stir it into the water as soon as it boils. Add the salt and boil 2-3 minutes. Turn the heat low and simmer for another 10 minutes. Then turn off the heat and let stand over hot water until all the water is absorbed. Serve with browned butter.

Millet is delicious as a substitute for rice or potatoes. For special occasions, brown it in a bit of butter. Also, try cooking in Hauser Broth instead of water. Excellent with fowl and chops.

## NATURAL BROWN RICE

White rice, with much of its flavor and food value polished away, has no place in the new-style cookery. We use the natural brown rice, which consists of the whole kernel with only the outer husk removed. Brown rice is an economical energy food which should replace the foodless white rice in every modern kitchen.

### BOILED RICE

1 cup natural brown rice                    1 tsp. vegetable salt
5 cups boiling water

Pick over the rice and remove any husks and foreign particles. Put in a wire strainer and rinse under cold running water to remove the dust. Bring the water to the boiling point, add the rice, and boil briskly for 5 minutes. Turn the heat low then and simmer for 20 minutes. Turn off the heat when the rice is soft, add the vegetable salt, and let stand over hot water until the remaining water is absorbed—about an hour. The grains will be whole and fluffy.

### BAKED RICE FONDU

1 cup boiled brown rice                     1 pimento, diced
½ cup grated cheese                         2 eggs, separated
1 cup milk                                  ½ cup ground pecans
1 tsp. vegetable salt

Mix together the rice, cheese, milk, salt, and pimento. Beat the egg yolks until thick and lemon-colored and combine with the rice mixture. Beat the egg whites until stiff but not dry and fold lightly into the rice. Turn into a well-buttered baking dish. Sprinkle ground nuts over the top and press them in a little till they are moistened. Bake in a moderate oven (350°F.) about 25 minutes, or until firm. Serve garnished with parsley.

3 servings.

## RICE CASSEROLE

| | |
|---|---|
| 1 cup chopped onion | 1 tsp. vegetable salt |
| 1 cup chopped mushrooms | 1 tsp. chopped pimento |
| 3 tbsp. butter | 1 egg |
| 1 cup cooked brown rice | ½ cup cream |
| 2 tbsp. chopped ripe olives | ½ tsp. paprika |

Sauté the onions and mushrooms in butter for 8 minutes. Mix with the rice, olives, pimento, and salt. Beat the egg and cream together and add to the rice. Turn into a well-buttered baking dish and sprinkle generously with paprika. Bake in a moderate oven (325°F.) 30-40 minutes, or until firm.

3 servings.

## RICE WAFFLES

| | |
|---|---|
| 1 cup cold cooked brown rice | ¾ cup milk |
| 1 cup sifted whole-wheat flour | 3 eggs, separated |
| 1 tsp. vegetable salt | 4 tbsp. melted butter |
| 1½ tsp. baking powder | |

Sift the flour, salt, and baking powder together. Add the milk. Beat the egg yolks and add, then the rice and melted butter. Beat the egg whites until stiff but not dry and fold in lightly. Bake in a hot waffle iron.

4 servings.

## OCONOMOWOC RICE CASSEROLE

| | |
|---|---|
| 2½ cups cooked brown rice | 1 cup grated American cheese |
| 2 eggs, slightly beaten | 2 tablespoons finely chopped onion |
| 2 cups rich warm milk | 1 tsp. vegetable salt |
| 2 cups finely chopped parsley | |

Place all the ingredients in a mixing bowl and lift lightly to mix in order to prevent mashing the cooked rice. Place in a buttered casserole and bake in a moderate oven (325°F) about 1 hour, or until set.

## WILD RICE

Wild rice is one of the elegancies of life. Unhappily it is expensive because it is not really rice, but the seed of a grass which grows wild in shallow lakes and marshy lands. But you should try one of these dishes on special occasions—you'll find it worth the money.

### QUICK WILD RICE

½ cup wild rice                                ½ tsp. vegetable salt
½ cup boiling water                            1½ tsp. butter

Add the rice to the boiling salted water. Cover and cook over a slow fire without stirring, if possible, for 15 minutes. Take off the cover, dot the butter over the top, and let stand a few minutes on a warm grid to dry out the steam. Serve with fowl or chops.

### FLUFFY WILD RICE

1 cup wild rice                                2 tsp. vegetable salt
2 cups boiling water                           2 tbsp. butter

Add the vegetable salt to the hot water. Pour it over the cleaned wild rice and set aside for 3 hours. The rice will swell to more than double its bulk. Now place over a very low flame and heat through thoroughly to dry out the rice. Do not stir. When the rice is hot and fluffy, dot with butter and serve.

### WILD RICE AND ALMOND PUDDING

⅜ cup seedless raisins                         ¼ tsp. garlic seasoning
1¼ cups shelled almonds                        1 tsp. vegetable salt
2 cups cooked wild rice                        ½ cup crumbled shredded wheat
⅔ cup minced onion                             1 cup cream
1 large green pepper, minced

Put the raisins and nuts through the fine knife of the food grinder and mix with the rice. Stir in the minced onion and green pepper and seasonings. Then add the cream and mix thoroughly. Last of all, lightly mix in the shredded-wheat crumbs. Turn into a well-buttered baking dish and bake in a moderate oven (350°F.) till firm, about 30-40 minutes. Serve with a thick lemon sauce or a tart applesauce.

5 servings.

### WILD RICE NUTBURGERS

2 cups cooked wild rice                        1 egg, slightly beaten
½ cup ground nuts

Combine the ingredients and shape into patties, using a heaping serving-spoonful for each and sauté in butter or olive oil. Or drop from the spoon onto a hot griddle, well oiled, and cook like flapjacks. Olive oil adds to the meaty flavor.

## WILD RICE HAMBURGERS

| | |
|---|---|
| 1½ tsp. olive oil | 2 cups cooked wild rice |
| ½ onion, finely chopped | 1 egg, slightly beaten |

Cook the chopped onion in the olive oil for 3 minutes. Mix with the rice and egg and form into patties, using a heaping servingspoonful for each. Cook on a hot griddle, well oiled. Serve with tomato sauce.

## MACARONI, SPAGHETTI, NOODLES

Whatever their size and shape, macaroni, spaghetti, and noodles are all brothers, made of wheat flour and water. Their size and shape are the only things that distinguish them one from another. The following recipes are for macaroni, but spaghetti and noodles may be used instead. Be sure to get macaroni made with whole-wheat or soya flour.

### BOILED MACARONI

Macaroni packages give directions for boiling, and if you do not own a heavy glass or stainless-steel cooking pot you will probably have to follow them. But a better way, which keeps the food elements on your plate instead of down the sink, is to use not quite 2 cups of water or Hauser Broth to 1 cup of macaroni. Bring the water to a boil in a heavy kettle. Turn in the macaroni and stir briskly a moment. Reduce the heat to a gentle boil and cover tightly. When the macaroni is soft—it will take 9-12 minutes, perhaps longer depending on the brand of macaroni—look to see if there is any water left. If there is it will be only a little. Turn up the heat and stir while the water boils away. The macaroni should be tender and dry without pouring away water.

One cup of spinach and parsley juice, mixed in equal amounts, used as part of the cooking liquid will enrich the macaroni and gives it an appetizing green color.

### BAKED MACARONI AND CHEESE

Fill a buttered baking dish with alternate layers of boiled macaroni, light sauce, and cheese—¼ to ½ pounds of grated cheese to 1 package of macaroni. Top with buttered crumbs and bake in a moderate oven (375°F.) until the crumbs are brown—about 25 minutes.

That is the basic recipe. To liven it up, add to 1 package of macaroni, 1 tablespoon of grated onion, ½ teaspoon of dry mustard, ½ green pepper chopped and sautéed in 1 tablespoon of butter, ½ cup of chopped green olives, and 3 tablespoons of chopped pimento.

And for a tomato dish, use tomato sauce instead of light sauce in the above recipe.

## MACARONI À LA KING

1 package macaroni, boiled
2 tbsp. butter
1½ cups sliced mushrooms
⅓ cup green pepper strips
⅓ cup pimento strips

3 cups light sauce
1½ tsp. vegetable salt
½ tsp. dry mustard
½ cup buttered crumbs

Melt the butter in a heavy skillet and sauté the mushrooms and green pepper strips until soft. Combine all the ingredients except the crumbs and turn into a well-buttered baking dish. Top with buttered crumbs and a dash of paprika. Bake in a moderate oven (375°F.) about 25 minutes, or until browned.

## TAMALE PIE

4 tbsp. olive or vegetable oil
1 clove garlic
1 large onion, chopped
1½ lb. ground top round
1 qt. Spanish sauce, or canned tomatoes with 1 green pepper chopped

Vegetable salt to taste
½ cup grated cheese
2 tbsp. whole corn meal
1 tsp. paprika
1 recipe corn-meal mush (1 cup corn meal to 3 cups water)

Heat the oil in a large heavy skillet. Add the garlic and chopped onion and cook until the onion is soft. Remove the garlic and add the ground beef. Sauté lightly just until the meat loses its red color. Add the Spanish sauce or canned tomatoes and green pepper, and vegetable salt to taste. Cover and cook over low heat for an hour. Then add the grated cheese, 2 tablespoons of corn meal, and the paprika. Stir until the dish is fairly thick. Butter individual baking dishes, fill with the meat mixture, and cover each with a thin layer of corn-meal mush. Bake in a moderate oven until the mush is firmly set and browned. Garnish with chopped ripe olives and a sprinkling of chopped parsley and paprika.

You may use a large casserole instead of individual dishes, but in that case you will want to add more corn-meal to the meat mixture to make it stiffer.

# CHAPTER 15

# *Bakery--Bread, Muffins, Waffles*

"ALL THE ORIGINAL FOOD constituents of the grain, with nothing removed"—so reads the Federal definition of whole-grain flours. And what a difference it makes in the food value when man ceases to distort and denude the products Nature prepared for his use! The briefest glance at the difference in protein and vitamin content in white flour and whole-grain flour should convince the most confirmed skeptic that he simply can't afford to eat the pallid refined product. Look at these figures:

|  | % of Protein | Vitamin B₁[1] | Riboflavin[1] | Niacin[1] |
|---|---|---|---|---|
| Enriched white flour | 11.2 | 366 | 45 | 1,358 |
| Whole-wheat flour | 12.1 | 485 | 115 | 6,500 |
| Wheat germ | 28.9 | 2,400 | 650 | 6,300 |
| Peanut flour | 56.8 | 750 | 350 | 25,000 |
| Soya flour | 49.2 | 750 | 400 | 5,500 |

The superior food value of whole-grain flours speaks for itself in these statistics. As for taste and attractiveness of the baked goods, have you smelled the nutty fragrance of a fresh-baked loaf of whole-wheat bread? If you haven't, try any of the recipes in this and the next chapter and see how much more delicious they are than the products of white flour.

[1] Expressed in micrograms per 100 grams.

## FLOURS

*Whole-Wheat Flours:* It used to be that whole-wheat flours needed help from white flours; they could not be used alone. But now we have newer processes of milling which produce a flour which can be used alone with great success in bread and even cakes. In many specialty and health food stores you can obtain whole-wheat pastry flour, an extra fine grind of the entire-wheat flour which is especially useful in making fine cakes and pastries. *In all your baking, sift your whole-wheat flour.* Any grade, even the very coarse, can be made light enough for baking if you will *sift, sift, sift*—at least 3 times and preferably 5 times.

For you who are just beginning to enjoy whole-wheat breads, here is a hint: Be sure the recipe is sweet enough. A little extra sweetness makes the flavor more agreeable. Especially if you wish to use whole-wheat in a recipe which calls for white flour. In that case substitute whole-wheat flour for white, cup for cup, only let your cup of whole-wheat flour be gently rounded, not level.

*Rye Flour:* Rye flour lacks one of the proteins necessary for the formation of gluten, the stick-together substance in flour which makes it rise under the influence of yeast. For that reason it is usually combined with wheat flour to give it lightness. Rye flour is gaining in popularity these days because people who are allergic to whole wheat suffer no discomfort from rye.

*Buckwheat Flour:* The flour made from buckwheat has a strong flavor and is principally used in pancakes in combination with whole-wheat flour.

*Soya Flour:* Like rye flour, soya flour lacks gluten-forming protein, hence cannot be used alone in bakery, nor will it thicken gravy. In yeast breads it must be combined with whole-wheat flour for good results; in quick breads and cakes it can be used up to half the total amount of flour. It has a mild, sweet flavor, reminiscent of nuts, so it does not obtrude on the taste of other ingredients. Its high-quality protein—you remember I said the soybean contains first-class protein—enriches any dish in which it is used. Not only does it add its own richness, but it makes the protein of wheat flour more efficient. Even 10 per cent soya flour in a whole-wheat-flour product *triples* the efficiency of the wheat flour. So try soya flour in lots of recipes. The only change you need make in a recipe for whole-wheat flour when you substitute part soya flour is to use a little more vegetable salt because of the mild flavor of the soya flour.

Unless the percentage of soya flour is more than 12½ per cent, or 2 tablespoons per cup of wheat flour, you need not change any other ingredient, not even shortening, nor the oven temperature. If for any reason you use more soya flour, remember that your baked goods will brown faster than usual. So I suggest that in any recipe you wish to enrich, you simply make 2 tablespoons out of every cupful, soya flour instead of whole-wheat flour. It won't change the flavor, but it will add richness, much as milk and eggs do. Also, its mineral ash is alkaline rather than acid like most flours.

And for those who watch the waistline, note that soya flour comes in two types—high-fat and low-fat. The first kind is 18-22 per cent fat, the second only 5-9 per cent.

On the practical side, here is another point—baked goods which contain soya flour keep their freshness longer than those without because soya flour holds moisture. The soft, velvety bloom of fresh-from-the-oven bakery is more pronounced in soya-enriched products than in others. Best of all the fresh bloom does not disappear when the bread or biscuits cool. Note, by the way, that soya bread makes wonderful toast because it browns so fast.

*Always sift soya flour—3 times at least and preferably 5 times.*

*Peanut Flour:* The rich food values of peanuts are well known to you all. At present you will probably have to go to a specialty store to find peanut flour, but things may change any minute after the results obtained in recent experiments on its effect in bread making. This flour also lacks gluten, so it must be combined with whole-wheat flour. Because it weighs less than wheat flour—1⅓ cups of peanut flour weighing the same as 1 cup of wheat flour—you will need to take account of the difference in converting recipes to peanut-flour products. *Sift your peanut flour like any other flour to give it lightness.*

*Other Special Flours:* Such special flours as rice, potato, and arrow-root are used principally in allergic diets in this country. They can be bought at health stores, foreign stores, and in some communities in large department stores. Rice and potato flour are pure starch and add no vitamin value to bread.

*Gluten Flour:* In diets where the intake of starch must be low, gluten flour is made by washing the starch out of wheat flour (see page 242). The tough gray mass left after the washing is largely gluten. When it is washed and dried and ground it is called gluten flour. By U. S. Government Standard gluten flour contains 160 calories in 1/3 cup. Its protein value is 43.48 per cent; fat, 1.37 per cent; carbohydrate, 42.72 per cent. Use this high-quality flour just as you would ordinary flour.

## BAKING POWDER

The dozens of trade names for baking powders all describe one of three kinds—tartrate powders, phosphate powders, or sodium-aluminum-sulphate phosphate. The last-named is not recommended in the new-style cookery.

The rising action of baking powder is caused by the release of carbon dioxide when the acid, supplied by the baking powder, is acted upon by liquid. The tartrate baking powders, in which the acid is supplied by cream of tartar or tartaric acid, begin to act the moment liquid touches them, so don't mix your dry ingredients with liquid until you are ready to cook the batter. Phosphate powders act a little more slowly.

## WHOLE-WHEAT BREAD

| | |
|---|---|
| 2 cakes compressed yeast | 1 tbsp. honey |
| 1 cup warm milk | 1 tbsp. vegetable salt |
| 3 cups Hauser Broth | 3 lbs. whole-wheat flour |
| 2 tbsp. vegetable shortening | (12 cups sifted) |

Dissolve the yeast in the warm milk. Add the vegetable broth, shortening, honey, and salt. Add the flour, enough to make a stiff dough, and mix thoroughly. Turn out on a lightly floured board and knead about 10 minutes, or until smooth and satiny.

Put the dough in a warm greased bowl, brush the surface very lightly with melted shortening to prevent a crust from forming, then cover lightly and let rise in a warm place (80° to 85°F.) for about 2 hours, or until the dough is doubled in bulk and will keep the impression of a finger when pressed.

Punch the dough down thoroughly in the bowl, fold the edges toward the center, and turn over so the smooth side is on top. Cover and let rise again about ½ hour, or until the dough has doubled in bulk. Then turn it out on the board, divide into three parts, and mold each third into a ball. Let the balls rest, closely covered, for 10 minutes, then shape into loaves.

Place each loaf in a greased loaf pan, about 9½ by 5½ inches, brush the tops with melted shortening, cover, and let rise about 1 hour, or until doubled in bulk. Bake in a hot oven (375°F.) for 45 minutes. Makes 3 loaves.

## WHOLE-WHEAT SOYA BREAD

1 package yeast (½ oz.)
½ cup lukewarm Hauser Broth
1 tsp. natural brown sugar
1 cup milk
2 tbsp. vegetable shortening

1 tbsp. vegetable salt
2 tbsp. blackstrap molasses
2⅔ cups sifted whole-wheat flour
⅔ cup sifted soya flour

Dissolve the yeast in the broth with the sugar. Scald the milk with the vegetable shortening. Measure the vegetable salt and the molasses into the mixing bowl, add the scalded milk, and cool to lukewarm. Sift together the whole-wheat and soya flours. Stir half the flour into the milk, add the yeast, then the rest of the flour. Beat until smooth. Cover and let rise in a warm place for 1½ hours.

When the dough has risen, flour a board lightly, turn out the dough onto the board, and knead for 5 minutes, using only enough flour to make it possible to handle the dough. Roll the dough between your palms to fit a medium-sized bread pan. Oil the pan and put in the dough so it fits into the corners. Set away again to rise for about half an hour, until it not quite doubles in bulk. Bake in a moderate oven (375°) about 40 minutes.

## WHOLE-WHEAT PARKER HOUSE ROLLS

2 tbsp. natural brown sugar
3 tbsp. butter
2 tsp. vegetable salt
1 cup sweet milk

1 cake compressed yeast
¼ cup lukewarm water
3½ cups sifted whole-wheat flour

Put the sugar, butter, and salt into the milk and scald in a double boiler. Cool to lukewarm. Dissolve the yeast cake in the lukewarm water and add to the cooled milk mixture. Stir in enough flour to make a soft dough. When light, add the remainder of the flour and mix thoroughly. Turn the dough out onto a lightly floured board and knead for 10 minutes, until the dough is smooth and satiny. Form it into a loaf and place it in an oiled bowl. Cover and let rise in a warm place (80° to 85°F.) until double in bulk—about 2 hours.

Roll on a floured board to 1/4 inch in thickness and cut into rounds with a cookie cutter. Crease the center of each round with a knife handle, brush one half with melted butter, and fold. Place the rolls on an oiled baking sheet, cover, and let rise until double in bulk—1/2 to 3/4 hour. Brush with melted butter and bake in a hot oven (400°F.) for 15 minutes.

## WHOLE-WHEAT STICKY BOTTOMS

Make a dough as for Parker House Rolls. Roll out 1/4 inch thick and brush with melted butter. Mix 1/4 cup of natural brown sugar and 2 teaspoons of ground cinnamon and dust the mixture over the buttered surface. Roll up the sheet of dough. Drop a dot of butter into each cup of a well-oiled muffin tin, and then dust into each one 1/2 teaspoon of the cinnamon and sugar mixture. Then cut the roll of dough crosswise into 1-inch slices. Place the slices in the muffin tins, cut side up, and let rise until double in bulk—1/2 to 3/4 hour. Bake in a moderate oven (375°F) for 30 minutes.

## CARAWAY RYE BREAD

1 cake compressed yeast
1/4 cup lukewarm water
2 cups milk
2 tbsp. natural brown sugar
2 tbsp. vegetable shortening

1 tsp. vegetable salt
6 cups sifted rye flour
1 1/2 cups sifted whole-wheat flour
2 tbsp. caraway seeds

Dissolve the yeast in the lukewarm water. Scald the milk with the sugar, shortening, and vegetable salt. Cool until lukewarm and add the dissolved yeast cake. Stir well. Gradually add 3 cups of the sifted rye flour, a little at a time, beating with an egg beater until the mixture is smooth. The dough will be too stiff for beating any more, so add the other 3 cups of rye flour with a spoon. Stir until the dough is smooth. Cover the bowl and set it in a warm place (80-85°F) to rise until double in bulk—about 2 hours.

Punch down with a spoon and turn out onto a lightly floured board. Knead in the sifted whole-wheat flour and the caraway seeds until the dough is smooth and satiny. Shape into 2 loaves and tuck into oiled bread pans or bake on a flat cookie sheet. Brush with melted butter and let rise again until the loaves are once more double in bulk—¾ hour to an hour. Bake in a hot oven (400°F.) for 15 minutes, then reduce the oven to 375°F. and bake another 45 minutes. When the loaves shrink from the sides of the pan, remove from the oven, turn out onto a cake cooler, and spread the crust with melted butter.

## RAISED COFFEE PUFFS

| | |
|---|---|
| 1 cake compressed yeast | 2 eggs, well beaten |
| ¼ cup lukewarm water | 3½ cups sifted whole-wheat flour |
| 1 cup milk | ¼ cup brown sugar |
| 1 tsp. vegetable salt | ½ tsp. cinnamon |
| 2 tbsp. natural brown sugar | ¼ cup chopped nutmeats |
| ½ cup butter or vegetable shortening | |

Crumble the yeast into the lukewarm water and dissolve it. Scald the milk and add the vegetable salt, 2 tablespoons of sugar, and butter. Let the milk cool to lukewarm, then add the yeast. Stir in the beaten eggs, add the flour, and mix well. Set the bowl in a warm place, cover, and let rise until light—1½ to 2 hours. Then drop by spoonfuls into buttered muffin tins, filling each cup half full. On top of each muffin sprinkle a topping made of the ¼ cup of brown sugar, the cinnamon, and the chopped nuts. Let rise again until double in bulk, then bake in a moderate oven (375°F.) for 25 minutes.

## PANCAKES ROBERTO

| | |
|---|---|
| 3 fresh eggs (or more) | ¾ cup sifted whole-wheat flour |
| 1 cup rich milk | ½ tsp. vegetable salt |

Beat the eggs and combine them with the milk. Sift together the flour and salt and add them to the milk and egg. Stir until completely smooth. Heat a large skillet or griddle and pour in a bit of vegetable oil. When good and hot, pour in ½ cup of batter. Tilt the pan quickly in all directions to get the pancakes really thin. This makes 6 delicious pancakes. Serve with maple syrup or apricot jam.

## SOYA NUT WAFFLES

2 eggs, separated
2 tbsp. melted butter
½ cup soya flour, measured after
   sifting 3 times
⅓ tsp. baking powder

⅓ cup finely chopped walnuts or
   pecans
½ cup sour cream
Pinch of baking soda

NOTE: The sifting of the flour is the trick with these waffles. Hold the sifter up high and let the flour fall in a peak. Do this 3 times. Then lightly skim the flour from the top of the peak into a measuring cup with a spatula. Do not pack down.

Beat the egg yolks well and add the melted butter. Then add alternately the soya flour sifted with the baking powder and the sour cream with the pinch of soda stirred into it. Save a little flour to coat the nuts and add them next. Beat the egg whites stiff but not dry, then fold in lightly. Bake in a hot waffle iron.

To double this recipe, use 3 eggs and double all the other ingredients.

## WHOLE-WHEAT FRUIT BREAD

3½ cups sifted whole-wheat flour
⅔ cup natural brown sugar
1 tsp. vegetable salt
4 tsp. baking powder
6 tbsp. shortening
2 eggs, beaten

1 cup milk
1 tbsp. grated lemon or orange rind
1 cup raisins or chopped figs, dates,
   or prunes
1 cup chopped nutmeats

Sift the flour 3 times, measure, and then sift with the sugar, salt, and baking powder. Cut in the shortening with 2 knives or a pastry blender. Beat the eggs, add the milk and lemon rind, and blend with the dry ingredients. Add the fruit and nutmeats, lightly floured. Turn into 2 oiled loaf pans, 6 inches by 3 inches. Bake in a moderate oven (375°F.) for about 1 hour.

## WHOLE-WHEAT BATTER BREAD

3 cups sifted whole-wheat flour
4 tsp. baking powder

2½ cups sweet milk
1 tbsp. honey

Sift the flour and baking powder together. Add the milk and honey and stir to a smooth dough. Turn out into oiled pans and bake in a moderate oven (350°F.) for 45 minutes.

## NUT BREAD

Add 1 cup of any chopped nuts to the batter for Whole-Wheat Batter Bread. Dust the nuts with flour before adding.

## RAISIN OR DATE BREAD

Add 1 cup of raisins or chopped dates to the Whole-Wheat Batter Bread, first dusting them with flour before adding.

## POPOVERS

2 eggs, well beaten
1 tbsp. sifted soya flour
½ cup sifted whole-wheat flour
1 tsp. natural brown sugar
¼ tsp. vegetable salt
½ cup milk
1 tsp. melted butter

Before you start to mix the popovers, put buttered muffin tins or individual custard cups in the oven to heat. Beat the eggs well. Sift together the flours, sugar, and salt and add to the eggs with half the milk. Beat until smooth. Add the remaining milk and the melted butter and beat again. Pour into the hot muffin tins, filling each half full. Bake in a hot oven (425°F.) for 15 minutes. Reduce the heat to 400°F. and bake for another 15 minutes. Resist the temptation to peek into the oven, for your popovers will not pop if you open the oven door at the wrong moment.

6 popovers.

## WHOLE-WHEAT MUFFINS

2½ tbsp. natural brown sugar
Butter the size of an egg, melted
1 tsp. vegetable salt
1 egg, well beaten
1 cup sweet milk
1½ cups sifted whole-wheat flour
2 tsp. baking powder

Cream together the sugar and butter. Add the salt and the beaten egg, then the milk. Sift the flour and baking powder together and add to the egg mixture. Beat the batter thoroughly to lighten it. Bake in a well-oiled muffin pan in a quick oven (400°F.) for 20 minutes.

## CORN MUFFINS OR CORNSTICKS

½ cup sifted soya flour
1½ tsp. baking powder
½ tsp. vegetable salt
2 tbsp. natural brown sugar
¾ cup whole corn meal
1 egg, well beaten
½ cup milk
¼ cup melted butter or vegetable
   shortening

Sift together the soya flour, baking powder, salt, and sugar. Add the corn meal. Add the milk to the well-beaten egg and combine with the dry ingredients. Mix only until blended. Stir in the melted shortening and pour into buttered muffin tins or cornstick pans. Bake in a hot oven (425°F.) for 20 minutes.

12 small muffins.

## REDUCING MUFFINS

1 fresh egg
½ cup Hauser Broth
¾ cup sifted gluten flour

¼ tsp. baking powder
¼ tsp. vegetable salt

Beat the egg and add it to the broth. Sift the flour and baking powder together and add to the broth. Beat until smooth. Pour the mixture into oiled muffin tins and bake in hot oven (400°F.) for about 15 minutes, or until muffins are a golden brown. For variety, add 1 tablespoonful blackstrap molasses.

## SOYA MUFFINS

1½ cups sifted soya flour
2 tsp. baking powder
1½ tsp. vegetable salt
2 eggs
3 tbsp. natural brown sugar

1 tbsp. grated orange rind
1 cup milk
1 tbsp. melted butter
¼ cup raisins, floured
¼ cup walnut meats, floured

Sift together the flour, baking powder, and salt. Separate the eggs and beat the yolks until very light and frothy. Beat the sugar into the egg yolks, add the orange rind, milk, and butter, and mix well. Pour the egg mixture onto the dry ingredients and mix. Add the raisins and the nutmeats, broken by rolling with a rolling pin. Mix thoroughly. Fold in the egg whites, beaten stiff but not dry. Pour into buttered muffin tins and bake in a slow oven (300° to 325° F.) 35 minutes, or until cooked through.

10 muffins.

## WHEAT-GERM MUFFINS

1 tbsp. melted shortening
1 tbsp. honey
½ cup sifted soya flour
¼ cup sifted whole-wheat flour
¼ cup wheat germ

½ tsp. baking soda
Pinch of vegetable salt
¾ cup buttermilk
1 tsp. vanilla or cinnamon if desired

Mix the honey and shortening together. Combine the sifted flours, wheat germ, soda, and salt and add alternately with the buttermilk. Beat thoroughly. Pour into buttered muffin tins and bake in a moderate oven (350°F.) for 35 minutes. Cool before serving.

## WHOLE-WHEAT BAKING POWDER BISCUITS

2 cups sifted whole-wheat flour  
1 tbsp. natural brown sugar  
5 tsp. baking powder  

1 tsp. vegetable salt  
¼ cup butter or vegetable shortening  
1 cup milk  

Sift the dry ingredients together several times. Work in the shortening with the fingertips. Cut in the milk with a knife, mixing very lightly. Form into small biscuits and place them on a buttered baking sheet. Bake in a hot oven (425°F.) for 15 minutes.

## BRAZIL-NUT BREAD

4½ cups sifted whole-wheat flour  
5 tsp. baking powder  
2 tsp. baking soda  
1½ tsp. vegetable salt  

1½ cups natural brown sugar  
1½ cups sliced Brazil nuts  
3 cups sour milk or buttermilk  

Mix the dry ingredients together. Add the nuts and mix thoroughly. Add the milk and stir well. Pour into 2 oiled loaf pans and bake about 1 hour in a slow oven (325°F.).

2 loaves.

## STEAMED SOYA BREAD

½ cup sifted soya flour  
1 tsp. baking soda  
1 cup whole-grain meals [1]  

⅜ cup blackstrap molasses  
½ tsp. vegetable salt  
1⅛ cups buttermilk  

Sift the soya flour and soda into a mixing bowl. Add the meals and the vegetable salt and mix. Make a depression in the center of the dry mixture and pour the molasses and milk into the whole. Mix carefully, stirring outward from the center as the dry ingredients take up the moisture. When thoroughly mixed, put into a buttered mold or No. 3 tin can, filling the can ⅔ full. Cover and steam until the center is cooked through—about 2 hours. Serve hot. Makes 1 loaf, 4 servings.

This bread makes delicious sandwiches when cold. Spread with cream cheese. It is also delicious toasted.

If desired, add ½ cup seeded raisins just before putting into the mold.

[1] Grains in any desired combination of corn, wheat, barley, rye, or crisp bread crumbs.

## SPOON BREAD

1 qt. rich milk
1½ cups yellow corn meal
1 tbsp. butter

½ tsp. vegetable salt
4 eggs, well beaten

Scald the milk and stir the corn meal into it slowly. Bring to a boil and cook, still stirring, to the consistency of thick mush. Drop in the butter and season with vegetable salt. Allow to cool. When the corn meal is lukewarm, beat in the eggs and pour the dough into a buttered baking dish. Bake in a moderate oven (350°F.) about 45 minutes, or until a golden brown. Serve hot with buffet suppers.

## STEAMED BROWN BREAD

1 cup coarse whole-wheat flour
2 tsp. baking powder
1 tsp. vegetable salt
½ cup raisins
½ cup chopped nuts

4 tbsp. blackstrap molasses
1 cup sweet milk
1 tbsp. melted butter or vegetable
shortening

Sift together the dry ingredients. Stir in the raisins and nuts, then add the molasses, milk, and melted shortening. Mix well. Pour into a covered 1-quart mold, well greased; or use any round tins—No. 2 tomato cans will do very well. The cans should be filled only ⅔ full. Steam for 2 hours.

1 loaf.

# SANDWICHES

## CREAM-CHEESE AND PEANUT-BUTTER SANDWICH

Mix equal parts of peanut butter and cream cheese with 1 tablespoon of mayonnaise and some chopped green pepper. A small amount of vegetable salt should be added. Spread on thin slices of whole-wheat bread.

## WATER-CRESS SANDWICH

Chop water-cress fine, add a few chopped walnuts, a little vegetable salt, and some mayonnaise. Put between buttered thin slices of rye bread.

## CALIFORNIA SANDWICH

Wash and dry Black Mission figs. Grind with pecans or walnuts until soft and mellow enough for spreading. Moisten with lemon juice. Spread on thin slices of whole-wheat bread.

## DEVILED-EGG SANDWICH

Mash hard-cooked egg yolks. Mix in lemon juice, vegetable salt, dry mustard, chopped chives to your taste. Moisten with mayonnaise.

## NUTRITIOUS SANDWICH SPREADS

Blend the soya flour and the other ingredients. Keep tightly covered in the refrigerator.

*Peanut Butter:* Combine ½ cup peanut butter, ½ cup soya flour, and ½ cup salad dressing or sandwich spread.

*Apple Butter:* Combine 1 cup well-seasoned apple butter with ½ cup soya flour.

*Egg Salad:* Combine ¼ cup salad dressing, ¼ cup soya flour, 2 chopped hard-cooked eggs, ¼ teaspoon salt, pepper, and if desired a little mustard and chopped celery.

*Cheese:* Combine a 3-ounce package of cream cheese or ½ pound of cottage cheese with ½ cup of soya flour. To heighten the flavor, add ¼ cup sweet red pepper relish, or add 2 tablespoons of salad dressing, ½ teaspoon of salt, and one of the following:

    2 tablespoons horse-radish.

    2 teaspoons onion pulp, 2 tablespoons finely chopped parsley.

    2 tablespoons chopped nuts.

# CHAPTER 16

# Bakery--Cakes, Pies, Cookies

## BUTTER CAKE

2 cups sifted whole-wheat flour
3 tsp. baking powder
¼ tsp. vegetable salt
1 cup natural brown sugar

½ cup butter
3 eggs, separated
¾ cup rich milk
1 tsp. vanilla

Sift together the flour, baking powder, and salt 4 times. Cream the sugar and butter together. Add the egg yolks, beaten until thick and lemon-colored. Add the dry ingredients alternately with the milk, starting and ending with flour. Beat the egg whites stiff but not dry and fold into the batter. Turn into 2 buttered 8-inch layer pans and bake in a moderate oven (375°F.) 25 to 30 minutes.

Use your favorite frosting, or sprinkle grated chocolate, coconut, or chopped nuts on the batter before baking.

## WHOLE-WHEAT POUND CAKE

1 lb. butter
2 cups natural brown sugar
6 eggs

2 cups sifted whole-wheat flour
Grated rind of 2 large oranges
Juice of 1 orange

Cream the butter until soft. Add the sugar gradually and cream together until light and fluffy. Add the egg yolks, 1 or 2 at a time, beating well after each addition. Sift the flour and add with the orange rind and juice. Beat the egg whites until stiff but not dry and fold them into the mixture. Turn into a buttered loaf pan and bake in a slow oven (300°-325°F.) about 1 hour.

## BEVERLY ANGEL CAKE

1½ cups natural brown sugar
½ cup strained orange juice
6 fresh eggs, separated
2 tsp. strained lemon juice

1 cup sifted whole-wheat flour
¾ tsp. cream of tartar
¼ tsp. vegetable salt

Combine the sugar and orange juice in a saucepan. Cook over low heat until the sugar has melted and the mixture is about to boil. Then cook without stirring until the syrup spins a thread when dropped from the edge of a spoon. Beat the egg whites until stiff but not dry, then beat in the syrup drop by drop. Beat the egg yolks well and add the lemon juice. Sift together the flour, cream of tartar, and vegetable salt, and sift at least six times. Add the yolk mixture, then fold in the whites. Pour into an unbuttered angel-food cake pan and bake in a moderate oven (325°F) for 1 hour.

## NUTRITIOUS SPICE CAKE

1 cup butter
1 cup natural brown sugar
3 eggs, slightly beaten
1 cup sour cream
1 cup raisins or chopped dates
1 cup nutmeats

2 cups sifted whole-wheat flour
2 tsp. baking powder
1 tsp. baking soda
1 tsp. allspice
1 tsp. cinnamon

Cream the butter and sugar  together. Add the slightly beaten eggs. Three times sift the flour with the baking powder, soda, and spices. Add to the batter the dry ingredients alternately with sour cream, starting with flour and ending with flour. Bake in a buttered square pan, 9 by 9 inches, at 350°F. for about 50 minutes.

If you prefer, this will make 2 dozen light and delicious small cupcakes. They make a delicious dessert when topped with whipped cream.

## DELICIOUS SOYA CAKE

2 eggs, well beaten
1 cup natural brown sugar
⅓ cup sifted whole-wheat flour
1⅓ cups sifted soya flour
1½ tsp. baking powder

½ tsp. vegetable salt
¾ tsp. cinnamon
1 tbsp. cocoa
⅔ cup milk
⅓ cup vegetable oil

Beat the eggs and add the sugar gradually while beating. Continue to beat until very light. Sift together the dry ingredients and add to the egg alternately with the milk. Stir in the vegetable oil. Pour into buttered shallow layer pans and bake in a moderate oven (350°F) for 45 minutes.

Preparation: 15-20 minutes.

2 8-inch layers.

## CREAM-CHEESE CAKE

| | |
|---|---|
| 2 tbsp. butter | ¼ tsp. vegetable salt |
| 2 tbsp. natural brown sugar | 1 lb. cream cheese |
| 4 cups graham cracker crumbs | 1 tsp. grated lemon peel |
| ½ cup natural brown sugar | 4 eggs, separated |
| 2 tbsp. sifted whole-wheat flour | 1 cup cream |

To make the crust, cream the butter and 2 tbsp. of sugar until very smooth. Add the finely rolled graham-cracker crumbs and mix thoroughly. Press the mixture evenly around the inside of a buttered 9-inch spring form mold.

For the filling, mix the sugar, flour, and salt. Soften the cheese with a wooden spoon, add the dry ingredients, and cream together thoroughly. Add the lemon peel and the egg yolk, unbeaten. Beat well and stir in the cream. Beat the egg whites until stiff but not dry and fold into the cheese mixture. Turn the cheese mixture into the dish on top of the crumbs. Bake in a slow oven (325°F.) about 1 hour, or until the center is firm.

## SANDWICH DATE CAKE

| | |
|---|---|
| 1½ cups sifted whole-wheat flour | 1½ cups stone-ground oatmeal |
| 1 tsp. baking soda | 1 cup natural brown sugar |
| ½ tsp. vegetable salt | ¾ cup butter |

Sift the flour, measure, and sift again with the soda and vegetable salt. Add the oatmeal and brown sugar, then cut in the butter with a pastry blender or two silver knives as in making pastry. Pour half the mixture into a buttered pan, 8½ by 11 inches. Pat down gently, then pour on the following date filling:

| | |
|---|---|
| 3 cups chopped dates | 1 tsp. vanilla |
| ¾ cup brown sugar | ¼ tsp. vegetable salt |
| ¾ cup hot water | |

Mix the dates, sugar, and water in a saucepan and cook until thick. Remove from the fire and add the vanilla and salt. Spread over the oatmeal mixture in the pan, then cover with the rest of the oatmeal. Bake in a moderate oven (350°F.) for 30 minutes. Serve plain or with whipped cream.

## DATE TORTE

4 eggs, separated
1 cup chopped nuts
1 cup natural brown sugar

1 cup chopped dates
½ cup sifted whole-wheat pastry flour
½ tsp. vegetable salt

Beat the egg yolks and stir in the sugar, nuts, dates, and salt. Fold in the flour, then the egg whites beaten stiff but not dry. Pour the mixture into a buttered cake pan, 8½ by 11 inches. Bake in a moderate oven (350°F.) for 25 minutes. When cool, cut in squares and serve topped with whipped cream.

## FAVORITE DARK FRUIT CAKE

1 lb. seeded raisins
1 lb. citron
½ lb. candied pineapple
½ lb. lemon peel
1 lb. candied cherries
1 lb. dates
1 lb. nutmeats
1 lb. currants
1 lb. whole-wheat flour, sifted

1 tsp. nutmeg
1 tsp. cloves
2 tsp. baking soda
1 lb. butter
1 lb. natural brown sugar
10 eggs, separated
1 cup blackstrap molasses
½ cup grape juice

Cut up the fruits, chop the nuts, and wash the currants and raisins. Mix with half the flour. Sift the rest of the flour with the soda and spices. Cream the butter, add the sugar, then the egg yolks slightly beaten. Add the molasses and grape juice, then the sifted flour, and then the floured fruits and nuts. Last, beat the egg whites until stiff but not dry and fold into the cake mixture. Turn into pans lined with buttered paper. Bake in a slow oven (300°F.) for 2 hours. Let cool in the pans, then store away.

NOTE: The baking time is given on the assumption that you will use regular large loaf pans—about 3 will hold this batch. If you use smaller pans, reduce the cooking time.

8 pounds.

## QUICK SERVICE CAKE

½ cup butter
1 cup natural brown sugar
2 eggs, well beaten
1 cup sifted whole-wheat flour
1 cup sifted soya flour
1 tsp. baking soda

2 tsp. baking powder
1 tsp. cinnamon
¼ tsp. vegetable salt
1 cup chopped nuts
1 cup chopped dates
1 small can crushed pineapple

Cream together the butter and sugar until light and fluffy. Add the eggs. Sift the flours with the dry ingredients, add nuts and dates, and stir and add to the mixture alternately with the pineapple. Mix thoroughly. Line the bottom of a buttered loaf pan with waxed paper and pour in the cake dough. Bake in a moderate oven (325°F.) about 1 hour.

Preparation: 15-20 minutes.

1 loaf.

## MODERN GINGERBREAD

| | |
|---|---|
| 1 tsp. baking soda | 1 egg |
| 1 tbsp. hot water | ½ cup milk or hot water |
| ½ cup blackstrap molasses | 1 cup sifted rice flour |
| 3 tbsp. butter | 1 cup sifted soya flour |
| 2 tbsp. natural brown sugar | 1 tsp. baking powder |
| ½ tsp. vegetable salt | 1 tsp. ginger |
| 1 tsp. grated orange peel | 1 tsp. cinnamon |

Put the soda and the tablespoon of hot water in a bowl and set aside until the mixture foams. Then add the molasses. Cream together the butter and sugar. Add the vegetable salt, orange peel, and egg. Beat well and add the milk or hot water. Sift together the flours, baking powder, and spices and add to the mixture. Pour into a buttered square loaf pan and bake in a moderate oven (325°F.) 40 minutes.

1 loaf.

## ICEBOX PUDDING

| | |
|---|---|
| ½ cup butter | ⅛ tsp. vegetable salt |
| ½ cup natural brown sugar or honey | ¼ tsp. vanilla extract |
| 3 eggs, separated | Graham-cracker crumbs, about 28 |
| 1 cup crushed pineapple | crackers |
| ½ cup chopped pecans | |

Cream the butter and add the sugar or honey. Cream them together thoroughly. Beat the egg yolks and add to the butter, then the pineapple, nuts, salt, and vanilla. Beat the egg whites until stiff but not dry and fold into the mixture. Spread about half the graham-cracker crumbs over the bottom of a pan, pour in the pudding, and top with crumbs. Chill in the refrigerator for at least 12 hours. Serve with whipped cream.

## PIES

### WHOLE-WHEAT PIE CRUST
#### (Hot-Water Method)

1 cup vegetable shortening or butter
½ cup boiling water

2 cups sifted whole-wheat flour
1 tsp. vegetable salt

Pour the boiling water over the shortening and stir until blended. Gradually add the sifted flour and salt and mix thoroughly. Put on ice about half an hour, then roll on a pastry sheet or a lightly floured board.

### SOYA-FLOUR PIE CRUST

1 cup vegetable shortening or butter
½ cup boiling water
½ cup sifted whole-wheat flour

1½ cups sifted soya flour
¼ tsp. baking powder
1 tsp. vegetable salt

Pour the boiling water over the shortening and blend well with a fork. Sift the flours, baking powder, and salt together. Gradually add to the water and shortening and mix thoroughly. Chill thoroughly before rolling. This pie crust is difficult to handle, so roll it on floured waxed paper or a pastry sheet and then invert on the pie plate and remove the waxed paper.

### CHEESE PIE CRUST

¼ lb. butter
2 cups sifted whole-wheat flour

1 package (3 oz.) cream cheese
⅛ cup water

Cream together the butter and cheese, add the flour and enough water to make a soft dough. Chill 30 minutes and roll on a pastry sheet.

### FLAKY WHOLE-WHEAT PIE CRUST
#### (Ice-Water Method)

1½ cups sifted whole-wheat flour
½ tsp. vegetable salt
½ cup vegetable shortening

2 tsp. butter
¼ cup ice water

Sift together the flour and salt. With a pastry blender or two silver knives, cut in the shortening and butter, working until the particles of dough are the size of peas. Add the ice water and mix lightly with a fork. Turn onto a lightly floured board and roll out.

1 2-crust pie or 2 pastry shells.


## BRAZIL-NUT PIE CRUST

1½ cups Brazil nuts                              Pinch of vegetable salt
2 tbsp. natural brown sugar

Grind the nuts through the nut-butter attachment of the food grinder. Thoroughly work in with the fingers the sugar and salt. Press around the bottom and sides of an 8-inch pie plate to make a crust of even thickness. Fill with lemon or any cream filling. For any custard filling, brush the crust with egg white, pour in the filling, and bake in a moderate oven (325°F.) until the custard is set—about ½ hour. Serve cooked or uncooked crusts cold.

Preparation: 15-20 minutes.

1 8-inch pie.

## ZWIEBACK PASTRY SHELL

Mix 1 cup of finely crushed Zwieback crumbs with ⅓ cup of melted butter, a pinch of cinnamon, and a few drops of lemon juice. Press the mixture evenly around sides and bottom of a pie tin. Chill before serving. Excellent for cheese pie.


## GRAHAM-CRACKER PASTRY SHELL

Melt ⅓ cup of butter in a pie pan, add 1 cup of graham-cracker crumbs, and mix thoroughly. Press the mixture evenly and firmly around the sides and bottom of the pan. Chill before filling.


## CONTINENTAL PIES

Continental pies can practically take care of the whole problem of dessert. You simply make Continental Pie Shells and fill them with any of your favorite fresh fruits. Always sprinkle the fruits with a bit of fresh lemon or lime juice and add honey to taste. Sometimes, for the sake of variety, use French Stewed Fruits. Add enough natural brown sugar and cook until thick. For very juicy fruits you may want to add 1 teaspoon of dry

# Bakery—Cakes, Pies, Cookies 199

agar-agar. This will thicken the juice enough without destroying the delicious flavor of the natural fruit.

Apricot, raisin, and prune pies can be made in a jiffy by soaking the dry fruit in warm water overnight. Next day they will be juicy and plump. Add a cup of orange or pineapple juice, natural brown sugar to taste, and cook·for 10 minutes, or until thick. Pour the thickened fruit into the pie shells, or mash the fruit and mix with whipped cream. Both are delicious.

You will make a hit with the man of your heart if you fill the pie shells with applesauce and cover with whipped cream—if he's as thin as Sinatra.

## CONTINENTAL PIE SHELLS

¼ lb. butter—margarine if you must
1 cup whole-wheat flour
1 tbsp. natural brown sugar
½ tsp. vegetable salt

Put all the ingredients into a bowl and mix with a fork or pastry blender. When well mixed, turn into a pie tin—do not roll—and press firmly against the bottom and sides. Bake in a medium oven (350°F.) for 15 minutes, or until golden brown.

1 pie shell or 6 tart shells.

## PEACH PIE

1 recipe whole-wheat pastry
4 cups sliced peaches
Juice of ½ lemon
¾ cup natural brown sugar
¼ tsp. vegetable salt
¼ tsp. nutmeg
1 tbsp. butter

Line a 9-inch pie plate with whole-wheat pastry. Sprinkle the peaches with lemon juice, then mix with the sugar, salt, and nutmeg. Spread over the pastry and dot generously with butter. Moisten the edge of the pie crust with cold water, put the top crust in place, and press the edges of the two crusts together with a fork. Prick the top crust to let the steam escape. Bake in a hot oven (450°F.) for 10 minutes, then reduce the temperature to 350°F. and bake for another 30 minutes. This prevents the juice from escaping, and no thickening is needed to spoil the flavor of the fruit.

## APPLE PIE

Follow the recipe for Peach Pie, using cinnamon instead of nutmeg if desired. Bake at 450°F. for 10 minutes, then another 40 minutes at 350°F.

## DUTCH APPLE PIE

4 large red apples
½ lb. chopped almonds or walnuts
¼ cup seeded raisins
¼ tsp. cinnamon

Juice and grated rind of 1 large lemon
¾ cup natural brown sugar
2 tbsp. butter
½ recipe whole-wheat pie crust

Wash but do not peel the apples. Shred with the peelings on, and sprinkle with the lemon juice, strained. Combine with the nuts, raisins, sugar, and cinnamon in a saucepan. Cook, stirring constantly for only 5 minutes, then let cool. Line a pie plate with thin whole-wheat pie crust and pour in the apple mixture. Dot generously with butter. Delicious served alone or with a bit of snappy cheese.

## DEEP-DISH APPLE AND CRANBERRY PIE

⅔ cup cranberries
3 tbsp. natural brown sugar

3 small cooking apples
3 tbsp. water

Place the cranberries in a buttered baking dish. Sprinkle with the sugar. Slice the apples into the dish and sprinkle the water over them. Spread the top with a crust made as follows:

2 tbsp. whole-wheat flour
1/16 tsp. baking powder
1/16 tsp. baking soda
1/16 tsp. vegetable salt

¼ cup rolled oats
¼ cup natural brown sugar
⅛ cup butter

Mix until thoroughly blended. Press into a thin sheet and make a layer over the apples. Bake in a moderate oven (350°F.) until the fruit is cooked through and the crust browned at the edges—about 30 minutes.

Preparation: 10-15 minutes.

4 servings.

## CHEESE PIE

½ recipe whole-wheat pastry
2 cups fresh cottage cheese
½ cup milk
½ cup cream
2 eggs, well beaten

¼ tsp. vegetable salt
Pinch of cinnamon
½ tsp. vanilla
½ cup natural brown sugar
2 tbsp. melted butter

Line a pie plate with pastry, building up the edge as for a pastry shell. Bake 8-10 minutes. Break up the cheese and mix in the milk, then the cream, beating until smooth. Add the well-beaten eggs and continue beating. Mix salt and cinnamon with the sugar, then with the vanilla and melted butter and add to the cheese mixture. Pour into the whole-wheat pastry shell and bake in a slow oven (250°F.) for 45 minutes, or until the cheese is set.

## CUSTARD PIE

½ recipe whole-wheat pastry
4 eggs, slightly beaten
½ cup natural brown sugar
½ tsp. vegetable salt

2½ cups rich milk
1 tsp. vanilla
Sprinkling of nutmeg

Line a pie plate with whole-wheat pastry. Beat the eggs slightly and stir in the natural brown sugar and vegetable salt. Add the milk and vanilla and blend thoroughly. Pour into the pastry shell, sprinkle with nutmeg, and bake in a moderately hot oven (425°F.), 25-35 minutes, or until a silver knife inserted in the custard comes out clean.

## COCONUT CUSTARD PIE

For a delicious Coconut Custard Pie, add 1 cup shredded coconut which has been doused with pineapple juice to Custard Pie before pouring into pastry shell.

## CALIFORNIA PRUNE PIE

1 recipe whole-wheat pastry
3 cups pitted soaked prunes
½ cup natural brown sugar

Grated rind of 1 large lemon
Cinnamon or nutmeg to taste

Line a pie plate with whole-wheat pastry. Mix the prunes, sugar, lemon rind, and spice and turn into the pie shell. Cover with lattice strips and bake in a moderate oven (375°F.) for 30-40 minutes, or until browned.

## GOLDEN APRICOT PIE

3 cups soaked dried apricots
1 recipe whole-wheat pastry

½ cup natural brown sugar
1 tsp. grated orange rind

Wash the apricots thoroughly and soak overnight in orange juice. Line a pie plate with whole-wheat pastry. Mix the apricots, sugar, and orange rind and turn into the pie shell. Cover with lattice strips and bake in a moderate oven (375°F.) for 30-40 minutes. For special occasions, serve with whipped cream.

## BUTTERSCOTCH CREAM PIE

2½ tbsp. sifted whole-wheat flour
¾ cup soy milk, or cow's milk if
    preferred
1 tbsp. butter
¾ cup natural brown sugar

1 egg yolk
⅛ tsp. vegetable salt
½ tsp. vanilla
Whipped cream
1 baked pie shell

Moisten the flour with about ⅓ cup of milk. Heat the remaining milk while preparing the butterscotch mixture, as follows:

Melt the butter in the top of a double boiler over direct heat. Add the sugar and cook, stirring constantly, until the sugar is melted and the mixture begins to puff up just before boiling. Stir in the hot milk, adding it by the spoonful at first. Beat the egg yolk into the moistened flour and slowly pour on it the hot mixture, stirring all the time. Mix thoroughly and return to the double boiler. Cook over boiling water for 15 minutes, stirring constantly until the mixture begins to thicken, then occasionally. Cool, add vanilla, and pour into a baked pie shell. When cold spread with whipped cream.

## DATE PIE

1 baked pastry shell or 6 tart shells
3 egg whites
¼ cup natural brown sugar
1½ cups finely chopped dates

1 tbsp. lemon juice
1 tsp. vanilla
¼ cup finely chopped nutmeats

Beat the egg whites stiff but not dry, then beat in the sugar. Fold in the dates, lemon juice, and vanilla and pour into the pie shell. Sprinkle the chopped nuts over the top and bake in a moderate oven (325°F.) for 25 minutes.

## BLUEBERRY PIE

1 recipe whole-wheat pastry
3 cups blueberries

½ cup natural brown sugar
⅛ tsp. vegetable salt

Line a 9-inch pie plate with pastry. Wash the berries and roll them lightly in flour. Turn into the pie shell and sprinkle with sugar and salt. Moisten the edge of the pie shell with cold water. Put on the top crust and press the edges of the two crusts together with a fork. Bake in a hot oven (425°F.) for 50 minutes.

## BERRY PIES

Follow the recipe for Blueberry pie, varying the proportions of sugar as follows:

Blackberries, 3/4 cup
Cherries, about 1 1/2 cups, depending on tartness
Raspberries, 1/2 cup
Rhubarb, 1 1/2 cups
Strawberries, 3/4 cup

## MY FAVORITE LEMON PIE

1 baked pie shell, Continental
3 fresh eggs, separated
2 tbsp. lemon juice
1 cup natural brown sugar

1/4 tsp. vegetable salt
1 tbsp. butter
Grated rind of 1 lemon

Beat the egg yolks well and put them in the top of a double boiler. Add the lemon juice, half the sugar, and the butter and vegetable salt. Cook until thick, stirring constantly. Remove from the fire and let cool while you beat the egg whites until stiff but not dry, beating in the other half of the sugar. Fold half the whites into the yolk mixture, pour into the Continental pie shell, and cover with the remaining whites. Brown in the oven.

## HONEY MERINGUE FOR PIES

Beat 2 egg whites until light and foamy. Gradually beat in 1/3 cup of honey, beating until the egg white will stand up in peaks when you remove the beater. Pile lightly on top of the pie and place under the broiler until brown.

## PUMPKIN PIE

1/2 recipe whole-wheat pastry
2 eggs, beaten
3/4 cup natural brown sugar
1 1/2 cups canned pumpkin
1/4 tsp. ginger

1 tsp. cinnamon
1 tsp. nutmeg
1/2 tsp. salt
1 cup light cream

Line a pie plate with whole-wheat pastry. Beat the eggs and add the sugar, then the pumpkin, spices, and salt. Stir in the cream last and turn into the pie shell. Bake in a hot oven (450°F.) for 10 minutes; then reduce heat to 350°F. for 30 minutes. Serve plain or topped with whipped cream.

## GOLDEN CARROT PIE

½ recipe whole-wheat pastry
2 eggs
½ cup natural brown sugar
1½ cups mashed cooked carrots
¼ tsp. ginger

¼ tsp. cloves
½ tsp. vegetable salt
1 tsp. cinnamon
1 tsp. nutmeg
1 cup cream

Line a pie plate with whole-wheat pastry. To make the filling, beat the eggs well, add the sugar, then stir in the mashed carrots and spices. Add the cream last, mix thoroughly, and pour into the unbaked pie shell. Bake in a hot oven (450°F.) for the first 10 minutes, then reduce the heat to 350°F. for another 30 minutes. Serve plain or with whipped cream.

# COOKIES

## SOYA COOKIES

¼ cup butter or vegetable shortening
⅛ cup natural brown sugar
1 egg, separated
¼ cup honey
Grated rind of ½ lemon

1½ cups sifted soya flour
2 tsp. baking powder
3 tbsp. finely chopped nuts
2 tbsp. brown sugar
½ tsp. cinnamon

Cream the butter and sugar together until fluffy. Beat in well the egg yolk and half the white. Add the honey and the lemon rind and mix thoroughly. Sift the flour with the baking powder and stir into the mixture. Knead with as little flour as possible to blend thoroughly. Roll out thin on a floured board. Spread the surface with the other half of the egg white, slightly beaten, and sprinkle evenly with nuts, sugar, and cinnamon well mixed together. Cut into about 40 rectangular pieces and transfer to a floured baking sheet. Bake about 12 minutes in a moderate oven (350°F.) until the dough is cooked. Transfer to a flat brown paper to cool, then store in a tightly covered box.

## VANILLA WAFERS

½ cup butter or vegetable shortening
⅓ cup natural brown sugar
1 egg, well beaten

¾ cup sifted whole-wheat flour
½ tsp. vanilla

Cream together the butter and sugar until fluffy. Beat in the egg thoroughly. Stir in the flour and vanilla and drop by teaspoonfuls onto a buttered baking sheet. Place far apart because the batter spreads during baking to twice its size. Bake in a moderate oven (375°F.) until the cookies are done and the edges browned, about 15 minutes. Upon removing from the oven, quickly transfer to a flat sheet of brown paper to cool. Then store in a covered box.

Preparation: 30-35 minutes.

2 dozen large cookies.

## CARROT MOLASSES COOKIES

½ cup sifted whole-wheat flour
¼ cup sifted soya flour
¼ tsp. vegetable salt
¼ tsp. cloves
½ tsp. cinnamon
¼ cup butter or vegetable shortening

¼ cup blackstrap molasses
½ cup brown sugar
1 egg, slightly beaten
½ cup mashed cooked carrots
¼ cup chopped nutmeats
½ cup seedless raisins

Sift together the flour, salt, and spices. Cream the butter and add the molasses and brown sugar, then the slightly beaten egg and the mashed carrots. Fold in the dry ingredients and the nuts and raisins. Drop by the spoonful onto a buttered cookie sheet. Bake in a moderate oven (375°F.) for 15 minutes.

## NUT CRISPS

¼ cup butter
½ cup natural brown sugar
1 egg
1 cup sifted whole-wheat flour

1 tsp. baking powder
¼ tsp. vegetable salt
¼ tsp. vanilla

Cream the butter, add the sugar, and cream until light and fluffy. Add the egg and mix well. Sift the flour 5 times, measure, add the baking powder and salt, and sift again. Fold into the mixture and add the vanilla.

Set the dough in the refrigerator to chill. Then roll in small balls, place on a buttered cookie sheet, and press flat with a fork. Put a half nutmeat on top of each cookie. Bake in a moderate oven (375°F.) 10-12 minutes.

## NUT SQUARES

1 egg, separated
½ cup natural brown sugar
½ cup chopped nutmeats

3 tbsp. sifted whole-wheat flour
Pinch of vegetable salt

Beat the egg yolk until thick and lemon-colored, adding the sugar gradually. Add the nutmeats and fold in the egg white, beaten until stiff but not dry. Mix lightly and drop by teaspoonfuls about 2½ inches apart on a buttered baking sheet. Spread a little so the mounds will run together during baking. Bake in a moderate oven (350° to 375°F.) until the centers are done and the thin edges brown. Cut apart where the cookies have run together immediately upon taking them from the oven. Transfer the squares to a flat brown paper to cool, then store in a tightly covered box.

Preparation: 10-15 minutes.

About 2½ dozen.

## SOYA SAND TARTS

| | |
|---|---|
| ¼ cup butter or vegetable shortening | 1½ cups sifted soya flour |
| ⅜ cup natural brown sugar | 2 tsp. baking powder |
| 1 egg, separated | 3 tbsp. finely chopped almonds |
| ¼ cup honey | 2 tbsp. natural brown sugar |
| Grated rind of ½ lemon | ½ tsp. cinnamon |

Cream the butter and sugar together until fluffy. Beat in the egg yolk and half the egg white. Add the honey and lemon rind and beat until thoroughly blended. Sift together the soya flour and baking powder and stir into the dough. Knead the mixture with as little flour as possible to blend thoroughly. Roll out thin on a lightly floured board. Spread the surface with the other half of the egg white slightly beaten, then sprinkle evenly with the almonds, 2 tbsp. of sugar, and cinnamon, well mixed together. Cut into about 40 rectangular pieces and transfer to a buttered baking sheet. Bake in a moderate oven (375°F.) about 15 minutes. Place on flat brown paper to cool, then store in a covered box.

Preparation: 45-50 minutes.

40 medium-sized cookies.

## COCONUT BALLS

| | |
|---|---|
| 1½ cups shredded coconut | 2 tsp. honey |
| 6 tbsp. natural brown sugar | 1 egg white |

Cook the coconut, sugar, and honey in the top of a double boiler, stirring frequently, until the shreds of coconut become transparent—10 to 15 minutes. Add the egg white, slightly beaten, and continue cooking, stirring occasionally, until the mixture feels sticky, which will take another 10 to 15 minutes. Spread out on a platter to cool. Put waxed paper over a baking sheet and on it deposit the coconut mixture by heaping teaspoonfuls. Bake in a moderate oven (325°F.) until nicely browned, about 20 minutes.

Quickly transfer to a platter or marble when removed from the oven. Store in a tightly covered box when cool.

Preparation: 10-15 minutes.

2½ dozen balls.

# CHAPTER 17

# Jams, Jellies, and Confections

CLEAR, SPARKLING JELLY which keeps its shape when molded, yet quivers when disturbed, is made from fruit which has the proper proportions of pectin, which makes the fruit juice jell, and acid, which gives it firmness. Now, not all fruits contain the right amounts of these substances. Apples, blueberries, blackberries, loganberries, crab apples, currants, grapes, some raspberries, plums, gooseberries, quinces, pears, and cranberries furnish enough pectin in themselves if the fruit is not quite ripe. Ripe quinces, pears, and apples do need extra pectin.

Strawberries, peaches, rhubarb, cherries, pineapple, apricots, some raspberries, and elderberries do not furnish their own pectin.

Commercial pectin, liquid or powdered, solves the difficulty; but many epicures think the jelly is a little tough. One way of adding pectin is to use combinations of one fruit low in pectin and one high in pectin. And here is a way to make your own added pectin:

*To Make Added Pectin:* Strip off the inside white peel of grapefruit and oranges. Tie the white peel in little cheesecloth bags and draw it through the boiling juice. When the juice, with sugar added, has been cooking about 3 minutes, when beads of jelly begin to cling to the cloth, the jelly is finished.

*To Test for Pectin:* The amount of pectin in any given fruit depends not only on the kind of fruit, but the degree of ripeness. Fruits which are not too ripe make the best jelly, remember. If you are in doubt whether a fruit will jell without extra help, stir 1 tablespoon of the juice into 1 tablespoon of alcohol. If one large, firm mass of jelly is formed, the fruit is rich in pectin and can be used alone for jelly. If several pieces, not so firm, are formed, the fruit is only moderately rich in pectin and will do better if combined with a pectin-rich fruit. If only small flakes of jelly form, or none at all, the fruit is poor in pectin and will not make jelly by itself.

If you make a good deal of jelly, it may pay you to buy a jellmeter, a gauge which registers the amount of pectin in fruit juice and how much sugar to use.

*Added Acid:* The only way to tell whether fruit juice needs added acid is to taste for sweetness. Juice for jelly making should be tart. If it is too sweet, add 1 teaspoon of lemon juice to each cup of fruit juice before heating.

*Sweetening for Jelly:* Honey is the ideal sweetener for jams and preserves and jellies. Be sure it's a mild-flavored honey such as clover or sage so the honey flavor will not dominate the fruit flavor. Natural brown sugar is also good. Remember that natural brown sugar should be packed firmly into the cup when measuring.

*Proportion of Sugar:* The amount of sugar to use depends upon the pectin content of the fruit.

Fruits rich in pectin—Use 1 cup sugar to 1 cup fruit juice

Fruits moderately rich in pectin—Use ⅔ cup sugar to 1 cup fruit juice

Fruits poor in pectin—Use ½ cup sugar to 1 cup fruit juice

*Proportion of Honey:* You need slightly less honey than sugar. Try ¾ cup mild honey to 1 cup of fruit juice when the juice is rich in pectin. For juices moderately rich or poor, use slightly less than the amount given for sugar.

### PRINCIPLES OF MAKING JELLY

The first step in making jelly is to extract the juice from fruits. The juice is then heated, sugar added, and the mixture boiled until it will jell. Jelly made with natural pectin, usually called "long-boil" method, has a variable boiling time. The juice is concentrated by boiling to the point where the juice will jell. This will take anywhere from 10 to 15 minutes, depending upon the amount of pectin in the particular juice you are using. As a rule the sugar is added when the juice has reached the boiling point. But you will find that your jelly will have a more delicate texture if you add the sugar not more than 3 minutes before the jelly point is reached. This will take a little experience to calculate. If more evaporation is desired, let the jelly stand in the sun a few days.

Another important rule is to make a small batch of jelly at any one time, not more than 6 or 8 cups of juice. Less cooking time will be required for a small amount, thus preserving not only the delicate flavor, but also the food value.

Have the jelly glasses hot and sterilized. Fill to within ⅛ inch of the top, holding the pot close to the glass while pouring to avoid air bubbles.

### EXTRACTING THE JUICE

*Hard Fruits* (apples, quinces, crab apples, etc.): Wash thoroughly and cut out any spoiled spots. Cut in quarters or eighths, keeping the peelings and cores. Put in a saucepan and add water barely to cover. Boil gently until the fruit is tender. Now the fruit must be strained through several thicknesses of cheesecloth or a Canton flannel bag. Use a strainer to hold the bag, or suspend it over a kettle in any way you like. The point is the juice must drip through of its own momentum. Never squeeze the bag or otherwise try to hurry the dripping or the jelly will be cloudy.

*Soft Fruits* (berries, grapes, and other juicy fruits): Place in a saucepan and crush slightly. Add only enough water to start the fruit cooking—about ¼ cup for 1 quart of fruit. Bring slowly to the boiling point and cook gently until most of the color has faded from the pulp. Put in a bag and strain as described for hard fruits.

### MAKING THE JELLY

Put the juice in a broad kettle which will leave plenty of room for it to boil up. Bring to a vigorous boil and boil several minutes. Add the sugar and stir until it is thoroughly dissolved. Continue to boil rapidly until the jelly point is reached, testing a small amount of juice frequently.

## THE JELLY POINT

To test for the jelly point, dip a spoon into the boiling juice, take it out, and let the juice drip slowly off the edge of the spoon. As the juice nears the jelly point, it will drip off the spoon in two separate drops about ½ inch apart. Continue to cook until it drips off in one sheet—in other words, until it will not separate into two separate drops.

Or, if you have a candy thermometer, use that instead of the jelly test. At sea level the jelly point is reached at 220°F. to 222°F. For higher altitudes, the temperature is 1.8° lower for each 960 feet of altitude.

## TO SEAL GLASSES

Pour a thin layer of melted paraffin over the surface of the jelly and let cool thoroughly. Cover the glasses and store in a cool place.

## KINDS OF JELLY

Apples, blueberries, blackberries, loganberries, crab apples, currants, and grapes make jelly when used alone. Most others are used in combination unless commercial pectin is added. Here are some combinations:

¼ blackberry, ¾ apple
½ black raspberry, ½ apple
⅔ black raspberry, ⅓ currant
⅓ red raspberry, ⅔ currant
½ blueberry, ½ apple
½ cherry, ½ apple
½ rhubarb, ½ apple

½ elderberry, ½ apple
¾ gooseberry, ¼ currant
½ peach, ½ apple
¼ plum, ¾ crab apple
½ quince, ½ apple
½ strawberry, ½ apple
⅓ quince, ⅓ cranberry, ⅓ apple

## NEW-STYLE BERRY JELLY

All juicy fruits and berries can be made into jelly this quick and easy way. Try a small quantity the first time. You will find this new method a great time-saver, and you'll like the richer and more delicate flavor of these tender jellies.

Extract the seeds from berries by putting them through a juice extractor. Strain the juice and measure it. Heat to the boiling point, turn off the heat, and stir in 1½ cups of natural brown sugar for each cup of juice. Stir until the sugar is dissolved, then pour into hot sterilized jelly glasses.

## JAMS

Jams are made of the whole crushed fruit cooked with sugar instead of just the juice as in jelly. Whenever possible cook the fruit without any added water. Three-fourths pound to 1 pound of natural brown sugar is added for each pound of fruit.

Fruits such as apricots and peaches need ¼ cup of water or lemon juice per quart of fruit. Gooseberries also need a little water, but most other berries can be cooked without any water.

Pare, core, and remove the seeds of hard fruits, then crush or chop. Hull berries, pit cherries, stem currants, etc. Put the fruit in a heavy kettle large enough to let the mixture boil up. Stir frequently as it cooks to prevent scorching. It will take 10 to 20 minutes to cook, depending on how hard the fruit is. Fruits rich in pectin will sheet off the spoon when done just as jelly does. Other fruits are done when the syrup is somewhat thick.

Add the sugar about 3 minutes before the jam is done. Skim if necessary, and pour immediately into hot sterilized jars or glasses. Seal jars immediately; pour melted paraffin over glasses. Cool, cover, and store in a cool place.

If you live in a climate where you can count on several sunny days in a row, try the new-style method of making jam described in the recipe below.

## CALIFORNIA SUNSHINE JAM

A new method of making berry jams is this: Wash the berries—not more than 4 boxes at once. Cut the berries in half and weigh them. Then weigh out an equal amount of natural brown sugar. Put the sugar over the berries and let stand 2 or 3 hours, or until the juice starts to run. Put over low heat until the sugar is thoroughly dissolved. Bring to a rolling boil and boil for just 1 minute. Set off the stove and let stand 5 to 10 minutes. Add the juice of 1 good-sized lemon. Pour out into a shallow pan or platter and put in the sunshine for 2 or 3 days, covered with a cheesecloth to keep out the dust. The jam should evaporate from ½ inch to 1 inch. Can or put in jelly glasses.

## CONFECTIONS
### CALIFORNIA FRUITS FOR CANDY

Dates, figs, raisins, and dried apricots are natural sweets. Serve them instead of acid-forming candies for children. It is the best way to keep them from eating unwholesome candies.

### CALIFORNIA FRUIT CANDY

4 oz. figs
4 oz. dates
4 oz. seedless raisins

2 oz. unblanched almonds
2 oz. pecans or walnuts

Put all the ingredients through a food chopper and mix well. Make into small balls and roll in natural brown sugar.

### FRUIT BALLS

Grind equal portions of figs, dates, prunes, and raisins. Grind ½ cup unblanched almonds or walnuts very fine and mix with the fruit. Heat enough honey to roll the fruit balls in and cover with shredded coconut.

### NEW ORLEANS CARAMELS

2 cups blackstrap molasses
1 cup natural brown sugar
1 cup rich cream

¼ lb. bitter chocolate
4 tbsp. butter
1 tsp. vanilla, if desired

Boil the ingredients together until they harden in cold water. Add the vanilla. Pour into a buttered flat baking dish and cut into small squares when nearly cold.

### YANKEE WALNUT FUDGE

2 cups natural brown sugar
1 tbsp. cocoa
Pinch of vegetable salt

1 cup rich milk
3 tbsp. butter
½ cup chopped black walnuts

Combine the sugar, cocoa, and salt. Add the milk and cook until a soft ball forms when a bit of syrup is dropped into cold water. Remove from fire, stir in the butter, and let cool. Then beat until creamy, stirring in the walnuts at the last, and turn onto a buttered platter.

## SOUTHERN PEANUT BRITTLE

Put 2 cups of natural brown sugar into a smooth iron frying skillet. Turn on the heat and start stirring the sugar with the bowl of a spoon, keeping the spoon flat. When the sugar is all melted, remove at once from the heat and stir in 2 cups of unsalted roasted peanuts. When the mixture begins to stiffen, pour it out onto an oiled surface and let it harden. Break it into pieces to serve. Easy to make and the children love it.

## DELICIOUS CANDIED PEELS

1 large grapefruit
2 golden oranges

1 cup natural brown sugar
1 cup water

Cut the grapefruit peel into slices about ½ inch wide and soak overnight in cold water. Add a few drops of lemon juice to prevent discolorations. Next morning put the peels in a saucepan and cover with water. Boil for 10 minutes, then pour off the water and add fresh water. Let boil another 10 minutes. Pour off the water again and make a syrup of natural brown sugar and 1 cup of water. Boil this for 5 minutes and place the fruit peels in this syrup. Let cook until peels look transparent. Drain and roll in coarse raw sugar.

# CHAPTER 18

# *Beverages*

THE WORD "beverage" suggests the comfort and stimulation of a steaming cup of coffee on a cold morning or the refreshment of a tall, frosty glass on a hot summer afternoon. But besides their obvious function, to relieve thirst, beverages are a delightful means of supplying vitamins and minerals. From milk we get calcium and phosphorus; from fruit juices and vegetable juices the B vitamins and vitamin C. Besides the morning orange juice, the luncheon tomato-juice cocktail, there are dozens of health-giving "liquid salads," as I like to call vegetable juices, growing more popular daily. A juice extractor (see page 229) is an investment which will pay high dividends in health and beauty.

## FRUIT JUICES

Ripe, sweet fruits freshly squeezed is the cardinal rule of fruit juices. Vitamin C is destroyed by exposure to air, so if for some reason you have to squeeze your oranges before you serve the juice, keep it in a tightly covered container in the icebox. Fruit juices are better unsweetened. Try it awhile and see how soon you learn to prefer the natural flavor.

Mixed vegetable juices are good, but fruit juices are better taken one at a time. Lemon juice and orange juice, for instance, neutralize each other so you do not get the full benefit of either.

# Beverages

A glance at the table below will show the nutritive value of fruit juices. A 6-ounce portion yields the following number of International Units of vitamin C:

| Juice | International Units of vitamin C |
|---|---|
| Fresh orange juice | 1700 |
| Fresh grapefruit juice | 1370 |
| Canned grapefruit juice | 1080 |
| Canned tomato juice | 900 |
| Fresh pineapple juice | 850 |
| Fresh lemonade | 368 |
| Canned pineapple juice | 360 |
| Fresh limeade | 190 |

## CANNED JUICES

Modern methods of canning preserve the vitamin content of fruit and vegetable juices to a very large extent. Fresh juices from first-quality fruits is the best, of course; but a good canned juice may offer more nutritive value than an inferior fresh one. Any suspicion of a "canny" taste can be eliminated by letting the canned juice stand in the open air for 15 to 20 minutes before using. Mixing a small quantity of good fresh juice with the canned product or simply adding a few drops of lemon juice helps to improve the flavor.

## LEMONADE

Lemon juice and its cousin, lime juice, are not adapted to drinking undiluted. But they are invaluable in lemonade and limeade and in fruit-juice punches.

The simplest and best lemonade is the juice of 1 lemon in 1 cup of cold water, sweetened with sugar or honey to taste. Using the rind as well as the juice not only adds flavor but is economical.

## LEMON PUNCH

½ cup natural brown sugar
½ cup water

Rind of 1 lemon, grated
½ cup lemon juice

Put the sugar, water, and lemon rind in a saucepan. Stir over low heat until the sugar is dissolved. Then boil 5 minutes without stirring and let cool. When ready to serve, add the lemon juice and 4 cups of water. Pour over ice in a pitcher or tall glasses. Or reheat and serve as hot punch.

## LIMEADE

Follow the recipe for Lemonade, using lime juice instead of lemon.

## MINT LEMONADE

Put some bruised mint leaves in the bottom of the pitcher before pouring in the lemonade. Garnish each glass with a sprig of mint.

## RASPBERRY LEMON PUNCH

Add 1 pint of crushed raspberries to the boiled sugar mixture in Lemon Punch while it is still hot. Strain, cool, and add lemon juice as described.

## HERB JUICES

A sprig of mint in a glass of iced tea is the bare beginning of what can be done with herb flavors in beverages. Put other fresh herbs through your juice extractor and add 1 teaspoon of the herb juice to a glass of fruit juice. Anise, for instance, will give the drink the flavor of absinthe. Try mint with grapefruit or pineapple juice. And experiment with serving the herb teas iced.

## BERRY JUICES

Don't neglect the berry juices—strawberry, loganberry, and raspberry make delicate, delicious drinks.

## COFFEE

Coffee is really not a food, but a stimulant. If your doctor has forbidden it to you, read no farther. This section is for us healthy people who can enjoy this favorite drink with no ill effects because we know how to make it correctly. The harmful element in coffee is not so much the caffein as the tannic acid; hence the least harmful coffee is the one which contains the least tannic acid. Of the various methods of making coffee, percolating is the least desirable, for the long cooking period draws out the tannic acid. Drip or filtered coffee contains less tannic acid than percolated. Use either a porcelain or an earthenware drip pot or a glass vacuum-method coffee maker and follow directions which come with your coffee maker.

My own method of making the best-flavored coffee is this:

1. Use a porcelain or crockery pot, never metal.
2. Use a heaping tablespoonful of coffee per cup; don't skimp.
3. Put the coffee in the pot and pour over it scalding hot water, which must be fresh water freshly boiled. When coffee tastes flat it is because the freshness has been boiled out of the water.
4. Steep the coffee in the water for 5 minutes by the clock.

With this method you will have a fragrant cup of coffee minus the tannic acid. And one cup of coffee can do a healthy person no harm. As with any other good thing, harm comes from overdoing it.

Any true coffee fiend has his own idea of what is a good cup of coffee, but they all agree that good coffee must have a tantalizing fragrance, a clear, sparkling surface, not a muddy one, and leave no dregs in the cup. In the matter of strength and flavor, however, you will want to experiment a little unless you have already done so. The flavor of coffee depends upon the varieties of coffee bean and how they are roasted. Commercial coffees are usually a blend of several varieties in different proportions. In general, the darker the beans, the more pronounced the flavor. The volatile oils which give coffee its rich aroma gradually evaporate upon exposure to air, and so coffee should always be fresh. I prefer to buy the whole beans and grind my own coffee fresh each time. Find a grocer who likes you and will sell you a good whole-bean coffee in small quantities.

Vacuum-packed coffee in tin cans remains fresh until the can is opened. After that it deteriorates like any other kind. However, no matter where you buy your coffee nor in what form, keep it in airtight containers, tightly covered. During the recent shortage many people claimed that coffee keeps better in the refrigerator with the can turned upside down. Try it and see for yourself.

## DECAFFEINATED COFFEE

For those who are sensitive to the stimulating effects of caffein, decaffeinated coffees are a blessing, particularly in the evening. Use them in the same proportions as ordinary coffee; or, if you want to fool your guests, use double the usual amount and they'll rave over your good coffee.

## VIENNA COFFEE

Initiates swoon over Vienna coffee. The secret is simple—have the coffee hot, hot, and heat the cream also. Or, if you want it particularly *Wienerisch,* put a couple of tablespoons of whipped cream in the cup and pour the coffee over it—again hot, hot.

## SMART AFTER-DINNER COFFEE

Make the same way as breakfast coffee, but use twice as much coffee per cup of water. Serve black in demitasse cups, without sugar or cream. But have some coarse raw sugar on your tray for those who like a bit of sweetening.

## ICED COFFEE

In making iced coffee the problem is not to let the coffee be too much diluted. Make regular-strength coffee and let it cool before pouring over ice, or make double-strength coffee and pour it hot over ice. If you find it still too diluted, try freezing coffee in the ice-cube tray to use for ice in the drinks. Placing one whole dark roasted coffee bean in each cube before freezing gives added flavor.

## TEA

A famous Chinese chemist says the Chinese people drink as much as twenty cups of tea a day with no bad effects. This is because their method of steeping eliminates most of the harmful tannic acid. Here is how they do it:

Scald an earthenware pot to warm it and throw out the water. Then put in the tea leaves, a pinch to each cup. Next, pour scalding water over the leaves just to cover and let stand 2 minutes by the clock. Pour this water off! It contains most of the tannic acid. Now pour freshly boiling water over the leaves and steep 3 to 5 minutes. Strain into cups and you will have the flavorsome bouquet of tea without its harmful ingredient.

## ICED TEA

Tea loses some of its flavor when it stands, so cold tea poured over ice is not the best way to make iced tea. Rather, fill tall glasses a third full of shaved ice or nearly full of cracked ice and fill with hot tea. Serve with lemon and sugar.

## HERB TEAS

Thousands who have given up coffee thrive on natural, fragrant herb drinks—peppermint tea, strawberry, vervain or verbena, papaya-mint, and lemon—use a bit of peel and flavor with honey. Follow the recipe for Peppermint Tea.

## PEPPERMINT TEA

Into boiling water put a pinch of peppermint tea per cup. Let simmer for 3 minutes to extract the peppermint oil. Serve with lemon and honey.

## GINGER TEA

Mix 1 tablespoon of blackstrap molasses with ½ teaspoon of ginger. Pour on gradually ½ cup of boiling water and boil for 1 minute. Add ½ cup of hot milk and serve.

## NEW ORLEANS CUP

Dissolve 2 teaspoons of blackstrap molasses in a cup of hot water. Flavor with a bit of lemon, or cream if you prefer. This is a healthful drink and pleasantly replaces some of the evil-tasting substitutes for coffee.

## PAPAYA-MINT TEA

Combine equal parts of papaya tea and mint tea and prepare as for Peppermint Tea. Or the mixture can be bought at some specialty shops.

## MILK

Milk is the perfect food for babies, but when the teeth come it is nature's sign that milk is not enough, and solid food should be eaten. This is not a statement intended to minimize the value of milk as a food. It contains first-class protein, calcium, phosphorus, and vitamins —just how much depends upon the feed of the cow from which it came. But milk is not the complete food which advertising agents would have us believe, and any milk drink is improved by the addition of blackstrap molasses, carrot juice, bananas, and such high-vitamin foods.

Especially for children, insist upon certified milk instead of pasteurized. Pasteurization destroys about 15 per cent of the vitamin $B_1$ of milk.

CHAPTER 19

# Fletcherized Foods for Children and "Skinnies"

IT'S NOT HOW much you eat but how much you assimilate which builds a strong body. Weak, run-down persons stuff themselves in an effort to gain strength, and more often than not merely add to their troubles. The vital elements of most foods are locked in minute cells which must be broken down to release their building elements. This breaking-down process should be well begun before the food reaches the stomach. As Horace Fletcher taught more than 75 years ago, every bit of food we put into our mouths should be so thoroughly chewed that it is the consistency of a fine, milky paste before it is swallowed.

But in these days of hurry and worry, proper mastication seems to be a lost art. For that reason I recommend the use of an electric food pulverizer, or Fletcherizer, which whips the food into a fine, almost colloidal consistency. Foods thus prepared have worked wonders for those who have tried in vain to gain strength and vitality. They are of tremendous value to the needlessly thin and weak who cannot get the good from what they eat; to those suffering from intestinal difficulties and all cases where the dietitian has prescribed a nonirritating diet; and also for spoiled youngsters who are finicky and hard to please.

## GENERAL DIRECTIONS

Put the liquid into the container. Cut the solids into ½-inch pieces. Fletcherize for a minute or so—the more difficulty you have with digestion, the finer the foods should be Fletcherized.

Most foods can be Fletcherized, but the protein foods such as nuts, cheese, egg yolks, and so forth, when mixed with fruit juices are the most nutritious combinations. Select the foods you know agree with you. Try all the different combinations, then stick to the ones you enjoy the most. I find that it is never necessary to take more than 3 glasses a day of these "builder-uppers." The Almond Milk is a great favorite in the famous Bircher-Benner Sanatorium in Switzerland.

THE FLETCHERIZER

## COMBINATIONS FOR FLETCHERIZED DRINKS

These are my favorite Fletcherized combinations:

*Almond Milk:* 1 cup orange juice, a handful of blanched unsalted almonds.

*Pecan Milk:* 1 cup unsweetened pineapple juice, a handful of unsalted pecans.

*Walnut Milk:* 1 cup unsweetened grapefruit juice, a handful of unsalted walnuts.

*Filbert Milk:* 1 cup unsweetened pineapple juice, a handful of unsalted filberts.

*Cashew Milk:* 1 cup orange juice, a handful of unsalted cashews.

*Coconut Milk:* 1 cup unsweetened pineapple juice, a handful of fresh or canned coconut. This tastes better strained.

*Cream of Soya Milk:* 1 cup water, 1 tablespoon soya flour,[1] 1 teaspoon honey, and a pinch of vegetable salt. *Or*
    1 cup pineapple juice, 1 tablespoon soya flour. *Or*
    1 cup orange juice, 1 tablespoon soya flour

*Vege-Nut Milk:* 1 cup unsweetened fruit juice, 1 heaping teaspoon soya flour, a few almonds or other nuts, and 1 teaspoon honey. This delicious combination is less expensive and excellent for children.

*Banana Eggnog:* 1 cup milk, 2 eggs, 1 banana, and 4 or more teaspoons honey. Put the milk in the container and start the machine, then add eggs, banana, and honey in that order.

*Fruit Nog:* 1 or 2 eggs, 1½ cups of any of these juices: orange, unsweetened pineapple, or apple, or grape.
    Put the juice into the container and start the machine. Then add the eggs. Run the Fletcherizer another 30 seconds and serve with a sprinkle of nutmeg on top.

*Pep Cocktails:* Combine 1 fresh egg with 1 cup of any of the following: orange juice, unsweetened grapefruit juice, unsweetened pineapple juice, or Hauser Broth.

*Calcium Cocktails:* 1 cup unsweetened pineapple juice, 1 tablespoon fresh cottage cheese. *Or*
    1 cup orange juice, 1 tablespoon cream cheese

---

[1] Be sure the soya flour you use in these drinks has been cooked—otherwise the raw starch may cause discomfort.

## FLETCHERIZED CREAM SOUPS

With the invention of that wonderful time-saving gadget the Fletcherizer, an entirely new way of making soups has been discovered. By first Fletcherizing the ingredients such as vegetables, nuts, fruits, legumes, and so forth, in Hauser Broth or milk, all you have to do is heat the soup to serving temperature, season, and serve immediately. It's a time-saver, but, more important, it gives the value of raw food with the advantage of hot food.

Almost any vegetable can be used to make a delicious Fletcherized cream soup. Cut the vegetables into small pieces before putting them in the machine.

If you do not like milk, make the soups in this section with Hauser Broth and top them with whipped cream.

Here are some of the favorite soups:

### CREAM OF ONION SOUP

Pour 1 cup of fresh milk into the Fletcherizer and add ½ cup of dry or green onion cut in ½-inch pieces. Fletcherize 2 minutes, then heat in the top of a double boiler until very hot but not at the boiling point. Turn off the heat and add vegetable salt and 1 teaspoon of butter. Serve at once sprinkled with minced parsley.

### CREAM OF PEA SOUP

Pour 1 cup of fresh milk into the Fletcherizer. Add ½ cup of freshly shelled young green peas. Fletcherize for 2 minutes and turn into a saucepan. Heat over low heat until the soup begins to simmer. Turn off the heat, season with vegetable salt and 1 teaspoon of butter, then serve at once. Add your favorite herbs and spices upon occasion to vary the flavor.

### CREAM OF BEET SOUP

Pour 1 cup of fresh milk into the Fletcherizer. Add ½ cup of young, tender raw beets cut in small pieces. Fletcherize for 3 minutes, then heat over a low flame to the simmering point. Hold at that heat for 2 minutes. Turn off the heat and season with vegetable salt, 1 teaspoon of butter, and any of your favorite herbs and spices.

## CREAM OF CARROT SOUP

Pour 1 cup of fresh milk into the Fletcherizer. Add ½ cup of young carrots cut in small pieces. Fletcherize for 2 minutes, then heat over low flame to the simmering point. Hold at this heat for 2 minutes. Turn off the heat and season with vegetable salt and 1 teaspoon of butter. Serve at once, sprinkled with chopped parsley or mint.

## CREAM OF PARSLEY SOUP

Pour 1 cup of fresh milk into the Fletcherizer. Add a handful of parsley cut up into ½-inch pieces. Fletcherize for 3 minutes, then place over low heat and bring to the simmering point. Turn off the heat and season with vegetable salt and 1 teaspoon of butter. Serve at once with a sprinkling of paprika.

## CREAM OF SPINACH SOUP

Follow directions for Cream of Parsley Soup, above, using a handful of spinach instead of parsley.

## CREAM OF SOYBEAN SOUP

Pour 1½ cups of tomato juice into the Fletcherizer. Add 1 cup cooked or canned soybeans and Fletcherize for 1½ minutes, then turn into a saucepan. Heat over low heat until the soup begins to simmer. Turn off the heat, season with vegetable salt, and add sweet cream to taste.

## CREAM OF ASPARAGUS SOUP

Pour 1 cup of milk or cream into the Fletcherizer. Add ½ cup diced fresh asparagus and 1 tablespoon of whole-wheat flour. Fletcherize for 2 minutes and turn into a saucepan. Heat over low heat until the soup begins to simmer. Turn off the heat, season with vegetable salt and 1 teaspoon of butter, and serve at once.

## CREAM OF MUSHROOM SOUP

Pour 1 cup of milk or cream into the Fletcherizer. Add a slice of onion, 3 fresh sautéed mushroom caps, a few sprays of celery leaves, and 1 tablespoon of whole-wheat flour. Fletcherize for 2 minutes and turn into a saucepan. Heat over low heat until the soup begins to simmer. Turn off the heat, season with vegetable salt and 1 teaspoon of butter, and serve at once.

## OTHER RECIPES FOR YOUR FLETCHERIZER

### CARROT MAYONNAISE

2 eggs
1 cup yellow olive oil or vegetable oil

½ cup diced raw carrots

Put the eggs into the container and start the motor. Pour the oil in slowly. When half the oil has been added, put in the carrots, then the rest of the oil. Run the machine until the mayonnaise is thick and creamy.

### HERB MAYONNAISE

Make your favorite herb mayonnaise by following the recipe for Carrot Mayonnaise. Simply add 2 tablespoons of chopped fresh parsley or chives or water cress. Or you can use dried herbs, but in that case add only ¼ teaspoon.

### HEALTH MAYONNAISE

1 egg
2 tbsp. honey
Juice of 1 lemon

Vegetable salt to taste
1 cup yellow olive oil or vegetable oil

Put all the ingredients except the oil into the container and start the motor. Run the machine until the mayonnaise is thick and creamy—about 30 seconds.

### BEVERLY HILLS LIVER PASTE

½ lb. fresh liver
Fresh butter
  1 large onion, chopped
  1 clove garlic, chopped
½ tsp. vegetable salt

1 tsp. soya or whole-wheat flour
Hauser Broth
1 tbsp. chopped parsley
1 tbsp. wheat germ

Get your butcher to give you the freshest liver, calves', chicken, or goose. Wash the livers and cut out all the tough spots. Melt a little butter in a hot skillet and brown the chopped onion and garlic. Take out the onion and garlic and save them, then sauté the liver in the butter, sprinkling it with vegetable salt as it finishes cooking. Add the onions and garlic when the liver is nicely browned but not tough.

Put all the solids in the pan into your Fletcherizer. Thicken the pan gravy with the teaspoon of flour and add enough Hauser Broth to make a rich gravy. Let the gravy cool and add it to the liver mixture in the Fletcherizer. When the mixture is nearly smooth, add the chopped parsley and the wheat germ. Blend for another 30 seconds and pour into a jar to cool. Melt enough butter to cover the top of the jar and act as a seal, then keep the jar in the refrigerator.

## MADE-IN-A-MINUTE DESSERTS

### MINUTE APPLESAUCE

Fletcherize for 1 minute 1 cup unsweetened cider or pineapple juice, 2 medium-sized unpeeled apples cut in small pieces, 1 tablespoon of honey, 1 teaspoon of fresh lemon juice, and a dash of cinnamon. Can be served raw, or heated with a bit of melted butter.

### MINUTE APRICOT SAUCE

Fletcherize together 1 cup unsweetened pineapple juice, ½ cup fresh, canned, or soaked dried apricots with a little honey, if desired. Serve in sherbet glasses with whipped cream.

### MINUTE PRUNE SAUCE

Fletcherize together 1 cup unsweetened grapefruit juice, 1 cup soaked dried prunes, pitted, and honey if desired.

### MINUTE CRANBERRY SAUCE

Fletcherize together 1 cup orange juice, 1 small unpeeled red apple cut in small pieces, and 1 or 2 tablespoons of honey. Add cranberries until the mixture thickens.

### MINUTE STRAWBERRY-RHUBARB SAUCE

Fletcherize together 1 cup unsweetened pineapple juice, 1 cup tender raw rhubarb cut in ½-inch pieces, ½ cup ripe strawberries, and 1 or 2 teaspoons of honey.

Delicious individual pies can be made with these minute sauces. Simply fill individual Continental pie shells and top with a bit of whipped cream. Try the *hot* minute applesauce in a Continental pie crust; it is even better than the pie that "mother used to make."

## FRESH BERRY ICE CREAM

1 pt. ripe berries
⅓ cup water
2 tbsp. honey

Juice of ½ lime
½ cup heavy cream
Pinch of vegetable salt

Combine the water, honey, lime juice, and salt and put in the container. Add the berries and Fletcherize for 1 minute. Whip the cream in the Fletcherizer for about 10 seconds—a second too much and it will turn to butter. Fold the whipped cream into the berries and freeze.

## PINEAPPLE SHERBET

1 cup diced canned pineapple
1 cup milk or cream

1 tsp. lemon juice
Honey to taste

Turn on the motor and put the ingredients into the container in the order named. Add ½ tbsp. gelatin which has been soaked in 4 tbsp. cold water. When the contents are thoroughly blended, pour into a refrigerator tray and freeze. For a fine texture, stir occasionally as the sherbet freezes.

# CHAPTER 20

# Juices for Health and Good Looks

"DRINK YOUR VEGETABLES" is an idea which was born in Carlsbad, Czechoslovakia. In a famous sanatorium there I saw a nurse extracting the juice from vegetables in a very primitive gadget. The "blood of the plant," she called it, and thousands of people with troubled digestions came to drink it from all over the world. When I saw what drinking the vegetable juices without the irritating bulk of the whole vegetable did for these people, I brought the juice therapy to America. That was in 1926, and in the years since then people all over this country have learned to enjoy drinking their vegetables.

One of the most important points in making vegetable juices is to get vegetables as fresh as possible. On Elizabeth Arden's beauty farm in Maine where I was nutritional director, we had the vegetables fresh-picked in the morning and juiced in a special gadget within twenty minutes. Even the spoiled ladies of the beauty farm drank with delight these juices with all their goodness—minerals, vitamins, enzymes, and no doubt other important food factors not yet discovered.

Why drink vegetables instead of eating them? you ask. It is true that the body can make use of the food elements of the whole vege-table, but a deficiency can be made up more quickly by drinking the fresh juices. Larger quantities can be taken, for one thing. Second, since the vitamins and minerals have already been extracted from the pulp, they can be more easily absorbed by the body. And, third, losses due to cooking are avoided.

People with weak digestions, who cannot stand the irritating fibers of vegetables, find the juices a gift from heaven. Older people who have trouble chewing, children who hate vegetables, and people on reducing diets all benefit from this concentrated goodness.

No more than a pint need be taken in a day unless your nutritionist specifies more.

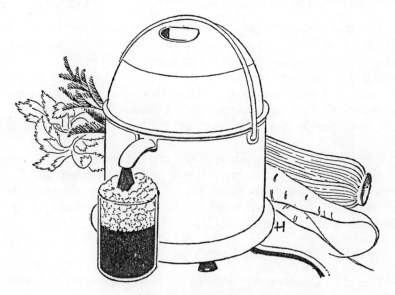

THE VEGETABLE JUICER

## VALUES OF VEGETABLE JUICES

All vegetables—and fruits—make healthful juices, but some taste better than others and hence make more palatable combinations. Carrot juice is the most popular with Americans. Next comes celery juice, and after that the green juices—spinach, parsley, and water cress. These green juices, however, are rather sharp and taste better when mixed with carrot or celery juice. A few drops of lemon, orange, or pineapple juice improves the flavor of vegetable juices and may be added to any of them.

In the sanatoriums of Europe the vegetable juices are served fresh from the garden, but for the ordinary healthy individual it is all right to chill them and serve them cold. Keep them in an airtight container while they are in the refrigerator.

## PREPARING VEGETABLES FOR JUICE MAKING

A special electric gadget for extracting vegetable juices is already in thousands of my student's homes. There is now a practically perfect one which extracts quarts of fresh vegetable juices on a moment's notice. It is as simple as making orange juice. This newest gadget is made of a wonderful metal which cannot affect the taste nor the chemistry of these fresh juices, which, of course, is very important. An investment in such a "health mine" will pay handsome dividends to any family.

Select the freshest vegetables you can get; the younger the better—dark golden carrots, dark green leaves, heavy, juicy celery and fat, ripe apples make delicious juices. Do not peel the vegetables; simply scrub them with a very stiff brush or a bit of steel wool, then cut them in pieces to fit the machine.

## REMOVING POISONOUS SPRAYS

Sometimes farmers spray vegetable plants with poisons to kill pests. When juices are made for people with sensitive digestion, all trace of such sprays should be removed. Simply place the washed fruits and vegetables in an earthenware pot filled with 1 per cent hydrochloric acid solution. Chemically pure hydrochloric acid can be purchased at your nearest drugstore and should be used in proportion of 1 ounce to 3 quarts of water. You can use this solution for an entire week. Keep the vegetables or fruits in the spray remover for about 5 minutes and rinse afterward. This simple method is used in sanatoriums here and abroad.

You with healthy digestions need give these sprays no thought, as the natural digestive juices automatically take care of any impurities.

## CARROT JUICE

This golden juice is really delicious. It should be drunk immediately as it comes from the juicer. California carrots make the sweetest juice. If you want to *keep* carrot juice it should be placed in the refrigerator. By adding a few drops of orange juice, it will keep its golden color for hours. *Here is what carrot juice contains*—lots of vitamins A, B, C, and G; also, a good combination of needed minerals including calcium, iron, and even iodine. The soothing substance in carrot juice makes it an ideal drink for people with irritated "innards" and dispositions. The large amount of natural sugar is responsible for the "lift" after you drink a glass of carrot juice—carrot juice blends well with all other vegetable and fruit juices. Three glasses a day with or between meals is a good start. Half carrot juice and half milk is a wonderful combination for youngsters who will not eat vegetables.

## CELERY JUICE

Men often prefer celery juice. Use all the green outside stalks for juice making since they contain more vitamins and minerals than the pale, inside hearts. Do not use the leaves since they make the juice unpleasantly bitter. Celery juice tastes best fresh but can be kept on ice for about 10 hours. Adding a few drops of lemon juice adds flavor and helps to keep that appetizing light green color. *Here is what celery juice contains*—a good supply of vitamins A, B, C, and E; also, a good amount of minerals, especially potassium, sodium, and chlorine. Celery juice makes an ideal "anti-acid" drink plus a favorite reducing "cocktail." Celery juice blends well with all other juices.

## APPLE JUICE

I describe apple juice here because it blends so well with the above celery and carrot juices. Do not peel the apples nor take out the seeds; simply slice them to fit into the machine and the juice will come forth—the like of which you have never tasted. Drink all you want while it is fresh and place the rest into the refrigerator. To prevent red or green apple juice from losing its attractive color, add a few drops of lemon juice. The large amount of pectin in apple juice makes it one of the most soothing and desirable drinks. *Here is what apple juice contains*—some vitamin A and

B, but much more C and G plus many desirable minerals. Fresh apple juice makes a welcome change for the usual glass of citrus juice in the morning.

## MY FAVORITE COCKTAIL

Equal amounts of celery, carrots, and apples make a most delicious and desirable cocktail. It contains practically all of the vitamins and minerals. It is one of the best tasting combinations and a great favorite from coast to coast. Three glasses a day contain practically all the vitamins and minerals needed for vital health and good looks. To keep this combination attractive looking, add a few drops of lemon juice and keep in the refrigerator. Try this as an appetizer in place of tomato juice.

## SPINACH JUICE

Dark, fresh, green spinach leaves make a good-looking dark green "wine." Unfortunately, spinach juice does not taste good alone so it has to be blended and combined. The spinach taste should never predominate in any cocktail and only a small handful is all that is necessary to get the benefits of this old favorite. *Here is what spinach juice contains*—lots of vitamin A, a little vitamin B, and a good amount of E and G. A good balance of minerals from potassium to iodine, but the calcium in spinach is not assimilated. Equal parts of carrots, celery, and spinach make a pleasant combination. The chlorophyll in spinach gives added health value.

## PARSLEY JUICE

One of the most neglected vegetables is coming into its own. Fresh dark green parsley makes a beautiful green juice but like spinach it has to be blended with other juices to make it tasty. *Here is what this unpretentious vegetable contains*—it is the richest source of vitamin A in the vegetable kingdom; contains some vitamin B, and lots of C; also, a little vitamin E. It is an outstanding source of iron and chlorophyll; all this makes it a tremendously rich source of vitamins and minerals. A small amount of parsley juice can be added to any of the other vegetable juices, but a blend with carrots, or celery, or both is the most pleasant.

## PINEAPPLE JUICE

Peel a fresh, ripe pineapple and cut into slices to fit the machine, and you will have a drink which is "fit for the gods." You don't know the goodness of this juice until you have tasted it fresh from the juicer. Pineapple juice is rich in bromelin, and is an excellent digestive aid. Fresh pineapple juice makes a delicious appetizer and mixes well with any other fruit or vegetable juices. *Here is what fresh pineapple juice contains*—some vitamin A, more B and C, and some vitamin G, plus 9 needed minerals including iodine. Try an appetizer of fresh pineapple juice flavored with a bit of water-cress juice. This is the famous combination I served to the Duchess of Windsor and it was a great hit.

## TOMATO JUICE

Fresh, sun-ripened tomatoes make a juice unlike any you have tasted. Cut tomatoes in slices to fit your machine. You will be amazed at the beautiful color of this juice, and to give it more character you can add a few drops of lemon juice. This also helps to preserve the color. If you like, you can add some onion or some celery. This makes a beautiful vegetable cocktail and can be served chilled as an appetizer. Be sure and add a bit of vegetable salt. Tomato juice mixes well with practically all other juices and adds flavor and savor. *Here is what tomato juice contains*—lots of vitamin A, a little vitamin B, and lots of C; so much so, fresh tomato juice can be called the "poor man's orange juice."

## GRAPE JUICE

You can take your own "grape cure" at home. Fresh juicy grapes make a beautiful, delicious tasting sweet "wine." All grapes in season are good. Simply wash them and drop them into the machine—seeds and all. The large amount of invert sugar assists the body in burning up its stored fat. A pint to a quart of fresh grape juice is a delicious addition to any "cure." *Here is what fresh grape juice contains*—small amounts of vitamins A, B, and C, and large amounts of all the important minerals.

## SPRING COCKTAIL

Put equal amounts of young tender rhubarb and fresh strawberries through the juice extractor. This makes a beautiful tinted, rose-colored juice. Flavor each glass with a teaspoon or two of honey. This is one of the cocktails which I used successfully on Elizabeth Arden's farm. One glass a day is enough and takes the place of grandmother's old-fashioned sulphur and molasses concoction.

## WATER-CRESS JUICE

Fresh dark green water cress makes a potent mineral- and vitamin-rich juice. Its taste, however, is too strong, and therefore it must be mixed and blended with such vegetables as carrots and celery. Equal amounts of water cress, celery, and carrots make a healthful cocktail. A few drops of lemon juice give it a lift, and help to preserve the natural color. *Here is what fresh water-cress juice contains*—it is very rich in vitamins A and C; contains some vitamin B, E, and G; plus nine minerals including iodine.

## OTHER VEGETABLE JUICES AND COCKTAILS

Remember, the above juices and mixtures are about the most popular combinations and it is a good idea to start with them. Do not over-do in the beginning. A pint a day is sufficient. However, all vegetables and fruits lend themselves for attractive cocktails. Remember always to combine the lesser flavorsome vegetables with such as carrots, celery, and apples.

*Apricot Juice* contains iron, copper, plus lots of vitamins A, C, and G. Tastes delicious and mixes well with all other juices.

*Beet Juice* contains ten minerals plus a fair amount of vitamins A, B, C, and G. Tastes unpleasant and should be mixed with celery, carrot, or pineapple juice (small amounts only can be taken).

*Cabbage Juice* contains calcium, sulphur, chlorine and is especially rich in vitamins A, B, and C. Should be combined with celery juice, or apple juice.

*Cucumber Juice* contains ten minerals plus a fair amount of vitamins A, B, and C. Tastes flat and should be mixed with apple juice.

*Dandelion Juice* contains chiefly potassium, iron and is especially rich in vitamins A, B, G, and some C. Tastes very bitter but makes an excellent spring tonic when mixed with celery and carrots.

*Papaya Juice* contains a fair amount of vitamins A, B, C, and a little D, plus papain, an excellent digestive. Can be made more tasty by mixing with orange juice.

*Radish Juice* contains ten minerals plus vitamins A, B, and C. Tastes unpleasant and should be blended with celery juice (only small amounts can be taken).

CHAPTER 21

# Yogurt, Brewers' Yeast, and
# Other Special Foods

## YOGURT

ONE PLEASANT WAY TO obtain many of the B vitamins is to drink milk fermented with Bulgarian milk cultures, as acidophilus milk and yogurt. These milks contain bacteria which live in the intestinal tract and make, or synthesize, B vitamins for themselves—those vitamins which are so necessary for health and good looks.

Yogurt is fast becoming a fashionable food since the publication of *Diet Does It*. In large cities now you can buy it from dairies in fifteen-cent bottles. If you are in the money, you can simply buy it regularly and eat to your heart's content. If you're not in the money, you can still eat to your heart's content because one fifteen-cent bottle will make quarts and quarts of yogurt for you and your relatives and your in-laws—if you like them enough. This is how you do it:

Simply heat a quart of milk to lukewarm, not boiling. Then take 2 tablespoons of yogurt from your little bottle and mix it into the warm milk, using a wooden spoon. Put the milk back into the quart bottle and set the bottle in a warm place—over a pilot light, near a radiator, over hot water, wherever is most convenient. It is much like setting bread dough to raise—you want a place which will keep the yogurt warm but not cook it. Let it stand there for 6 to 8 hours, until the milk curdles and solidifies like junket. As soon as it is firm, put it on ice, otherwise it will get too thick.

When this quart is gone, make another quart, using another 2 tablespoons from your little bottle, and so on until the little bottle is used up. Then you buy another fifteen-cent bottle and start again.

If the dairies in your town have not yet begun to make yogurt, you can still have it. Go to a health food store and buy a bottle of yogurt culture, then follow directions on the package.

Any kind of milk can be used to make yogurt—whole milk, skim milk, powdered milk, or evaporated milk mixed with water. If you are on a reducing diet, enjoy your yogurt without a twinge of conscience by using milk with the fat removed.

## BREWERS' YEAST

This golden powder is one of the great food discoveries of our time. Its popularity is steadily growing, but not nearly enough people yet take advantage of this modern food. Possibly some of you have a prejudice against the taste of yeast; but you need not avoid brewers' yeast on that account. One of the big breweries now makes a yeast with celery flavor which is perfectly delicious.

Brewers' yeast comes in powdered or tablet form. Eat the tablets out of hand, of course. Sprinkle the powder over cereals and vegetables like wheat germ. Add it to meat loaves, stews, gravies, bread, waffles, cookies, and so forth.

I am giving you an analysis so you can see for yourself how many good food elements lie in this modest powder:

| Vitamins | Amino Acids | Minerals |
|---|---|---|
| vitamin $B_1$ | lysine | phosphorus |
| (thiamine) | tryptophane | potassium |
| vitamin $B_2$ | histidine | magnesium |
| (riboflavin) | phenylalanine | silicon |
| vitamin $B_6$ | leucine | calcium |
| (pyridoxine) | methionine | copper |
| choline | valine | manganese |
| pantothenic acid | glycine | zinc |
| nicotinic acid | alanine | aluminum |
| (niacin) | aspartic acid | sodium |

| Vitamins | Amino Acids | Minerals |
|---|---|---|
| p-aminobenzoic | glutamic acid | iron |
| acid (paba) | proline | tin |
| biotin | hydroxproline | boron |
| (vitamin H) | tyrosine | gold |
| "filtrate factor" | cystine | silver |
| | arginine | |

When you add brewers' yeast to recipes, you need make only one change in the original recipe—increase the vegetable salt ¼ teaspoon for each ¼ cup of yeast added. Here are some suggestions for recipes and the amount of yeast to add to each:

| Food | Amount of Yeast |
|---|---|
| Liver loaf | ¼ cup |
| Stuffed heart | ¼ cup |
| Beef loaf | ¼ cup |
| Stuffed peppers | ¼ cup |
| Hungarian goulash | 3 tbsp. |
| Cheese fondu | 2 tbsp. |
| Baked beans | 3 tbsp. per cup of beans |
| Liver paste | 3 tbsp. |
| Pancakes and waffles | 1 tbsp. |
| Peanut-butter cookies (5 doz.) | ⅞ cup |
| Molasses cookies (5 doz.) | ½ cup |
| Ginger snaps (5 doz.) | ¼ cup |
| Gingerbread | ⅓ cup |
| Pumpkin pie | 2 tbsp. |
| Boston brown bread | ⅓ cup |

## SOYBEANS

The "honorable soybean," the "meat without bones" familiar to the Orient for centuries, is now coming into its own in our Western diet. We have been feeding soybeans to cattle for a hundred years, but have only now discovered how nourishing and delicious they can be on our tables.

Soybeans are one of the few vegetables which contain first-class protein. They have 30 to 50 per cent protein which approaches in quality the protein of meat, eggs, milk, and cheese. Hence soy products can take the place of 20 to 25 per cent of the meat in many recipes without reducing the protein value of the dish. Also, soybeans contain the B vitamins in quantities comparable to those in meat, eggs, and milk, so that if you use soy products to stretch your meat or eggs, the vitamin B content is not reduced. Soybeans are rich in phosphorus and iron and contain some calcium, as well as copper, sodium, potassium, and magnesium. Soybean sprouts, if eaten raw, are a good source of vitamin C.

*Soybean Oil:* The oil of soybeans is extracted and put into such products as shortenings, cooking oils, margarine, salad oils, and mayonnaise.

*Soya Flour and Grits:* Soybeans are ground fine into flour or coarse into grits, which resemble corn meal in consistency. Both flour and grits come in 1-pound packages and larger. Store them just as you would any other packaged food—cool and dry.

*Soy Flakes:* The flakes are made after the oil is removed, hence are high in protein and low in fat. Soy flakes resemble rolled oats, and like grits come in different degrees of fineness. They increase the nutritive when added to oatmeal or other cereals.

*Soy Meats:* Split or coarsely ground soybeans, called soy meats, are chiefly used instead of roasted peanuts in cakes and candies. They can also be cooked and eaten like navy beans.

*Soybeans as a Vegetable:* So far vegetable soybeans are raised only in home gardens for family and local use. In most parts of the country they make an excellent garden crop. They grow in much the same land as corn and are planted like corn. Department of Agriculture bulletins will tell what varieties to plant and how and when.

*Soybean Milk:* A liquid which looks something like milk can be extracted from soybeans. It has much the same food elements as cow's milk, but in smaller amounts. With a little salt and sugar to season it, soy milk can be drunk as a beverage, or it can be used in making custards, soups, breads, cakes, sauces, and such drinks as cocoa. The pulp which is left over is nutritious but has very little flavor. But it can be used with foods which have a strong flavor—in macaroons, for instance. To use it, cook in a double boiler for about an hour, add

½ teaspoon of salt to each pint of mash, and moisten with soy milk if necessary. Store in a covered jar in a cool place.

*Soybean Curd or Tofu:* A curd can be made either by adding lemon juice to soy milk or by letting it ferment naturally. Using lemon juice makes a firm curd, the "bean curd" of Chinatown. Natural fermentation results in a texture like cream cheese. Soy cheese, or Tofu, or soy curd—it comes under all three names—can be purchased in cans, in flat cakes in Chinese stores, or made at home.

## SOYBEAN SPROUTS

You can grow your own bean sprouts in a flower pot or strainer and have a year-round fresh vegetable which can be eaten raw or cooked. A flower pot 6 to 7 inches in diameter and 6½ to 7 inches high is the right size for ½ cup of dried beans. Cover the hole in the bottom of the pot with rust-proof wire netting or cheesecloth. Sort the dried beans and discard shriveled ones. Soak the good beans overnight in 1½ cups of lukewarm water. In the morning drain the beans, put them in the flower pot, and cover them with a damp cheesecloth. Put a piece of damp cardboard over the top of the pot and weight it down. Keep the pot in a dark place at about 78° to 80°F. Three times a day pour water over the soybeans, draining it off immediately. Take care not to break the tender sprouts as they appear. Every evening sprinkle the beans with a chlorinated lime solution to keep down mold. (1 teaspoon of calcium hydrochloride to 3 gallons of water makes enough solution to treat 5 to 6 pounds of beans. It can be stored to use with later plantings.)

The sprouts are ready to use when they are 2 to 3 inches long. Both beans and sprouts are eaten—remove the loose skin from the beans by washing thoroughly. The sprouts can be used raw in salads, cooked in various ways, or used in omelets, stews, fricassees, and chop suey. They lose their crispness if they are put into hot dishes more than a few minutes before serving.

The best varieties of beans for sprouting are Mung, Peking, Cayuga, and Otootan, but other varieties are satisfactory. One-half cup of dry beans of some varieties will make 5 or 6 cups of sprouts; other varieties make only 2 to 3 cups of sprouts.

## BOILED SOYBEAN SPROUTS

Boil the sprouts gently in a small amount of salted water in a covered pan for 10 to 12 minutes. Season with salt, paprika, and a little butter.

## FRIED SOYBEAN SPROUTS

Melt a small amount of fat in a skillet. Add the sprouts and a little hot water, cover, and cook for 10 minutes, stirring frequently. Leave the cover off for the last few minutes to let the sprouts brown. Season with vegetable salt. Combine with onions if desired.

## GREEN SOYBEANS

Boil the beans in the pod, or allow the pods to stand in boiling water for 5 minutes, then cool. The beans can then be easily squeezed out.

Wash the shelled soybeans and boil lightly in salted water, 1 cup to 1 pint of beans, for 15 to 30 minutes.

Or, if preferred, boil in the pod 25 to 30 minutes, cool, and shell. The shelled beans can be cooked 5 to 10 minutes before serving if desired.

Serve with butter and vegetable salt or with crisp bacon. Cold cooked soybeans are excellent in salads.

## BAKED SOYBEANS

| | |
|---|---|
| 1 cup dried large soybeans | 1 onion, thinly sliced |
| Hot Hauser Broth | 1¼ tsp. vegetable salt |
| 4 tbsp. vegetable oil | ¼ lemon cut in thin slices |
| 2 tbsp. blackstrap molasses | Juice of ¼ lemon |

Wash the soybeans and put them in a kettle in which you can boil them next day. Pour 3 cups of water over them and soak for 24 hours. Bring to a boil in the same water and cook slowly, adding hot Hauser Broth as needed to keep the beans covered. Simmer for 3 to 4 hours, until the beans are a light tan. Transfer to a covered baking dish and add the oil and molasses. Bake in a moderate oven (325°F.) for 1-2 hours, depending on the age and quality of the beans, until they are brown and well done. Stir occasionally during the baking and keep the beans in liquid until the last half-hour. At that time add the onion, salt, and the lemon juice and slices. Return to the oven until the top is brown. Serve in the baking dish and garnish with chopped parsley or onion tops.

4 servings.

## SOYBEAN MILK

This food is used by millions of Orientals. When milk disagrees, soybean milk often makes an excellent substitute. Soybean milk can now be bought in cans, or you can make it at home as follows. Soak 1 cup of large soybeans for 24 to 48 hours; then grind them through a meat chopper, or put them in a Fletcherizer until very fine. Add 5 to 6 cups of warm water and boil for about 15 minutes. Strain through fine strainer; add a pinch of vegetable salt and 1 tablespoonful honey. This milk can be used exactly the same as cow's milk.

## SOYBEAN PARSLEY CROQUETTES

| | |
|---|---|
| 1 tbsp. olive oil | ¾ tsp. vegetable salt |
| ¾ cup finely chopped onion | 2 tbsp. minced parsley |
| 1 cup leftover soybeans | 1 tbsp. melted butter |
| 1 cup cooked brown rice | 1 egg, separated |

Put the oil in a heavy skillet. Cook the onions in the oil with the pan covered until they are soft. While the onions cook, put the rice and soybeans through the medium knife of a food grinder. Combine the two mixtures, add seasonings, and the egg yolk slightly beaten. Mix all thoroughly. Divide into heaping servingspoonfuls and mold into the desired shape. Roll in whole-wheat or soya flour. Blend the egg white with 1 tablespoon of water and dip each croquette in the mixture. Then roll in whole yellow corn meal or in dry whole-wheat crumbs. Place in a buttered baking pan and bake in a hot oven (425°F.) about 15 minutes or until browned. Turn once if necessary to brown both sides. Serve with tomato or any desired sauce.

Preparation: 25 minutes.

6 croquettes.

## SOYBEAN NUT CROQUETTES

| | |
|---|---|
| 1 cup baked soybeans, mashed | 1 tbsp. vegetable salt |
| 1 cup cooked brown rice | Soya flour |
| 2 tbsp. chopped nutmeats or green olives | 1 egg, separated |

Combine all ingredients except the egg white, using enough soya flour to make a mixture which is firm enough to mold. Divide into heaping servingspoonfuls and mold into the desired shape. Blend thoroughly the egg white and 1 tablespoon of water. Roll each croquette first in soya flour, then dip in the egg white, and roll in whole yellow corn meal or in whole-wheat crumbs. Place on a buttered baking pan and bake in a hot oven (425°F.) until brown, about 15 minutes. Turn once during baking if necessary to brown both sides. Serve with a garnish of parsley if the loaf is made with olives, or a tart jelly if it is made with nuts.

Preparation: 20-25 minutes.

6 croquettes.

## VANILLA SOYA ICE CREAM

1½ tsp. flaked agar-agar
1 cup soy milk, warmed
¼ cup honey

⅛ tsp. vegetable salt
¾ cup heavy cream
¾ tsp. vanilla

Soak the agar-agar in the warmed milk for 20 minutes, then place over hot water until dissolved—about 10 minutes. Remove from the heat, add honey and salt, and let cool. Whip the cream stiff and add the vanilla. Stir the agar-agar solution frequently as it cools. When it begins to stiffen, quickly beat in the whipped cream and transfer to a freezing tray. Freeze until firm, stirring well once when partly frozen.

NOTE: If the agar-agar mixture stiffens too much before the whipped cream is added, melt it again over boiling water and cool again.

Preparation: 20-25 minutes.

4 servings.

## TO MAKE GLUTEN DOUGH

If you want to make gluten steaks and chops, the easier course is to buy them ready made at a health food store because it is a lot of trouble to make gluten dough for yourself. However, you may want to try it, so here is the process:

Mix 3 cups of flour with 1 cup of cold water and work it into a dough. Ordinary white flour can be used for this since all the minerals in whole-wheat flour will be washed away anyhow. Pull and knead the dough until it is rubbery, then let it stand for 10 minutes. Put it in a bowl large enough so you can work it while cool water runs over it to carry away all the starch. Keep working it until the water runs clear. Then squeeze out all the remaining water and work in ½ teaspoon of vegetable salt. Place in the refrigerator overnight in a covered vessel.

This is the basic recipe for gluten dough, from which vegetarians make many delicious protein dishes.

## GLUTEN STEAKS OR CHOPS

Cut the gluten dough into the size of a minute steak or lamb chop. Season with finely chopped onion, parsley, and vegetable salt, and a pinch of your favorite herbs. Steam the steaks over Hauser Broth, chicken soup, etc., as you would cook dumplings. Then dip in egg and roll in wheat germ, place in a heavy skillet with hot vegetable oil or butter, and sauté to a golden brown.

CHAPTER 22

# *You Can Eat Seven Years Onto Your Life*

⌒

BY SIMPLY CHANGING your diet to the right kinds of food—such as I give you in this book—I believe you can increase your life span by 10 per cent. The first factor which should guide you in your "live longer" eating regimen is the fact that "skinnies," or underweight people, as a rule live longer. One of the most exciting of recent food experiments was made by Dr. H. C. Sherman, well-known nutritionist, who finds that a balanced low-calorie diet is the first requirement for what he calls "the preservation of the characteristics of youth." This includes abundant vitality, a clear skin, and a natural enthusiasm for life. So down with that waistline and off with those extra chins, especially if you are over forty. Start now to learn to like low-calorie natural foods and stop drowning your system in denatured starches and sweets and other fattening foods.

With a "live longer" diet you will eat more good proteins to keep your muscles firm and your arteries pliant. You can load up on fruits and vegetables; they are living, sun-drenched foods, the best natural vitamin insurance. When you do eat starches and sweets, take the natural sugars, the nutty brown whole-grain breads and cereals.

## VITAMINS AND MINERALS—YOUR HEALTH INSURANCE

There is much discussion about vitamins these days which we need not go into here. What I want to impress upon you is that they are important—especially when taken in the form of food. No matter what your jealous in-laws think, I assure you that all vitamins, discovered and undiscovered, are needed for good health and good looks. Especially vitamins A, B₂, and calcium, says Dr. Sherman, are needed for longer life.

To help you thread your way through the bewildering subject of vitamins, I give you here a capsule course in the important vitamin and mineral foods—their richest sources and what they can do to and for you. But always remember two things when you cook—that good food contains the vital factors for good health and good looks, and that it should be prepared in ways which will preserve the most possible vitamins and minerals.

## YOUR KEY TO VITAMIN-RICH FOODS

### VITAMIN A

Vitamin A is one of those used in large amounts in the longevity experiments. But vitamin-A foods have many important functions besides prolonging life. On the outside, it helps to give you a beautiful skin and bright eyes. On the inside, it helps to build up your system's resistance. This important vitamin is found only in animal products such as liver, kidney, butter, and fresh eggs, but chiefly in fish-liver oils. However, if your own liver is in good form, it can make its own vitamin A from the yellow and green vegetables and fruits—carrots, apricots, spinach, parsley, and many others.

Fortunately vitamin A is not easily destroyed in cooking, but short-cooking, described on pages 3-5, helps to make the vegetables more attractive and healthful.

### FOODS FOR VITAMIN A

Include not less than 10,000 units—still better, 20,000 units—each day. I know these are not the minimum amounts, but after all what we want is maximum, not minimum, health; and I believe it is wise to

use maximum amounts of vitamins whenever possible. Check your
daily intake by the following list:

| Excellent Sources | Serving | Units |
|---|---|---|
| Kale | ⅞ cup | 17,500 |
| Liver (calf) | 8 oz. | 12,590 |
| Broccoli | ⅔ cup | 10,800 |
| Turnip greens | 1 cup | 10,000 |
| Spinach | ¾ cup | 9,375 |
| Collards | ⅔ cup | 7,000 |
| Potatoes, sweet | 1 medium | 5,250 |
| Squash, Hubbard | ⅞ cup | 5,000 |
| | | |
| Good Sources | | |
| Pumpkin | ¾ cup | 3,000 |
| Apricots | 2 whole | 2,880 |
| Carrots | ¾ cup | 2,520 |
| Peaches, yellow | 2 halves | 1,400 |
| Prunes | 5 fruit | 1,250 |
| Tomatoes | 1 whole | 1,250 |
| Kidney, lamb | 4 oz. | 1,150 |
| Beans, green | ¾ cup | 750 |
| Peas, green | ½ cup | 750 |
| Butter | 2 tbsp. | 720 |
| Cantaloupe | ½ | 600 |
| Asparagus | 6 6-inch stalks | 525 |
| Cheese, Cheddar | 1½x1½x1¼ inches | 500 |
| Corn, yellow | 1 8-inch ear | 500 |
| Egg | 1 | 500 |
| Soybeans, fresh | ½ cup | 150 |

## ENRICHING YOUR MEALS WITH VITAMIN A

*A small piece of liver or heart* (about ¼ pound) chopped up with
your beef for hamburger or meat loaf enriches with 25,000 units.

*Adding a cup of chopped spinach, parsley, or turnip greens* to your
soups or stews enriches them with 10,000 additional units.

*Eating sweet potatoes in the wintertime* instead of white potatoes
is a simple way of enriching.

*Two ounces of yellow American cheese* sprinkled over your salad
bowl enriches with 1,000 units.

*A scant cup of finely chopped carrots* added to your salad bowl enriches with 2,500 units.

*Egg yolks used instead of white flour for thickening gravies* are excellent for enriching. Each egg adds 500 units.

With a little experimenting you will soon be able to add thousands of extra units of vitamin A to your meals.

### The Vitamin B Family

This important vitamin family keeps growing in members and importance. There are at least twenty known members now, each and every one important in its own right. The most famous, of course, is vitamin B₁, which bears the unromantic name of thiamine chloride. It plays a large part in making people energetic and preventing tiredness, and some also say it keeps the heart in good form.

The second member of the B family is vitamin B₂, better known as riboflavin. It is needed for a good healthy skin and young-looking eyes. This is another of the vitamins Dr. Sherman fed liberally in his longevity experiments.

Pyridoxine, or vitamin B₆, is rapidly making a name for itself because of its power to keep the nerves relaxed.

Niacin amide promotes the health of the blood and aids digestion.

Pantothenic acid, the much-glamorized anti-gray-hair factor, and para-amino-benzoic acid, which helps the glands, are among the better-known members of this illustrious family. Some of the lesser-known members are folic acid, which helps the hair keep its natural color, and biotin, necessary for production of energy and sound mental health.

There are still other members of the B family which are not yet completely understood, but all are essential to good health and looks. And here is the best news of all—this whole wonderful B family is contained in natural foods. Wheat germ, dried brewers' yeast, and blackstrap molasses are some of the richest sources. Another way of adding B vitamins to the diet is by eating Bulgarian yogurt.

*Vitamin B dissolves in water,* just as salt does. For that reason the water in which vegetables are cooked should never, never be poured off. Your entire B family is lost when the water goes down the sink. Baking soda destroys riboflavin and should never be used in vegetable cookery.

## Foods for Vitamin B₁

Vitamin $B_1$ must be taken into the body each and every day because it is not stored in the system. The average man and woman needs between 600 and 800 units each day. Check your intake for the last twenty-four hours by this table:

| Excellent Sources | Serving | Units |
|---|---|---|
| Liver, beef or lamb | 8 oz. | 250 |
| Kidney, lamb | 4 oz. | 196 |
| Lamb, lean | 8 oz. | 196 |
| Veal, lean | 8 oz. | 168 |
| Peanuts | ⅓ cup | 165 |
| *Good Sources* | | |
| Chicken, dark meat | 8 oz. | 156 |
| Soybeans, fresh | ½ cup | 132 |
| Chicken, white meat | 8 oz. | 85 |
| Lima beans, dried | ⅓ cup | 84 |
| Lima beans, green | ½ cup | 84 |
| Codfish | 8 oz. | 70 |
| Navy beans, dried | ¼ cup | 64 |
| Potatoes, white | 1 | 62 |
| Oatmeal | 1 cup | 57.5 |
| Brussel sprouts | 1 cup | 57 |
| Cauliflower | 1 cup | 56 |
| Kale | ⅞ cup | 55 |
| Corn, yellow | 1 8-inch ear | 50 |
| Oysters | ⅓ cup | 49 |
| Turnip greens | 1 cup | 46 |
| Lentils | 2 tbsp. | 42 |
| Milk, whole | 1 cup | 37 |
| Prunes | 5 fruit | 30 |
| Bacon | 4 8½-inch strips | 26 |
| Egg | 1 | 25 |
| Wheat bran | ½ oz. | 15-54 |

### ENRICHING YOUR MEALS WITH THE B FAMILY

The richest sources, for practical purposes, of the vitamins of the B family are brewers' yeast, wheat germ, and organ meats such as liver, kidney, sweetbread, etc. The cheaper beef and lamb liver are just as rich as the expensive calves' liver.

*Using blackstrap molasses,* the blackest you can get, in place of white sugar, is an excellent way of fortifying cakes, cookies, milk, and beverages. Being a vegetable juice boiled down, blackstrap molasses is a very rich source of B vitamins.

*Add two tablespoons of dried brewers' yeast* with celery flavor to your gravies, stews, broths, meat loaves, etc. It's an excellent way of enriching with all the B family.

*Sprinkle a tablespoon or two of wheat germ* over all your hot and cold cereals to make them more delicious and add B vitamins at the same time. Put a few tablespoons in whatever you bake, including waffles and pancakes. Use it in place of bread crumbs to coat foods. Wheat germ also makes gravies richer and more delicious.

*A lazy way of getting B vitamins* is to chew a handful of brewers' yeast tablets. They are a godsend after a cooked-to-death meal and don't really taste bad.

### FOODS FOR RIBOFLAVIN

Adults should have 3 to 5 milligrams of riboflavin each day. Here are the richest sources:

| Sources | Serving | Milligrams |
|---|---|---|
| Beef liver | ¼ lb. | 2 |
| Brewers' yeast | 1 tbsp. | 1 |
| Milk, whole | 1 qt. | 2 |
| Yogurt | 1 qt. | 2 |
| Wheat germ | ½ cup | 0.8 |

## Enriching Your Meals with Riboflavin[1]

*Chop up beef liver* or any other liver and mix it into meat patties, meat loaf, or make a liver paste.

*Add brewers' yeast* to gravies, stews, or tomato juice.

*Sprinkle wheat germ* over your green salads.

*Drink several glasses of yogurt* each day.

## Vitamin C

People with all sorts of strange allergies will find vitamin C their best friend. It's another of the vitamins which enhance your looks, and stave off old age, and build up resistance. Fortunate indeed are those who can eat all they want of fresh fruits and vegetables—citrus fruits, green peppers, and tomatoes.

*Vitamin C is easily destroyed in cooking;* therefore all vegetables should be short-cooked and cooking utensils covered tightly. Never use soda to keep green vegetables green. A few drops of lemon juice added to the vegetables while cooking guards against loss of vitamin C and helps preserve the green color. Always prepare your vitamin C fruits and vegetables at the last possible moment because destruction of the vitamin begins the moment a cut surface is exposed to air. As long as foods are kept in the refrigerator, deterioration is not rapid.

## Foods for Vitamin C

Use vitamin C foods freely. The average adult needs between 1,500 and 2,000 units a day. Check your intake by this list:

| Excellent Sources | Serving | Units |
|---|---|---|
| Broccoli | ⅔ cup | 2,400 |
| Kale | ⅞ cup | 2,185 |
| Liver, calves', beef, or lamb | 8 oz. | 1,725 |
| Cauliflower | 1 cup | 1,500 |
| Cantaloupe | ½ | 1,200 |

[1] For less well-known members of the B family, see *Diet Does It*. The therapeutic values of all known vitamins are discussed there.

| Excellent Sources | Serving | Unit |
|---|---|---|
| Mustard greens | 1 cup | 1,200 |
| Peppers, red | 1 3-inch piece | 1,150 |
| Spinach | 1½ cups | 1,125 |
| Strawberries | ¾ cup | 1,000 |
| Brussel sprouts | 1 cup | 1,000 |
| Grapefruit | ½ cup | 850 |
| Cabbage | 1 cup | 845 |
| Orange | 1 medium | 800 |
| Pineapple | 1 cup | 750 |
| Turnips | ¾ cup | 720 |
| Beet greens | 1 cup | 700 |
| Collards | ⅔ cup | 700 |
| Peppers, green | 1 3-inch piece | 677 |
| Soybeans, green | ½ cup | 600 |
| Turnip greens | 1 cup | 600 |
| Parsnips | ¾ cup | 540 |
| Tomato | 1 | 475 |
| Lima beans, green | ½ cup | 450 |
| Asparagus | 6 6-inch stalks | 432 |
| Potatoes, sweet | 1 medium | 425 |
| Endive | ½ cup | 400 |
| Sardine | 1 large | 360 |
| Avocado | ½ | 340 |
| Peaches, yellow | 1 | 281 |

| Good Sources | | |
|---|---|---|
| Apples | 1 (2½ inches in diameter) | 279 |
| Banana | 1 | 275 |
| Rhubarb | 1 cup | 270 |
| Artichokes | 1 (3 inches in diameter) | 262 |
| Cranberries | 1 cup | 260 |
| Beans, green | ¾ cup | 225 |
| Raspberries | ⅔ cup | 225 |
| Peas, green | ½ cup | 225 |
| Potatoes, white | 1 | 220 |
| Watermelon | 1 4-inch slice | 210 |
| Water cress | ½ cup | 200 |
| Squash, Hubbard | 1¾ cups | 150 |
| Currants, red | ½ cup | 150 |
| Lettuce, head | ½ head | 50 |

## Enriching Your Meals with Vitamin C

Citrus fruits—lemons, limes, grapefruit, and oranges—are excellent for enriching your meals with vitamin C.

*Make your salad dressing with lemon juice.* One ounce of lemon juice alone enriches your meal with 350 units of vitamin C.

*Sprinkle lemon juice on fish* and mix lemon juice with butter and a bit of parsley to use on chops and steaks.

*An inexpensive and excellent way* to enrich your meals is by using more parsley. Not only for decoration, but chop it and eat it. One ounce of freshly chopped parsley added to your stews, salads, hamburgers, or over your potatoes (mashed—in the modern manner—baked, or boiled) gives you over 1,000 extra units of vitamin C.

## Vitamin D

More than any other vitamin, vitamin D has to do with strong, healthy bones and hard white teeth. Also it helps to keep the nerves relaxed. And yet few foods have enough of this vitamin to supply our daily needs, and so it is a good investment to use vitamin D milk and other foods enriched with vitamin D. During the winter months it is wise to add to your diet that richest of all vitamin D foods—cod-liver, haliver, and shark-liver oils in capsule form. When you see the low vitamin D contents of the foods in the following list, you will see the reason for this.

Fortunately nature has given us a source of vitamin D in the sun. The skin contains a substance, provitamin D, which is changed to vitamin D by the action of sunlight—that is sunlight which is not robbed of ultraviolet rays by smoke, dust, or window glass. Artificial sunlight produced by the carbon arc lamp and the ultraviolet rays of the mercury-vapor quartz lamp will also produce vitamin D through their action on the skin.

## FOODS FOR VITAMIN D

The average adult should have 1,000 units daily of vitamin D.

| Excellent Sources | Serving | Units |
|---|---|---|
| Mackerel | 8 oz. | 1,400 |
| Sardines | 3 oz. | 1,350 |
| Salmon | 8 oz. | 1,058 |
| Egg yolk | 1 | 100 |
| Vitamin-D milk | 1 pt. | 67-200 |
| Liver, beef | 8 oz. | 104 |
| | | |
| *Good Sources* | | |
| Halibut | 8 oz. | 30 |
| Butter | 1 oz. | 30 |
| Cream | 1 oz. | 12 |
| Cheese, Cheddar | 1 oz. | 10 |
| | | |
| *Richest Sources* | | |
| Irradiated yeast | 1 tablet | 1,000 |
| Cod-liver oil | 1 tablet | 350 |
| Haliver oil | 1 tablet | 600 |

## ENRICHING YOUR MEALS WITH VITAMIN D

*Enrich your salad oil* with vitamin D by this simple expedient: Pour the oil into a nice bright tin pan, to a depth of half an inch. Set the pan where the noonday sun can pour on the oil for about 2 hours. (Ordinary window glass filters out the ultraviolet rays which make vitamin D, remember.) Then pour the vitaminized oil into a dark bottle. This simple process is the humble forerunner of a scientifically applied process now used in the University of Wisconsin.

*Orange, lemon, and grapefruit peels* contain vitamin D because they are constantly exposed to the sun. Use grated citrus peel whenever possible in baking or other cooking. It's delicious in stewed dried fruits, for instance.

## VITAMIN E

This is the vitamin about which a hot debate is raging. It is sometimes called the sex or personality vitamin, a name which may be justified in that all healthy individuals need it for reproduction and glandular health. The modern nutritionist will insist upon large amounts of it for prospective mothers.

Using whole-grain breads and cereals is a good insurance against deficiency of vitamin E. Wheat germ is the richest natural source of this vitamin, but it is also contained in avocado oil, corn oil, soybean oil, peanut oil, and in smaller amounts in lettuce, tomatoes, carrots, egg yolks, and nuts.

## PROTEINS BUILD YOU UP

"Does man gain in vigor, happiness, and longevity when larger amounts of protein are eaten?" The question was put to Dr. James McLester, well-known specialist in diet and nutrition. A decided "yes" was his answer. And so the wise man or woman will eat larger amounts of the good proteins which I shall list below.

### Good Protein Foods

The daily requirement of protein for the average man is 70 grams; for a woman, about 60 grams. During adolescence and periods of rapid growth the amount is as high as 100 grams for boys and 80 grams for girls. Check your intake of protein for twenty-four hours by the following table:

| Food | Amount | Grams of Protein |
|------|--------|------------------|
| Beef | Average serving | 17 |
| Chicken | Average serving | 18 |
| Heart | Average serving | 11 |
| Kidney | Average serving | 11 |
| Lamb chop | 1 medium | 10 |
| Liver | Average serving | 19 |
| Steak | Average serving | 21 |
| Turkey | Average serving | 21 |
| Milk, whole | 1 qt. | 30 |
| Yogurt | 1 qt. (de-fatted) | 33 |
| Cheese | 1 piece, 2x1x1 inches | 12 |
| Cottage cheese | 3 tbsp. | 10 |
| Cream cheese | 1½ tbsp. | 8 |
| Egg | 1 | 6 |

| Food | Amount | Grams of Protein |
|------|--------|------------------|
| Fish | Average serving | 12 |
| Salmon, canned | ⅓ cup | 22 |
| Tuna fish, canned | 2 tbsp. | 12 |
| Shrimp | 6 medium | 8 |
| Peanuts | 2 tbsp. | 10 |
| Peanut butter | 2 tbsp. | 14 |
| Walnuts | ½ cup | 8 |
| Pecans | 10 meats | 3 |
| Lima beans | ½ cup | 8 |
| Navy beans | ½ cup | 6 |
| Soybeans, dried | ½ cup | 51 |
| Lentils | ½ cup | 9 |
| Peas, dried | ½ cup | 7 |
| Barley, whole | ½ cup cooked | 8 |
| Buckwheat, whole | ⅓ cup | 12 |
| Rice, brown | ¾ cup | 3 |
| Shredded wheat | 1 biscuit | 3 |
| Wheat germ | ½ cup | 4 |

## BE A MISER ABOUT MINERALS

Minerals are just as important as vitamins; in fact, they frequently do their good work together. Many important body functions are performed by the minerals, one of the most important being to maintain the acid-alkaline balance of the blood. Therefore an unforgivable sin in cooking is to throw away the water in which vegetables are cooked, for this water is full of valuable minerals.

### ACID-ALKALINE BALANCE

When the body burns up food, the minerals remain as an ash; they will not burn. This ash is acid or alkaline, depending on which minerals have been eaten. Now, the blood must remain neutral or very slightly alkaline, and the minerals in food help to maintain this condition. A well-balanced diet is one which supplies more than enough alkaline ash to counteract the acid ash, and thus preserve a proper acid-alkaline balance. Whenever excessive acidity exists, the acid foods should be cut down and more fruits and vegetables eaten.

## ACID FOODS

Meat, fish, poultry, and cereals are the acid-forming foods. The following list gives the percentage of acidity in 100-gram portions.

| Food | % of Acid |
|------|-----------|
| Oysters | 30 |
| Egg yolk | 26.69 |
| Chicken | 17.01 |
| Beef | 13.95 |
| Veal | 13.52 |
| Oatmeal | 12.93 |
| Eggs, whole | 11.10 |
| Rice | 8.1 |
| Crackers | 7.81 |
| Whole-wheat bread | 7.3 |
| Corn, dried | 5.95 |
| Egg white | 5.24 |
| Peanuts | 3.9 |

## ALKALINE FOODS

Generally speaking, fruits, vegetables, nuts, and milk are alkaline in their reaction, another good reason why these foods should be used liberally in the well-balanced diet. Even lemons and oranges are alkaline-forming. Here are some of the best-liked foods and their percentage of alkalinity per 100-gram portion:

| Food | % of Alkalinity |
|------|-----------------|
| Lima beans, dried | 41.65 |
| Beans, dried | 23.87 |
| Raisins | 23.83 |
| Almonds | 12.38 |
| Beets | 10.86 |
| Carrots | 10.82 |
| Celery | 7.78 |
| Melon | 7.47 |
| Chestnuts | 7.42 |
| Lettuce | 7.37 |
| Potatoes | 7.19 |
| Peas, dried | 7.07 |
| Currants, dried | 5.97 |

| Food | % of Alkalinity |
|---|---|
| Oranges | 5.61 |
| Bananas | 5.56 |
| Lemons | 5.45 |
| Cauliflower | 5.33 |
| Peaches | 5.04 |
| Cabbage | 4.34 |
| Apples | 3.76 |
| Radishes | 2.87 |
| Turnips | 2.68 |
| Milk, cow's | 2.37 |

## CALCIUM FOODS

Foods which supply calcium are of tremendous importance besides being responsible for strong bones and sound teeth. In combination with vitamin D, calcium helps to keep us relaxed and calm. Most American menus are woefully short of this important mineral unless some of these calcium-rich foods are included:

American cheese
Swiss cheese
Cottage cheese
Creamed cheese
Yogurt
Leafy vegetables

Buttermilk
Whole milk
Blackstrap molasses
Lemons
Oranges
Hazel nuts

## IRON FOODS

Many people are listless because they suffer from a deficiency of iron. If any mineral can be called the glamour mineral, it is iron. Iron makes red blood, increases vitality, and gives you that plus personality. Here are the best iron foods:

Blackstrap molasses
Liver
Turnip greens
Wheat germ
Kidney
Dates
Beet tops

Apricots
Dandelions
Spinach
Prunes
Raisins
Whole-wheat bread

## IODINE FOODS

This mineral could be called the beauty mineral, for it is necessary to the healthy functioning of the glands, good-looking hair, and an unblemished skin.

Most meals are sadly deficient in iodine, especially for people who live in the middle of America around the Great Lakes region, or in the Northwest. Rains and floods seem to wash this important mineral into the ocean, so we have to go there to get sufficient iodine.

Every time you eat sea food of any kind you are getting a bit of this important element, and now sea vegetables and sea greens are being used by many who live near the ocean, and in dried or powdered form by those who live away from the ocean. Thousands of people are using an iodized vegetable salt in place of the ordinary white salt, which gives them small amounts of organic iodine.[1]

Here is a list of the best iodine foods:

Oysters                     Sea greens
Shrimp                      Sea water
Lobsters                    Iodized vegetable salt
Salt-water fish

## A "LIVE LONGER" MENU

Your "live longer" menu, applying the principles we have been discussing in this chapter, would look something like this:

*Upon arising:*
Drink a glass of your favorite fresh fruit or vegetable juice. Drink it through a straw. Wait 30 minutes and follow with a good breakfast.

*Breakfast:*
Raw or cooked Swiss Breakfast served with rich milk, not cream, and sweetened with honey or blackstrap molasses. If you prefer, 1 or 2 fresh eggs any way except fried. One or 2 slices of whole-wheat or

---

[1] For information about other mineral foods, see *Diet Does It.*

rye bread buttered lightly. If you like coffee, have *café au lait* (half hot milk and half coffee).

*Midmorning:*

A glass of yogurt or carrot juice or a cup of hot broth. Take your choice.

*Noon:* It is preferable to have your big meal at noon.

A salad of chopped raw vegetables with lemon juice and oil dressing; broiled liver or chops, or meat loaf. One or 2 short-cooked vegetables. One potato cooked in the jacket—unless you are overweight. Fresh or honeyed fruit. Papaya and mint tea with honey.

*Midafternoon:*

A glass of yogurt or orange juice if you are hungry.

*Evening:*

A simple one-dish meal such as: thick vegetable soup served with dark bread: or milk toast made with whole-grain bread; or a dish of yogurt and 1 large mealy baked potato. A cup of herb tea.

*Before retiring:*

A glass of fruit juice or yogurt with 2 tablespoons of brewers' yeast.

# CHAPTER 23

# *Special Menus and Diets*

─────────⌣─────────

## GOOD-HEALTH MENUS

FOR THE LUCKY normal eaters with no special problems of diet, there need be little restriction except possibly a certain cutting down of starches. In all meals I have included a first-class protein to give strength and stamina and keep the body slim and trim.

It is permissible, even desirable, to have your largest meal at noon instead of at night.

*Extra Vitamins:* Right after breakfast, with your beverage, is the best time to enrich your daily diet with whatever vitamins your nutritionist has prescribed. In all my good-health diets I include about 10,000 units of vitamin A and 1,000 units of vitamin D in the form of yeast concentrate. Also, sometime during the day it is wise to include 2 tablespoons of brewers' yeast—this can be taken in juices or embodied in any kind of food. I find the new brewers' yeast with celery flavor the most desirable.

If you get hungry between meals, eat a piece of fruit or drink a glass of vegetable juice.

*Some New Beverages:* Instead of having coffee with every meal, try one of the fragrant herb teas. The French people love their *tisane* and swear that it helps them digest their sometimes overrich meals. Here in America you can have your choice of fragrant peppermint tea, delicious strawberry tea, or that great favorite, papaya tea. Treat your family to a cup of papaya tea combined with mint tea and listen to them rave.

Here are seven good-health menus. On the basis of these make up your own on the same principles:

## MENU I

*Breakfast:*
  1 large glass prune and grapefruit juice (equal amounts mixed)
  Soya waffle with brown sugar and butter.

*Luncheon:*
  Salad bowl (your favorite chopped vegetables plus 1 cup shredded American cheese with lemon-oil dressing)
  Whole-wheat toast
  Baked apple with raisins and cream
  Beverage

*Dinner:*
  Green salad with French dressing
  Lamb stew with young potatoes and vegetables
  Cheesecake
  Beverage

## MENU II

*Breakfast:*
  1 glass orange juice
  Hot Swiss Breakfast
  Beverage

*Luncheon:*
  Wild rice nutburgers
  Mixed green salad bowl sprinkled with wheat germ
  Fresh or honeyed fruit
  Beverage

*Dinner:*
  Vegetable-juice cocktail
  Beef Stroganoff
  Brown rice
  Fruit salad
  Beverage

## MENU III

*Breakfast:*
  ½ grapefruit
  Eggs with crisp bacon
  Rye-bread toast
  Beverage

*Luncheon:*
  Cottage cheese and prune salad
  Soya muffins
  Beverage

*Dinner:*
  Waldorf salad sprinkled with toasted wheat germ
  Broiled salt-water fish
  Stewed or broiled tomatoes
  Potatoes boiled in their jackets and sprinkled with parsley
  Apricot pie
  Beverage

## MENU IV

*Breakfast:*
  ½ grapefruit
  Soft-cooked egg
  Soya muffins with honey butter
  Beverage

*Luncheon:*
  Hot broth
  Hamburger with parsley and wheat germ
  Whole-wheat toast
  Fresh or honeyed fruit

*Dinner:*
  Chopped water-cress salad
  Cheese soufflé
  Short-cooked spinach with lemon juice
  Short-cooked carrots sprinkled with mint
  Broiled grapefruit sweetened with blackstrap molasses
  Beverage

## MENU V

*Breakfast:*
    1 glass tomato juice
    Scrambled eggs
    Corn bread with honey butter
    Beverage

*Luncheon:*
    Baked lima beans
    Stewed tomatoes
    Whole-wheat crackers
    Beverage

*Dinner:*
    Mixed green salad
    Broiled chicken
    Short-cooked beet greens
    Sweet potatoes
    Apricot soufflé
    Beverage

## MENU VI

*Breakfast:*
    Fresh fruit juice
    Whole-wheat pancakes with maple syrup
    Beverage

*Luncheon:*
    Mushroom soup
    Stuffed pear salad with French dressing (mix cream cheese and wheat
        germ and stuff the pear)
    Melba toast
    Beverage

*Dinner:*
    Chopped celery, carrot, and raisin salad with cream dressing
    Ground round steak mixed with parsley and wheat germ
    French-fried potatoes
    Cauliflower
    ½ grapefruit
    Beverage

## MENU VII

*Breakfast:*
  Fruit juice
  Raw Swiss Breakfast
  Beverage

*Luncheon:*
  Tuna-fish salad with celery
  Rye bread
  Applesauce
  Beverage

*Dinner:*
  Cucumber and tomato salad
  Broiled liver with crisp bacon
  Parsley potatoes
  Green beans
  Prune pie
  Beverage

### MENUS TO HELP YOU GAIN WEIGHT

It is much better to be a little underweight than overweight. On the other hand, a little padding of fat in the right places helps to protect health and create those nice aesthetic curves.

If you wish to gain weight, you should do everything in your power to gain health. It is therefore important to eat larger amounts of those foods which will keep you relaxed, for tension often prevents people from gaining sufficient weight. Practically all vitamins and minerals are needed for such relaxation, but calcium and vitamin D are of special importance.

Should your appetite be poor, check up and see if you eat enough of the vitamin B foods. If not, be sure and add extra amounts of brewers' yeast, and also try and eat at least one very ripe banana every day. Ripe bananas when mixed with milk or fruit juice, or simply eaten with meals, help you to get more good out of the foods you eat. That is why more and more bananas are used in baby diets.

Last but not least, be sure to use some vegetable oils. They are

especially important in weight gaining because they not only supply
extra calories, but give you vitamins B₆, E, and K, plus the important
fatty acids. Peanut oil and corn oil are richest in these fatty acids.
However, all vegetable oils are valuable. Use them for salad dressings
and for cooking.

Do not stuff yourself, but rather eat smaller meals more often. It is
wise to include a midmorning, midafternoon, and before-retiring
snack. Here are some menus to help you gain weight and health:

## MONDAY

*Breakfast:*
  1 large glass sweet fruit juice
  Swiss Breakfast (raw or cooked) with cream
  1 glass vitamin D milk, or *café au lait* (half coffee and half hot milk)

*Midmorning:*
  1 banana whipped into 1 glass milk, or 1 glass yogurt, or 1 glass carrot
    juice
  1,000 units of vitamin D yeast concentrate

*Luncheon:*
  Fruit salad with peanut-oil mayonnaise
  2 scrambled eggs
  Whole-wheat toast with butter
  1 glass vitamin D milk

*Midafternoon:*
  1 tablespoon blackstrap molasses in 1 glass milk, or 1 ripe banana whipped
    into 1 glass pineapple juice

*Dinner:*
  Hot vegetable broth
  Broiled liver with crisp bacon
  Short-cooked spinach sprinkled with hot peanut or olive oil
  Apple pie with cream
  Papaya-mint tea sweetened with honey

*Before retiring:*
  1 tablespoon brewers' yeast stirred into 1 glass yogurt, or 1 tablespoon
    blackstrap molasses stirred into hot milk

### TUESDAY

*Breakfast:*
  1 glass pineapple juice
  Cooked cereal with cream sprinkled with wheat germ and dates
  1 glass vitamin D milk, or *café au lait* (half coffee and half hot milk)

*Midmorning:*
  1 banana whipped into 1 glass milk, or 1 glass yogurt, or 1 glass carrot juice
  1,000 units vitamin D yeast concentrate

*Luncheon:*
  Chopped egg and celery salad with lemon and peanut-oil dressing
  Rye-bread toast, buttered
  1 glass hot or cold milk flavored with blackstrap molasses

*Midafternoon:*
  1 tablespoon blackstrap molasses in 1 glass milk, or 1 ripe banana whipped into 1 glass pineapple juice

*Dinner:*
  Broiled fish
  Stewed tomatoes
  Baked potato
  Green mixed salad with peanut-oil and lemon dressing
  Baked apple with cream
  Papaya-mint tea sweetened with honey

*Before retiring:*
  1 tablespoon brewers' yeast stirred into 1 glass yogurt, or 1 tablespoon blackstrap molasses stirred into hot milk

### WEDNESDAY

*Breakfast:*
  1 large glass orange juice
  1 soft-cooked egg
  2 slices whole-wheat toast with butter and honey
  1 glass vitamin D milk, or *café au lait* (half coffee and half hot milk)

*Midmorning:*
  1 banana whipped into 1 glass milk, or 1 glass yogurt, or 1 glass carrot juice
  1,000 units vitamin D yeast concentrate

*Luncheon:*

Tuna-fish and celery salad with peanut-oil mayonnaise
Rye bread
1 glass hot or cold milk flavored with blackstrap molasses

*Midafternoon:*

1 tablespoon blackstrap molasses in 1 glass of milk, or 1 ripe banana
whipped into 1 glass pineapple juice

*Dinner:*

Chopped cabbage and raisin salad with sour-cream dressing
Chopped round steak mixed with wheat germ and parsley
Beet greens
Stewed apricots with cream
Papaya-mint tea sweetened with honey

*Before retiring:*

1 tablespoon brewers' yeast stirred into 1 glass yogurt, or 1 tablespoon
blackstrap molasses stirred into hot milk

## THURSDAY

*Breakfast:*

Cooked cereal with wheat germ, honey, and cream
Whole-wheat toast
1 glass vitamin D milk, or *café au lait* (half coffee and half milk)

*Midmorning:*

1 banana whipped into 1 glass milk, or 1 glass yogurt, or 1 glass carrot
juice
1,000 units vitamin D yeast concentrate

*Luncheon:*

Large fruit salad sprinkled with chopped nuts
Whole-wheat crackers
1 glass yogurt with cinnamon and honey

*Midafternoon:*

1 tablespoon blackstrap molasses in 1 glass milk, or 1 ripe banana whipped
into 1 glass pineapple juice

*Dinner:*

Waldorf salad
Beef Stroganoff

Buttered green beans
Green salad
Apple pie
Papaya-mint tea sweetened with honey

*Before retiring:*
   1 tablespoon brewers' yeast stirred into 1 glass of yogurt, or 1 tablespoon
   blackstrap molasses stirred into hot milk

### FRIDAY

*Breakfast:*
   Stewed apricots
   Crisp bacon
   Whole-wheat toast and butter
   1 glass vitamin D milk, or *café au lait* (half coffee and half hot milk)

*Midmorning:*
   1 banana whipped into 1 glass milk, or 1 glass yogurt, or 1 glass carrot
   juice
   1,000 units vitamin D yeast concentrate

*Luncheon:*
   Cottage cheese salad with pears or pineapple
   Rye crackers
   1 glass hot or cold milk flavored with blackstrap molasses

*Midafternoon:*
   1 tablespoon blackstrap molasses in 1 glass milk, or 1 ripe banana whipped
   into 1 glass pineapple juice

*Dinner:*
   Steak with onions
   Cauliflower sprinkled with wheat germ and browned in butter
   Cucumber salad
   Baked custard
   Papaya-mint tea sweetened with honey

*Before retiring:*
   1 tablespoon brewers' yeast stirred into 1 glass yogurt, or 1 tablespoon
   blackstrap molasses stirred into hot milk

## SATURDAY

*Breakfast:*

1 large glass orange juice
Scrambled eggs
Corn muffin with honey butter
1 glass vitamin D milk, or *café au lait* (half coffee and half hot milk)

*Midmorning:*

1 banana whipped into 1 glass milk, or 1 glass yogurt, or 1 glass carrot juice
1,000 units vitamin D yeast concentrate

*Luncheon:*

Pancakes Roberto with brown sugar and butter
Fresh or stewed fruit
1 glass vitamin D milk

*Midafternoon:*

1 tablespoon blackstrap molasses in 1 glass milk, or 1 ripe banana whipped into 1 glass pineapple juice

*Dinner:*

Tomato-juice cocktail
Broiled steak with onions
Cauliflower sprinkled with cheese
Potato in jacket
Sliced banana with cream
Papaya-mint tea sweetened with honey

*Before retiring:*

1 tablespoon brewers' yeast stirred into 1 glass yogurt, or 1 tablespoon blackstrap molasses stirred into hot milk

## SUNDAY

*Breakfast:*

Honeyed apricots
Whole-wheat waffle
Crisp bacon
1 glass vitamin D milk, or *café au lait* (half coffee and half hot milk)

*Midmorning:*

 1 banana whipped into 1 glass milk, or 1 glass yogurt, or 1 glass carrot juice

 1,000 units vitamin D yeast concentrate

*Luncheon:*

 Stuffed tomato with cottage cheese, wheat germ, and celery

 Whole-wheat crackers

 1 glass vitamin D milk (hot or cold and flavored with blackstrap molasses)

*Buffet supper:*

 Cole slaw with cream dressing

 Cold cuts

 Cranberry sauce

 Baked sweet potatoes

*Before retiring:*

 1 tablespoon brewers' yeast stirred into 1 glass yogurt, or 1 tablespoon blackstrap molasses stirred into hot milk

## EASY REDUCING DIETS

I had intended this book to be fun, showing how really good food can be prepared in the modern healthful manner. But every day I am besieged by fat ladies and gentlemen who have all sorts of mistaken ideas about reducing—subconsciously they hate to give up their "smashed potato" diets. So I have decided to give you here a week of menus which will help to build you down, my Seven-Day Painless Reducing Diet. Also, for those who do not need such strenuous reducing, my Be More Beautiful Diet, a one-day house-cleaning regimen.

These menus can be followed with little or no hardship, and you will be amazed at the way the fat rolls off. Follow these menus until you are your own slim self again. Or you can make up your own menus by remembering to have two or three first-class protein foods every day. Proteins have a dynamic action which helps to burn up unneeded calories; and at the same time they keep the skin and muscles firm. This is a principle which must never be overlooked in any reducing diet. Don't use any such extras as gravies, mayonnaise, sugar, and so forth. They are the foods which prevent you from losing weight. Use the reducing dressings on your salads. I find the Vegetable Reducing Dressing most delicious, also the Yogurt Dressing. Mineral-oil dressing, it has been proved, is definitely harmful. Smart people no longer use cream and sugar in their coffee. Try your coffee black for a week and you will never go back to the fattening cream and sugar. But if black coffee doesn't appeal to you, try *café au lait,* which is half coffee and half hot milk.

Here, then, are the menus, in which I have used those foods which are plentiful and easy to get. In just seven days you can be slimmer and trimmer, so get going and good luck. Before you begin, and as you progress, check your weight by the tables on page 276.

## MY SEVEN-DAY PAINLESS REDUCING DIET

### MONDAY

*Breakfast:*
½ grapefruit
Black coffee

*Midmorning:*
Glass of buttermilk, yogurt, tomato juice, or hot broth

*Luncheon:*
2 hard-cooked eggs
Chopped carrot salad
Beverage

*Midafternoon:*
1 cup tea with lemon, or 1 glass lemonade, or 1 cup clear broth

*Dinner:*
1 cup clear broth
2 slices lean lamb or beef
Combination salad of cucumbers, tomatoes, and celery
Demitasse

*Before retiring:*
This is a good time to take your vitamins or 1 tablespoon brewers' yeast in 1 glass fruit juice, vegetable juice, or yogurt

## TUESDAY

*Breakfast:*
  1 sliced orange
  Black coffee

*Midmorning:*
  1 glass buttermilk, yogurt, or tomato juice, or 1 cup hot broth

*Luncheon:*
  1 large hamburger with lots of chopped parsley and onion
  ½ head lettuce sprinkled with lemon juice and vegetable salt
  Beverage

*Midafternoon:*
  1 cup tea with lemon, or 1 glass lemonade, or 1 cup clear broth

*Dinner:*
  Carrot and celery sticks
  Large slice of lean roast beef
  ½ cup spinach
  ½ broiled grapefruit
  Demitasse

*Before retiring:*
  This is a good time to take your vitamins or 1 tablespoon brewers' yeast
    in 1 glass fruit juice, vegetable juice, or yogurt

## WEDNESDAY

*Breakfast:*
  Baked apple or applesauce
  Black coffee

*Midmorning:*
  1 glass buttermilk, yogurt, or tomato juice, or 1 cup hot broth

*Luncheon:*
  2 eggs à la mode (2 boiled or poached eggs topped with ½ cup stewed
    tomatoes)
  Chopped carrot and apple salad
  Beverage

*Midafternoon:*
  1 cup tea with lemon, or 1 glass lemonade, or 1 cup clear broth

*Dinner:*

 Fruit salad
 2 broiled lean lamb chops
 ½ cup green beans sprinkled with parsley
 Demitasse

*Before retiring:*

 This is a good time to take your vitamins or 1 tablespoon brewers' yeast
 in 1 glass fruit juice, vegetable juice, or yogurt

## THURSDAY

*Breakfast:*

 ½ grapefruit
 Black coffee

*Midmorning:*

 1 glass buttermilk, yogurt, or tomato juice, or 1 cup hot broth

*Luncheon:*

 2 slices broiled liver
 Chopped cabbage and green-pepper salad
 Beverage

*Midafternoon:*

 1 cup tea with lemon, or 1 glass lemonade, or 1 cup clear broth

*Dinner:*

 Vegetable juice cocktail
 1 large veal chop
 Fresh celery
 Applesauce
 Demitasse

*Before retiring:*

 This is a good time to take your vitamins or 1 tablespoon brewers' yeast
 in 1 glass fruit juice, vegetable juice, or yogurt

## FRIDAY

*Breakfast:*

 Fruit or tomato juice
 Black coffee

*Midmorning:*

 1 glass buttermilk, yogurt, or tomato juice, or 1 cup hot broth

*Luncheon:*
   Eggs à la mode (two poached eggs covered with ½ cup chopped spinach)
   Celery and carrot sticks
   Beverage

*Midafternoon:*
   1 cup tea with lemon, or 1 glass lemonade, or 1 cup clear broth

*Dinner:*
   1 cup Hauser Broth
   1 large slice broiled fish (sole, whitefish, or halibut)
   ½ cup stewed tomatoes and celery
   ½ grapefruit, fresh or broiled
   Demitasse

*Before retiring:*
   This is a good time to take your vitamins or 1 tablespoon brewers' yeast
      in 1 glass fruit juice, vegetable juice, or yogurt


## SATURDAY

*Breakfast:*
   Sliced orange
   Black coffee

*Midmorning:*
   1 glass buttermilk, yogurt, or tomato juice, or 1 cup hot broth

*Luncheon:*
   3 tablespoons cottage cheese mixed with chives or onions on a bed of
      lettuce
   Raw celery and carrots
   Beverage

*Midafternoon:*
   1 cup tea with lemon, or 1 glass lemonade, or a cup clear broth

*Dinner:*
   Broiled grapefruit
   2 slices roast lamb
   ½ cup spinach, string beans, or broccoli
   Baked apple
   Demitasse

*Before retiring:*

This is a good time to take your vitamins or 1 tablespoon brewers' yeast in a glass of fruit juice, vegetable juice, or yogurt

## SUNDAY

*Breakfast:*

2 scrambled eggs
1 slice whole-wheat toast
Tea or black coffee

*Midmorning:*

1 glass buttermilk, yogurt, or tomato juice, or 1 cup hot broth

*Luncheon:*

Large salad bowl (chopped lettuce, celery, water cress) mixed with ½ cup cold meat or chicken
Baked apple or applesauce
Beverage

*Midafternoon:*

1 cup tea with lemon, or 1 glass lemonade, or 1 cup clear broth

*Dinner:*

1 cup broth
½ broiled chicken
½ cup cauliflower
4 stewed apricots
Demitasse

*Before retiring:*

This is a good time to take your vitamins or 1 tablespoon brewers' yeast in 1 glass fruit juice, vegetable juice, or yogurt

## BE MORE BEAUTIFUL DIET

After too much feasting during holidays, when you begin to feel stuffy or when your best dinner dress sticks out in the wrong places, why not do, as many of the beautiful ladies out here do—declare a holiday. Stop overeating and go on one of these simple housecleaning diets. It is just for one day, and even the weaker sisters can give up stuffing for that long. Take your choice—many prefer the liquid diet.

However, you may feel less sorry for yourself on the more solid Beauty Day.

## ONE-DAY BEAUTY DIET

*Breakfast:*
Sliced orange or ½ grapefruit
Black coffee if you insist, but herb teas are preferable

*Midmorning:*
Your choice of any fresh fruit (except bananas)

*Luncheon:*
Chopped carrot and cottage-cheese salad sprinkled with lemon (no oil dressing)
1 cup vegetable broth, or papaya-mint tea sweetened with honey

*Midafternoon:*
Your choice of any fresh fruit (except bananas)

*Dinner:*
Spinach short-cooked and sprinkled with lemon
Fresh fruit salad
1 dish yogurt
Demitasse or herb tea

*Before retiring:*
If hungry, more fruit or fruit juice, or hot papaya-mint tea

## ONE-DAY HOLLYWOOD LIQUID DIET

*Breakfast:*
1 large glass orange or grapefruit juice
Your choice of 2 cups hot peppermint or papaya tea with honey or, if you *must*, 1 cup black coffee

*Midmorning:*
Your choice of 1 large glass celery, carrot, or apple juice, or all 3 combined—if no fresh vegetable juices are available, drink orange or grapefruit juice instead

*Luncheon:*
2 cups Hauser Broth
1 glass yogurt with cinnamon, nutmeg, or blackstrap molasses

## THE SMALLER YOUR WAISTLINE, THE LONGER YOUR LIFELINE

### AVERAGE WEIGHT FOR WOMEN

| Age | 4 feet, 8 inches. | 4 feet, 9 inches. | 4 feet, 10 inches. | 4 feet, 11 inches. | 5 feet, 0 inch. | 5 feet, 1 inch. | 5 feet, 2 inches. | 5 feet, 3 inches. | 5 feet, 4 inches. | 5 feet, 5 inches. | 5 feet, 6 inches. | 5 feet, 7 inches. | 5 feet, 8 inches. | 5 feet, 9 inches. | 5 feet, 10 inches. | 5 feet, 11 inches. |
|---|---|---|---|---|---|---|---|---|---|---|---|---|---|---|---|---|
| 15 | 101 | 103 | 105 | 106 | 107 | 109 | 112 | 115 | 118 | 122 | 126 | 130 | 134 | 138 | 142 | 147 |
| 20 | 106 | 108 | 110 | 112 | 114 | 116 | 119 | 122 | 125 | 128 | 132 | 136 | 140 | 143 | 147 | 151 |
| 25 | 109 | 111 | 113 | 115 | 117 | 119 | 121 | 124 | 128 | 131 | 135 | 139 | 143 | 147 | 151 | 154 |
| 30 | 112 | 114 | 116 | 118 | 120 | 122 | 124 | 127 | 131 | 134 | 138 | 142 | 146 | 150 | 154 | 157 |
| 35 | 115 | 117 | 119 | 121 | 123 | 125 | 127 | 130 | 134 | 138 | 142 | 146 | 150 | 154 | 157 | 160 |
| 40 | 119 | 121 | 123 | 125 | 127 | 129 | 132 | 135 | 138 | 142 | 146 | 150 | 154 | 158 | 161 | 164 |
| 45 | 122 | 124 | 126 | 128 | 130 | 132 | 135 | 138 | 141 | 145 | 149 | 153 | 157 | 161 | 164 | 168 |
| 50 | 125 | 127 | 129 | 131 | 133 | 135 | 138 | 141 | 144 | 148 | 152 | 156 | 161 | 165 | 169 | 173 |
| 55 | 125 | 127 | 129 | 131 | 133 | 135 | 138 | 141 | 144 | 148 | 153 | 158 | 163 | 167 | 171 | 174 |

### AVERAGE WEIGHT FOR MEN

| Age | 5 feet, 1 inch. | 5 feet, 2 inches. | 5 feet, 3 inches. | 5 feet, 4 inches. | 5 feet, 5 inches. | 5 feet, 6 inches. | 5 feet, 7 inches. | 5 feet, 8 inches. | 5 feet, 9 inches. | 5 feet, 10 inches. | 5 feet, 11 inches. | 6 feet, 0 inch. | 6 feet, 1 inch. | 6 feet, 2 inches. | 6 feet, 3 inches. | 6 feet, 4 inches. | 6 feet, 5 inches. |
|---|---|---|---|---|---|---|---|---|---|---|---|---|---|---|---|---|---|
| 15 | 109 | 112 | 115 | 118 | 122 | 126 | 130 | 134 | 138 | 142 | 147 | 152 | 157 | 162 | 167 | 172 | 177 |
| 20 | 119 | 122 | 125 | 128 | 132 | 136 | 140 | 144 | 148 | 152 | 156 | 161 | 166 | 171 | 176 | 181 | 186 |
| 25 | 124 | 126 | 129 | 133 | 137 | 141 | 145 | 149 | 153 | 157 | 162 | 167 | 173 | 179 | 184 | 189 | 194 |
| 30 | 128 | 130 | 133 | 136 | 140 | 144 | 148 | 152 | 156 | 161 | 166 | 172 | 178 | 184 | 190 | 196 | 201 |
| 35 | 130 | 132 | 135 | 138 | 142 | 146 | 150 | 155 | 160 | 165 | 170 | 176 | 182 | 189 | 195 | 201 | 207 |
| 40 | 133 | 135 | 138 | 141 | 145 | 149 | 153 | 158 | 163 | 168 | 174 | 180 | 186 | 193 | 200 | 206 | 212 |
| 45 | 135 | 137 | 140 | 143 | 147 | 151 | 155 | 160 | 165 | 170 | 176 | 182 | 188 | 195 | 202 | 209 | 215 |
| 50 | 136 | 138 | 141 | 144 | 148 | 152 | 156 | 161 | 166 | 171 | 177 | 183 | 190 | 197 | 204 | 211 | 217 |
| 55 | 137 | 139 | 142 | 145 | 149 | 153 | 158 | 163 | 168 | 173 | 178 | 184 | 191 | 198 | 205 | 212 | 219 |

*Midafternoon:*
Your choice of 1 large glass celery, carrot, or apple juice, or all 3 combined—if no fresh vegetable juices are available, drink orange or grapefruit juice instead

*Dinner:*
Hauser Broth, all you want
1 glass yogurt with cinnamon, nutmeg, or blackstrap molasses
Demitasse or papaya-mint tea sweetened with honey

*Before retiring:*
Check up on your elimination. If in doubt, use some laxative herbs and drink down with a bit of fruit or tomato juice

## GOOD FOOD FOR GOOD DOGS

Right from the start I must confess I haven't fed nearly as many dogs as I have human beings, but with the pets I have had and still have, I have always had good luck.

There was Faust, the handsome police dog, with the fiery eyes and wonderful fur coat. He thrived on his diet until some cruel person ran over him in Chicago.

Ricky, my Sealyham, who traveled with me for years—and is known to thousands—got to be a wise old man (he was more than a dog). He would now be 15 years old if Lana Turner's Great Dane hadn't bitten him in two.

There were others, more Sealyhams, an Afghan, Sunny the chocolate-brown poodle, and Buster an uncertain mixture who adopted me and my friend when we were walking in the hills of Beverly. All these pets remained healthy and hearty and I believe one of my secrets is that I never gave any of them anything that I could not eat myself.

Dogs are not like pigs and should not be given a pig's diet of a lot of old bread with greasy gravy. I don't even believe that a dog can be at his best when he constantly gets canned or dehydrated foods.

I am convinced that our dogs can live longer and always be in top form if we feed them more intelligently. A good veterinary once told me that 90% of all dog diseases could be eliminated if people would stop giving their dogs sweets, too much starch, and instead gave them a balanced diet rich in proteins, minerals, and vitamins.

Here, I believe, is a well proportioned menu for any pet: 60% Meat —20% Vegetables—20% Starch.

*The meat* should be as fresh as possible. Cheap cuts are just as good as expensive ones, but best of all are the organ meats such as heart, kidneys, liver, and tripe. The meat should be ground up or cut in small pieces. Raw meat is best but for variety's sake slightly heat the meat, but do not fry.

*The vegetables* are best when raw and finely chopped. Chopped carrots are probably the best all-around vegetable for dogs. Carrots have a beneficial effect upon the "innards" of man and beast. However, all raw chopped vegetables can be used.

*The starch* should be of the whole variety. Whole wheat, whole rye, or whole corn are favorites. Broken up bits of whole-wheat bread, rye bread, and corn breads are a good choice. The whole-wheat biscuits which can be bought in any grocery store and stored, are liked by all dogs.

*Mix together* the fresh meat, the freshly chopped vegetables, and the whole starch and moisten with some soup stock, broth, milk, or gravy (remove the fat). When well mixed this looks like a nice big hamburger which *you* would want to eat and that is as it should be. If you can't afford such a dish for your Buster then you can't afford to have a dog.

*Occasionally add* one or two egg yolks, or one or two tablespoons of wheat germ, or one tablespoon of dry vegetable broth, or a clove of garlic.

*My prize pet meal* can be used for enriching your pet's diet. Here's how to make it:

| | |
|---|---|
| 1 cup dried brewers' yeast | 1 cup fine bone meal |
| 1 cup wheat or corn germ | 1 cup dried sea greens |

Mix the 4 dry ingredients together. Put in a tin can or bottle. Keep dry and covered. Mix 1 or 2 tablespoons of this mixture with the rest of the meal. Mix it up well, the first few times until your pet "cries for it." If you have a pampered one, let him go hungry until he will eat it.

*Here is what it does:* The brewers' yeast and wheat germ are wonderful for his skin and coat, the bone meal furnishes lots of calcium for his teeth, and sea greens (dried vegetables from the ocean) add a little iodine and other minerals necessary for a balanced diet.

One meal a day is best for grown dogs.

## LUCKY-DOG STEW

1 lb. fresh chopped meat
1 lb. whole wheat or oatmeal
1 bunch carrots

1 bunch celery
1 large onion

Chop up vegetables fine and mix with meat and the whole wheat. Put in a large kettle and cover with 3 quarts of water. Let boil slowly for 2 or 3 hours until the wheat kernels are tender and soft. The stew must not have too much liquid nor must it be too thick. Add salt and enrich with pet meal. This is enough food for several days. Put balance in refrigerator.

## SPECIAL DISHES FOR SPECIAL OCCASIONS

1. Mix cottage cheese with chopped carrots—⅔ cottage cheese and ⅓ chopped carrots. Enrich with 1 tablespoon of pet meal and mix well.
2. Milk and 2 egg yolks, mixed with whole-wheat biscuits.
3. Mix cottage cheese with tomato juice; enrich with 2 tablespoons of wheat germ.
4. Bits of rye bread soaked in yogurt and enriched with 1 tablespoon of brewers' yeast.
5. Whole-wheat biscuits saturated with ½ milk and ½ broth and enriched with 1 tablespoon of pet meal.

When our pet has an off day, when he scratches too much and when his breath is too "doggie," try one of the above dishes. Dogs are smarter than we are. They stop eating the minute they don't feel tops. All they want is plenty of water, so don't worry if your pet refuses all foods occasionally. As a matter of fact, we would all be healthier and probably live longer if we had an occasional fast day.

CHAPTER 24

# How to Buy and Use Health Foods

IN THE INTRODUCTION I spoke of the whole-grain flours and cereals, the natural sweetenings, and the nonirritating condiments which we use in the new-style cookery. For those of you who are making your first acquaintance with them, I give here some further information about them. If you live in a small town you will probably have to seek out a specialty store or a health food store in order to buy them. In some of your larger cities department stores may have a counter where you can buy whole-grain flours, natural sugars, and vegetable salt. Don't give up if the first store you try does not have them all. Keep looking until you have located the source in your town—or keep asking until you have helped create a demand. Remember that the stores supply what the customers demand, and if enough people insist upon having natural foods, eventually the stores will stock them.

## SWEETENINGS

In health and specialty shops you can get *raw natural crystal sugar,* with nothing taken away and nothing added. This is the best form in which to use sugar, but if you can't get it, use *brown sugar* in purified form which can be obtained under various trade names—Grans, for instance. And remember that brown sugar should be packed tight in the cup when measuring.

*Honey* is nature's sweetening. Be sure you buy the uncooked variety. Pure uncooked honey will always crystallize when put in the refrigerator.

*Molasses* comes light, medium, and dark. We prefer the dark blackstrap because it is richest in food elements and flavor. Always insist upon unsulphured molasses.

## FLOURS AND CEREALS—see pages 170 and 180-182.

## FOODS WHICH FORTIFY

We hear much these days about "fortified" and "enriched" foods. The use of these words implies that such foods are even richer than in their natural state. As a matter of fact, however, many good food elements have been removed from these so-called "enriched" foods, and only one or two replaced. The food in its natural form is far richer in minerals and vitamins.

There are some natural foods so rich in minerals and vitamins that when they are added to a dish, the food is really enriched, and in a natural manner. They are:

*Brewers' Yeast:* A single tablespoon of brewers' yeast contains $2\frac{1}{2}$ milligrams of vitamin $B_1$ and the rest of the B complex in proportion. Add it to beverages or put it in cooked dishes as suggested on page 237.

*Wheat Germ:* The germ of wheat contains all the B vitamins, vitamin E, iron, and first-class protein. A half-cupful will supply $2\frac{1}{2}$ milligrams of vitamin $B_1$. Sprinkle it on cereal, use it instead of crumbs for coating food, mix it into meat and vegetable loaves, or eat it as cereal. Mix with two-thirds whole-wheat flour in baking.

*Corn Germ:* Corn germ is as good as wheat germ, its protein being of the first class.

*Blackstrap Molasses:* This is the third of the "super foods" which give you concentrated supplies of vitamins and minerals in natural form. It contains all the B vitamins except $B_1$ and is high in iron, copper, calcium, and magnesium. Have it on your table as regularly as salt. Use it to sweeten cereals, to flavor milk, and in place of jam or jelly. It will give you some idea of the value of blackstrap molasses to realize that it is a vegetable juice concentrated by boiling down until it is sixty times richer than the original juice in minerals and in all vitamins stable to heat.

*Sweet Peppers:* Chopped sweet peppers, green or red, not only add color to a dish, but supply added vitamin C. An ounce of peppers contains 1350 International Units of vitamin C.

*Parsley:* You may think of parsley as a green sprig laid over meat—and sent back to the kitchen with the empty plates. Every time you do that, you throw out good vitamin C, for parsley contains 1050 International Units of vitamin C per ounce. Therefore parsley potatoes, parsley carrots, parsley-decorated fish are not only garnished and flavored, they are fortified with vitamin C. Always chop your parsley and sprinkle it liberally over the dish.

## SEASONINGS

*Vegetable Salt:* For years French and Italian chefs have used unrefined sea salt for cooking and flavoring. Later they added vegetables to the salt to make it more palatable. In America for the last twenty years fastidious cooks have used such flavorsome salt, known as "vegetable salt," which is a combination of sea salt, earth salt, and about ten dehydrated vegetables, plus—what is very important—a bit of organic iodine. Vegetable salt adds flavor and savor to foods, with additional health protection.

*Onion Powder, Garlic Powder:* Onion and garlic powders on your pantry shelf will make it easier to give a fillip to a dish without bothering to cut up the fresh onion or garlic.

*Okra Powder:* This is wonderful for thickening soups and gravies without the curse of added calories. The fresh okra will do the same thing, of course, but it is much harder to deal with.

*Anise:* Anise seed will give a delicate licorice flavor to coffee cakes, sweet rolls, cookies, candies, and sweet pickles.

*Bay Leaves:* Use with a delicate hand in stews, soups, boiled fish, fish chowder, pot roasts, and any tomato mixture. A whole bay leaf will season quantities—you will never need more than a half or a quarter of a leaf at a time.

*Caraway Seed:* Use in rye bread, sauerkraut, new cabbage, liver, kidneys, and in fish chowder.

*Cardamom Seed:* Sprinkle on Danish pastry, bun breads, coffee cakes, sliced oranges, cookies, or use in grape jelly.

*Cassia:* Use in pickling, for puddings, stewed fruit, baked goods, mincemeat.

*Celery Seed:* Put in fish, potato salad, tomato dishes, salad dressings, stews, hamburgers.

*Cinnamon:* See *Cassia.*

*Cloves:* Use whole in pickled fruits, spiced sweet syrups; ground in baked goods, puddings, potato soup, borsch, and stews.

*Coriander:* Try in apple pie, pea soup, gingerbread, cookies, cakes, sweet biscuits, poultry stuffing, mixed green salads.

*Curry Powder:* To flavor curry sauce, meat, fish, eggs, chicken, cream soups, tomato soup, French dressing, chicken soup, clam and fish chowders.

*Dill Seed:* To give the Swedish touch, use in sauerkraut, salads, soups, fish and meat sauces, gravies, and green apple pie.

*Fennel:* Resembles anise in flavor. Use in pastries, apple pie, sweet pickles, candies, and boiled fish.

*Fines Herbes:* Use in stews, soups, meat and fish stuffings, for garnishing, in omelets, fish sauces, over grilled meat, and in broth. To make: Chop separately ½ onion, 2 scallions, 2 sprigs parsley, ½ small leek, and 1 tablespoon of marjoram leaves.

*Ginger:* Use the root in chutneys, conserves, stewed dried fruits, and applesauce. Add ground ginger to cakes, puddings, pies, cookies, and canned fruits.

*Mace:* Ground mace goes with pound cakes and all yellow cakes, chocolate dishes, and oyster stew. Mace blades are added to fish sauces, preserves, stewed cherries, fruit jellies, gingerbread, and biscuits to be served with salads.

*Marjoram Leaves:* Dried marjoram leaves go with lamb, stews, soups, and poultry seasonings. See under Herbs for the uses of fresh marjoram.

*Mustard, Dry:* Add to meats, sauces, gravies, and salad dressings.

*Nutmeg:* Freshly grated nutmeg is used in baked goods, sauces, puddings, and with some vegetables.

*Orégano:* A wonderful substitute for hot red peppers, chili, and other sharp spices. Use in Mexican dishes instead of chili.

*Paprika:* Sweet paprika is an excellent source of vitamin C. Use it both for garnish and for flavor, wherever a recipe calls for pepper.

*Poultry Seasoning:* This is a prepared mixture of spices and dried herbs. Use it if you prefer, but first try the suggestions under Herbs.

*Tumeric:* This root of the ginger family is generally used with mustard to flavor meats and eggs.

## FINE HERBS MAKE FINE COOKS

England and Switzerland are the two countries where all sorts of fragrant herbs are cultivated and used with reverence. The English herb gardens are justly famous, and if you have ever been in one of those picturesque herb shops in London, you will be impressed what their simple herbs can do to and for you. In Switzerland whole valleys are devoted to herb culture. You can see the peasants cutting the herbs and carefully drying them in the morning sun. The Swiss insist that their herbs are better because they grow slower and higher up in the mountains where the sun and soil makes the herbs richer in minerals and vitamins.

Here in America many of our great cooks had a tradition of using herbs in cookery as strong as any European one. Then, no one knows just why, we lost the fine art of enriching with herbs. But now as mysteriously as it departed, the use of flavorsome herbs is coming back with a "bang." Whole books are devoted to the growing of herbs; how and when to plant and how to dry them. Most of the books mention 25 to 30 herbs available in this country which can make your dinners culinary triumphs, but for our purpose, you need not start on so large a scale.

Mint, thyme, sage, marjoram, rosemary, and basil are the basic six herbs preferred by Americans, and these will add a wealth of flavor to your simplest dishes. You can buy them from the grocer or in specialty shops. Still better, you can grow them. Even a window box will do. Start with these six and gradually add others. Before long you will add more and more varieties and herbal delights.

Two important points in the use of herbs: Don't let your seasoning become monotonous by using the same herb all the time. Second, remember that herbs should *enhance* the flavor of food, not drown it. Go easy—not too much in any one dish and don't flavor every dish with herbs. For any one meal, two herb-flavored courses, perhaps salad and soup, are sufficient.

*Dried or Fresh Herbs:* If you are a poor city dweller and don't even possess a window box for growing herbs, buy them—but buy the freshest and the most carefully dried you can find. Buy them whole in the leaf if possible and have the fun of crumbling them between your palms when you are ready to use them. Herbs already pulverized soon become flat even when kept in jars. If you have to buy them pulverized, buy small amounts and replenish them more often. However, there is no comparison between the flavor of crisp green herbs and the best dried variety; so get going, and have fun and grow at least a few of your own herbs. Seeds of all those listed below are available in this country and do well in this climate.

## ANISE (*Pimpinella asinum*)

This feathery plant is one of the most ancient herbs. The green leaves are a piquant addition to salads; the seeds are used in baking—coffee cakes, sweet rolls, cookies, candies, and also in sweet pickles or mixed into fresh cheeses. The flavor resembles licorice. And still another use: Pliny said that a bunch suspended near the bed assured the sleeper a youthful look in the morning. Someone please try it and report!

Anise is an annual. Sow in late spring in a sunny place. Good average garden soil is all you need.

### BASIL (*Ocimum Basilicum*)

From spring to early fall basil flourishes in Italian gardens. Its leaves are used in stews and soups and gravies, to flavor meat, salads, cottage cheeses, and sauces. And try it in fruit drinks.

Basil is an annual, and it does all the better for frequent cutting. When the ground warms up in the spring, plant it in a sunny place in average soil. The spot should be well drained.

### CARAWAY (*Carum carvi*)

Caraway seeds in bread, rolls, coffee cakes, and cookies are classic. Use them also in cream cheese; or strewn over sauerkraut, new cabbage, liver, and kidneys; or mix them into canapé spreads. Add the plumed tips of the green herb to salads, in moderation.

Caraway is a hardy biennial. Sow in a dry, sunny place in the middle of spring.

### CHIVES (*Allium Schoenoprasium*)

These hardy perennials can be bought in grocery and vegetable stores. Buy a pot and keep it on your window sill; cut them often; they will spring up again from their stems. They can be used as freely as onions —especially in salads, omelets, sauces, cheeses, and with potatoes.

### DILL (*Anethum graveolens*)

The young, tender leaves of this plant beloved by Italians give character to salads, eggs, cheeses, meat, fish, potatoes, avocados, and beans. The Swedes make a delicious dill sauce, and of course, everyone knows the dill pickle.

Dill is an annual. Sow in late spring in a sunny place. Ordinary garden soil is all you need.

### FENNEL (*Foeniculum vulgare*)

Mix the tender leaves with salad greens or use them to garnish fish. Cook the seeds with fish and soups, put them in bread, and use them to flavor drinks.

This is a European perennial treated as an annual. Sow in spring in ordinary garden soil. If the season is long enough, sow a second crop in midsummer.

Florence Fennel (*Foeniculum dulce*) resembles celery somewhat and is eaten the same way.

## PARSLEY (*Petroselinum sativum*)

Parsley has been called the "crown of cookery." But our way of posing it on top a dish for garnish, then returning it uneaten to the kitchen is not the kind of crowning that was meant. Either cook parsley into the food or add it the last two minutes of cooking so the flavor blends with the dish. Use in salads, soups, stews, cottage cheese, meats, vegetables.

Parsley is a biennial. Sow in spring in ordinary garden soil, then wait patiently for it to spring up. Parsley germinates very slowly. The Italian fern-leaved variety is tenderer than the ordinary kind.

## ROSEMARY (*Rosmarinus officinalis*)

Rosemary, with its blue flowers in honor of the Virgin, is a sweet, fragrant herb for use in pickles, jam, and sweet, bland sauces. Use it also with meats, poultry, stuffings, and greens.

Rosemary is a perennial. Plant the seeds indoors in January or February. In late spring transplant the seedlings in a dry, sunny place, well drained and sheltered.

## SWEET MARJORAM (*Origanum majorana*)

This pretty, fragrant plant with its flowers springing from little knobs is used for sauces, salads, meats, poultry, cheeses, soups, and fish. Use fresh young leaves as salad greens.

Sweet marjoram is a perennial, but in northern climates it has to be treated like an annual. Sow the seeds indoors in late January or February then transplant the seedlings to the garden in late spring. Plant 5 or 6 inches apart in a sunny place. When the plant flowers, cut off the entire plant then dry the leaves and tips for flavoring use.

### Spearmint (*Mentha spicata*)

Use in salads and salad dressings, cottage cheese, pea soup, broths, and with potatoes. The familiar mint tea is only one of the beverages with which mint goes well.

Spearmint is a hardy perennial. Plant root cuttings in rich moist soil—and then keep your eye on it or it will over-run the garden.

### Sage (*Salvia officinalis*)

Dried sage is one of the few herbs which have survived the long drouth in this country. Everyone knows it in the ubiquitous poultry seasoning. But try the fresh sage sparingly in beans, cottage cheese, stews, veal, duck, or geese. For turkey or chicken, try instead of sage a mixture of savory, thyme, and sweet basil.

Sage is very hardy perennial which can be propagated either from seeds or from cuttings. Set the cuttings in sand in the spring, or sow the seeds in a dry, spare soil.

### Summer Savory (*Satureia hortensis*)

This is the "bean herb" in Germany, the standard spicing for turkey and chicken in England. Use both leaves and flowers in poultry stuffings, salads, rice, fresh peas, string beans, lima beans, and broad beans.

Summer savory is an annual. Sow in late spring in a sunny place. When the seedlings come up, thin them so they stand 5 or 6 inches apart. After the plant flowers, cut off the entire plant and dry the leaves and tips.

### Tarragon (*Artemisia dracunculus*)

Tarragon is a valuable herb, but so powerful it drowns out everything else unless it is used sparingly. Cook young tops with other greens; use the leaves in salads, soups, dressings, fish sauces, stews, and preserves. Cook with meats. Mince it into tartar sauce, chop it on fish.

Tarragon is a perennial, hardy only if well protected. It propagates only from cuttings. Set them out in the spring in a partly shady place. In the fall cut the plants back and protect them either by hilling or by covering with litter held in place by branches.

## THYME (*Thymus vulgaris*)

There are many varieties of this ancient plant—orange, lemon, caraway are only a few of the many thyme scents. But the real kitchen herb is the simple Common Thyme. Use dried leaves in soups, sauces, stuffings, cheese. Cook thyme with poultry, veal, rabbit, fish. Use the flavor in pot cheeses, salad dressings, and salads.

Thyme is a perennial which grows from seed or rooting. Sow in late spring in a well-drained sunny spot; or plant the rooted sections of the creeping stems.

## FATS

Lard is never used in the new-style cookery. Butter, cream, margarines, and pure vegetable oils and shortenings, contrary to popular opinion, are quite completely digested and supply necessary food elements. Vegetable oils supply vitamins $B_6$, E, and K, and essential fatty acids. Peanut oil is the richest source of essential fatty acids; corn oil the richest in vitamin $B_6$. Use all the vegetable oils—not only for salad dressings, but to prepare short-cooked vegetables.

*French-Frying:* While frying is the least desirable way to prepare food, there is nothing against it for those with normal digestion—*if* a pure, wholesome vegetable oil is used and if the foods are cooked quickly so they do not absorb too much fat. Peanut oil is excellent. Use a deep, straight-sided pan into which a wire basket fits. Fill with enough fat to cover the food, but never more than two-thirds full or the fat may bubble over. Heat the fat gradually, and never let it smoke. Too-hot fat smells up the house, makes the food bitter, and leaves it more difficult to digest. A frying thermometer is a great help in keeping the fat at the right temperature, which is from 360°F. for uncooked mixtures such as fritters, to 385°-390°F. for French-fried potatoes, onions, eggplant, etc. If you have no thermometer, put a few cubes of stale bread in the fat and keep track of how long it takes them to brown. If the bread turns light brown in 60 seconds, the fat is between 360° and 375°F. If it takes 40 seconds, the fat is 375°-385°F. And if it takes only 20 seconds, the fat is very hot—385°-395°F.

*Sautéeing:* Food lightly browned in a very little fat is sautéed. Butter is excellent for this if you can afford it. Margarine is not good—its smoking temperature is too low. Use vegetable shortening or oil if you don't use butter.

*Shortenings:* For baking use vegetable shortenings or butter. Not all fats have the same ability to make doughs and batters tender, so many people prefer to use part butter if not all, both for shortening property and for flavor.

*Care of Fats:* All fats should be kept in a cool, dark place. Solid fats such as butter and vegetable shortenings do better in the refrigerator. Oils are likely to solidify in an automatic refrigerator.

Fat used for French-frying can be used over and over if it is not overheated and if it is properly cared for. After you have finished cooking, put a few slices of raw potato in the fat and cook them for a few minutes to absorb any foreign flavors which may have got into the fat. Then strain the fat through several thicknesses of cheesecloth to remove all the crumbs. Keep well covered in a cold, dark place.

### COATINGS FOR FOOD

Foods which are to be French-fried or sautéed are often covered with a coating to absorb the surface moisture. An egg coating is good because it hardens instantly and forms a coating which keeps the food from absorbing fat. Dip the food first in crumbs, then in egg beaten with 1 tablespoon of water, then in crumbs. Or dip first in seasoned flour, then in egg, then in crumbs.

*Seasoned Flour:* To 1 cup whole-wheat flour, add 1-2 teaspoons vegetable salt and ¼ teaspoon of paprika.

*Crumbs:* Crush or grind whole-wheat bread, dry, or crackers. Sift the crumbs and use the fine ones for coating, the coarse ones for buttered crumbs, soufflés, etc. One cup of crumbs and 1 egg will coat about 4 chops, cutlets, etc.

*Buttered Crumbs:* For covering baked dishes which call for buttered crumbs, melt ¼ cup of butter to each cup of crumbs. Mix the crumbs thoroughly into the butter until all are coated with butter.

## OVEN TEMPERATURES

Oven temperatures are described as slow, moderate, hot and very hot, as well as giving the degrees Fahrenheit. The equivalents in degrees are as follows:

Slow—250°-300°
Moderate—325°-375°
Hot—400°-450°
Very hot—anything over 450°

By all means you should have an oven thermometer if your oven has no heat control. But just in case you can't get one, here is a practical oven test which will give you some idea of how hot your oven is:

Sprinkle a teaspoon of flour on a piece of brown paper and put it in the oven. If the flour browns very lightly in 5 minutes, you have a slow oven. If it turns golden brown in 5 minutes, the oven is moderate. If it turns dark brown in 5 minutes, the oven is hot, and if it turns dark brown in 3 minutes, the oven is very hot. A sheet of unglazed white paper will do as well as the flour.

## TABLE OF YIELDS

How much to buy or prepare for a given amount of prepared food is not always easy to guess. The following table gives the yields of certain common foods.

| Food | Measure or Weight | How Much to Expect |
|------|------------------|--------------------|
| Apples | 1 lb. (3 medium) | 2½-3 cups, sliced or diced; 1½ cups applesauce |
| Apricots, dried | 1 lb. | 3 cups cooked |
| Bananas | 1 lb. (3 medium) | 2 cups sliced |
| Beans, dried | 1 lb. | 2½ cups raw, 6 cups cooked |
| Berries | 1 qt. | 3½ cups raw |

| Food | Measure or Weight | How Much to Expect |
|---|---|---|
| Bread crumbs: | | |
| Soft fresh | 3 ½-inch slices | 1 cup |
| Fine dry | 6 ½-inch slices | 1 cup |
| Butter | 1 lb. | 2 cups |
| Cheese, American | 1 lb. | 4 cups grated |
| Cherries | 1 lb. | 2¾ cups, stemmed and pitted |
| Coconut | 1 lb. shredded | 5 cups |
| Corn meal | 1 lb. | 3 cups |
| Cream | ½ pt. | 1 cup; 2 cups whipped |
| Currants, dried | 1 lb. | 3 cups |
| Dates, pitted | 1 lb. | 2½ cups |
| Egg whites | 8-10 | 1 cup |
| Egg yolks | 12-14 | 1 cup |
| Figs, dried | 1 lb. | 2⅔ cups, chopped |
| Flour, whole-wheat | 1 lb. | 3½ cups |
| Grapefruit | 1 | ⅔-¾ cup juice; 1¼ cups diced pulp |
| Lemon | 1 medium | 3 tbsp. juice; 1½ tsp. grated rind |
| Nutmeats | 1 lb. | 4½ cups; about 3½ chopped |
| Orange | 1 medium | ½ cup juice; 1 tbsp. grated rind |
| Peaches | 1 lb. | 2-2½ cups sliced |
| Pears | 1 lb. | 2½ cups cooked |
| Pineapple | 1 medium | 3 cups diced |
| Plums | 1 lb. | 2 cups cooked |
| Potatoes | 1 lb. (3 medium) | 1½ cups sliced |
| Prunes | 1 lb. | 4 cups cooked (2 cups pitted) |
| Raisins | 15-oz. package | 3¼ cups seeded; 3 cups seedless |
| Rhubarb | 1 lb. | 2 cups cooked |
| Rice | 1 lb. | 2 cups raw; 6 cups cooked |
| Sugar, brown | 1 lb. | 2¼ cups firmly packed |
| Tomatoes | 1 lb. | 3-4 medium |

## SOME USEFUL HINTS

1. *To Cut Butter for the Table:* Use a sharp, thin knife and dip it in hot water after each stroke, or wrap the blade of a silver knife in waxed paper before slicing.

2. *To Make Onion Juice:* Cut a small piece from the blossom end of the onion and scrape the cut surface with the edge of a spoon or a fine grater.

3. *To Sour Milk:* If you have no sour milk on hand, add 2 teaspoons of lemon juice to 1 cup of sweet milk and stir over very low heat a minute or two until the milk curdles.

4. *To Grate Orange or Lemon Rind:* Rub the whole orange or lemon over the grater before you cut it to squeeze the juice. Don't rub so hard you get the bitter white inner peeling—just the colored outer peel.

5. *To Grind or Chop Sticky Fruits:* Heat the food grinder thoroughly in boiling water to make the fruit slip through easily. Or heat the knife or scissors you use for chopping.

6. *To Peel Onions:* Scald the onions with boiling water and rinse with cold before peeling, or hold them under cold water while peeling if you wish to peel without tears.

7. *To Coat with Seasoned Flour:* Put the seasoned flour and the food to be coated into a paper bag. Close the top of the bag and shake vigorously.

8. *To Measure Fat:* To measure half a cup of fat when it is not to be melted, fill the cup half full of water, then put in chunks of fat until the water reaches the top of the cup. Pour off the water, and you have half a cup of fat left.

9. *To Open Sealed Jars:* Let hot water run over the jars or knock the edge of the top against a hard surface.

10. *To Measure Syrup, Molasses, or Honey:* Rinse in cold water or grease the spoon or cup in which you measure.

11. *To Smother a Grease Fire:* If the grease on your broiler catches fire, turn off the heat and close the oven door tightly. If the fire doesn't go out at once, smother it with salt.

12. *To Keep Cookies Soft*: Put a piece of bread in the cookie jar with macaroons, molasses cookies, or other kinds of soft cookies.

13. *To Wash off Eggs*: Soak all dishes with egg or egg batters on them in cold water before washing in hot. Milk also washes off better in cold water.

14. *Hot Pans and Kettles*: Never pour cold water in hot skillets or kettles. It may make them buckle. Either use hot water or wait till the pan cools.

15. *To Eliminate Garlic Odor from the Breath*: Chew a sprig of parsley or a few coffee beans.

16. *If Onions Disagree*: Try using shallots.

# Index

# Index

# Index

# Index

Vegetables (*Cont'd*):
  lima beans, short-cooked, 7
  okra, stewed, 11
  onion rings, French-fried, 13
  onions, stuffed, 121
  parsnips, French-fried, 13
  peas, short-cooked, 11
  peppers, stuffed, 121
  potato chips, sweet, 14
  —— crisps, Irish, 15
  potatoes, 14-6
  ——, sweet, 16-7
  preparing for juicer, 230
  quick-frozen, 6
  rutabagas, French-fried, 13
  sauces for, 135-6
  selecting, 5-6
  short-cooked, 4-12
  soybeans, green, 240
  soybean sprouts, 239-40
  spinach, short-cooked, 11-2
  squash, acorn, 12
  ——, baked Hubbard, 12
  to remove poisonous sprays, 230-1
  vitamin loss, 3-4, 6, 7, 19
  zucchini, 12
  (*See also* Meat substitutes)
Vegetable salads, 19-27; *for specific recipes see under* Salads
Vegetable Salisbury steaks, 126
Vegetable salt, 282
Vegetable soups, 43-52; *for specific recipe see under* Soups
Vegetable stew, chick pea and, 126
Vegetable toast, eggs on, 107
Vegetarian meat loaf, 129-30
Velouté sauce, *see* Mixed sauce
Vitamin A, 244-6
  enriching with, 245
  foods for, 245
Vitamin B1, 246-8
  enriching with, 248
  foods for, 247
  in flours, 179
Vitamin C, 249-51
  amount in lemon juice, 251
  enriching with, 251
  foods for, 249-50
  in fruit juices, 215
  in parsley, 282
  in vegetables, 6, 7
Vitamin-C butter, 137
Vitamin D, 251-2
  enriching with, 252
  foods for, 252
Vitamin E, 252-3
Vitamins:
  extra, 259

in brewers' yeast, 236-7
in vegetable juices, 231-4
prevent loss in vegetables, 3-4, 6, 7, 19

Waffles, rice, 175
Waffles, soya nut, 186
Waldorf salad, 30
Walnut milk, 222
Water-cress butter, 137
Water-cress juice, 233-4
Water-cress salad, cabbage and, 22
Water-cress sandwich, 190
Weight-gaining menus, 263-9
Weight-losing menus, 269-77
Weight tables, 276
Wheat germ:
  food value of, 179
  fortifying with, 281
Wheat-germ muffins, 188-9
Whip, Oregon prune, 161
Whip, Pasadena apricot, 161
White sauce, *see* Light sauce
White stock, 54
Whole-wheat bread, 182-3
  batter, 186
  fruit, 186
  soya, 183
Whole-wheat bakery, 179-82
Whole-wheat baking powder biscuits, 189
Whole-wheat biscuits for dogs, 278, 279
Whole-wheat flour:
  food value of, 179
  how to use, 180
Whole-wheat muffins, 187
Whole-wheat Parker House rolls, 183-4
Whole-wheat pie crust, 197-8
Whole-wheat pound cake, 192
Whole-wheat sticky bottoms, 184
Wild duck, broiled, 96
Wild rice, 175-7
  and almond pudding, 176
  —— mushroom stuffing, 103
  fluffy, 176
  hamburgers, 177
  nutburgers, 176-7
  quick, 176
  stuffing, 103

Yankee walnut fudge, 212
Yields, table of, 291-2
Yogurt:
  enriching with, 249
  how to make, 235-6
Yogurt reducing dressing, 37
Yogurt sauce, 140

Zucchini, 12
Zwieback pastry shell, 198